Mexican Cookery
Barbara Hansen

CONTENTS

ANOTHER BEST-SELLING COOKERY VOLUME FROM HPBooks®

Publisher: Rick Bailey; Editorial Director: Elaine R. Woodard
Editors: Carlene Tejada, Carroll Latham; Art Director: Don Burton
Book Assembly: Aspen Green, Tom Jakeway; Typography: Cindy Coatsworth, Joanne Porter, Kris Spitler
Book Manufacture: Anthony B. Narducci
Food Stylist: Mable Hoffman; Photography: George de Gennaro Studios

The author wishes to thank Richard Merrill, Instituto Moderno de Lenguas Extranjeras, Leon, Guanajuato; Maria Marquez de Merrill; Bertha Delfin de Rodriquez; Tity Rodriquez Delfin; Escuela Industrial Adolfo Lopez Mateos, Veracruz; Humphreys Family Center, Garfield Community Adult School, East Los Angeles, and the many cooks in Mexico and the southwestern United States who contributed to this book.

Published by HPBooks, Inc., P.O. Box 5367, Tucson, AZ 85703 602/888-2150
ISBN 0-89586-038-4
Library of Congress Catalog Card Number 80-80168 ©1980 HPBooks, Inc.
Printed in U.S.A.
8th Printing
Cover Photo: Enchiladas de Pollo (Deluxe Chicken Enchiladas), page 80

¡BIENVENIDOS!

Welcome to Mexican cooking! Mexico's food is as exciting and colorful as its art and music, as dramatic as its history and as appealing as its lively, warm-hearted people. It is also immensely practical, good for you and so varied that monotony is impossible. Yet what is known beyond the Mexican border about this entrancing food scarcely amounts to the crumb of a *tortilla*. *Tacos*, *tamales* and *enchiladas* are tasty ambassadors. But these and the few other dishes featured by Mexican restaurants outside the country only hint at greater riches.

Over the centuries, resourceful Mexican cooks have made the most of whatever the land produced. Squash flowers go into soups, and squash seeds are ground for sauces; banana leaves are wrapped around barbecued meats and *tamales;* *nopales*, or diced cactus, are added to salads and stews; and avocado leaves flavor some dishes. Native herbs and plants such as *cilantro* and *epazote* are not dismissed as weeds, but used to give some dishes their distinctive flavors. And the most basic of all Mexican ingredients—corn and *chiles*—are used with incredible variety.

Some cuisines reach their peak in ornate dishes requiring complicated sauces and expensive ingredients. But the simplest Mexican dishes are as notable as *fiesta* specialties that take hours to prepare. The aromas and flavors of fresh corn *tortillas*, really good refried beans, rice seasoned to perfection, and the wonderful soft rolls called *Bolillos* (French Rolls), page 161, are difficult to surpass.

On my first trip to Mexico, I was struck by the charm and ingenuity of the food. The basket of *pan dulce*, or sweet bread, served for breakfast in Guanajuato was a revelation. Plump, sweet Guanajuato strawberries smothered with thick cream and sprinkled with coarse sugar were something to sigh over. And why did no one at home spice and sweeten coffee in the manner of *Café de Olla* (Clay Pot Coffee)—served in rustic pottery mugs? The recipe is on page 20.

Mexico's Many Cuisines

It's difficult to generalize about Mexican food, because there is not one cuisine—but many. Dishes vary markedly from region to region. Each town and city has its own version of regional specialties and individual cooks add their own touches. Although intriguing dishes are found throughout the country, Puebla, Veracruz, Oaxaca and Yucatán are especially noted for their cuisines. Puebla, Veracruz and Oaxaca are also the names of large cities within their respective states.

PUEBLA

Mole Poblano (*Mole* Puebla-Style), page 116, is considered the national dish of Mexico. This baroque creation consists of turkey or chicken in a dark sauce flavored with chocolate and a multitude of *chiles* and spices. What could be more imaginative than *Chiles en Nogada* (*Chiles* in Nut Sauce), page 64, fresh *chiles* stuffed with meat and fruits, topped with a creamy nut sauce and sprinkled with pomegranate seeds? This dish was created in the city of Puebla in 1821 to honor General Agustín Iturbide after he had signed the treaties proclaiming Mexico's independence from Spain. Its colors represent the red, white and green of the Mexican flag.

VERACRUZ

A spectacular drive leads from Puebla to the city of Veracruz where you can find a wealth of seafood. Famous *Huachinango a la Veracruzana* (Red Snapper Veracruz-Style), page 128, originated here. You'll also find succulent *tamales* wrapped in banana leaves, an abundance of tropical fruits and possibly the best coffee in the world. Papantla, just north of Veracruz, gives us Mexico's heady vanilla. It is produced from orchid pods harvested by the Totonac Indians.

OAXACA

The cooking of Oaxaca—pronounced wah-HA-ka—is not as easy to uncover because it flourishes in homes—not in restaurants. The only Oaxacan cookbook I could find was a handwritten heirloom belonging to a local family. However, a few restaurants offer typical dishes. Oaxaca is noted for the variety and excellence of its *moles*, for chocolate, coffee and cheese. A Oaxacan version of string cheese called *quesillo* comes in thin strips rolled into coils. It is here that the potent, smoke-flavored liquor called *mezcal* is distilled from the maguey plant.

YUCATÁN

Mexico's most distinctive cuisine is probably that of Yucatán. One specialty is *Pollo Pibil* (Baked Chicken), page 120, chicken coated with seasoned red paste, wrapped in banana leaves and cooked in pits dug in the ground. Also typical are *Sopa de Lima* (Lime & Tortilla Soup), page 45, and *Panuchos Mérida* (*Panuchos* Mérida-Style), page 100, small tortillas topped with black beans and garnishes. Lebanese restaurants in Mérida, Yucatán's capital, add even more variety by serving Arabic pocket bread instead of *tortillas* or *bolillos* with a meal.

NORTHERN MEXICO

The northern part of the country is the region of flour *tortillas*, *tamales* wrapped in *hojas*, or dried corn husks, instead of banana leaves, and the spicy meat and *chile* dishes that spilled over into the southwestern United States. Flour *tortillas* originated in the state of Sonora, and enormous *tortillas* so thin they are almost transparent can be found there and in neighboring Arizona.

PACIFIC COAST

The west coast of Mexico abounds in seafood. In Ensenada, you can have *chorizo* made with abalone, excellent lobster dishes and *tacos* containing deep-fried, batter-coated nuggets of fish. Turtle is a Baja California specialty, while Mazatlán offers a great variety of shrimp dishes including *Coctel de Camarones Mazatlán* (Shrimp Cocktail Mazatlán-Style), page 126. Acapulco is noted for *ceviche*, an appetizer of marinated fish. *Ceviche de Alberto* (Alberto's Marinated Fish), is on page 125.

UNITED STATES BORDER

The regional character of Mexican food can also be seen in the United States. California, Arizona, New Mexico and Texas rest on the Mexican border and each has its own approach to Mexican food.

RESTAURANT FARE

Mexican combination plates, common in the United States, are overwhelming and often heavily sauced meals: *enchiladas, tacos, tamales, chiles rellenos*, rice and beans—all on one plate! No one eats that way in Mexico. *Tacos* and *tamales* are snack foods. The main meal, served in the early afternoon, consists of several courses from soup through dessert. Many restaurants offer the *comida corrida*. This fixed-price luncheon with a set menu of several courses demonstrates how Mexican people really eat.

Lunch one day at Doña Elpidia's, a home-style restaurant in the city of Oaxaca, started with an appetizer plate of *chicharrones*, or pork cracklings, barbecued ribs and an *empanada*, or turnover, filled with sautéed onion, a little *chile* and the herb, *epazote*. Next came a soup of vermicelli in tomato juice. *Arroz a la Mexicana* (Rice Mexican-Style), page 140, followed as a separate course. The waitress then brought a plate of *Mole Colorado de Oaxaca* (Oaxacan Red *Mole*), page 112. Beans cooked with bacon and served in their broth appeared after the meat. Dessert was the small orange fruit, *tejocote*, served in syrup. A cup of strong, fragrant coffee ended this sumptuous but modestly priced *comida*, or luncheon.

Lunch was simpler at the Nevería Gypsy, a little cafe on the main plaza of Tlaxcala. Here the menu included broth containing a choice of rice or pasta followed by a pork chop in tomato sauce with *chiles*, a plate of beans and, for dessert, *Arroz con Leche* (Rice Pudding), page 172.

At Prendes, a restaurant in the city of Veracruz, I had cream of corn soup followed by *paella*-style rice and *Pescado Alemán* (Fish German-Style), page 132, with *bolillos, chiles* and lime wedges on the side. Dessert was *Flan Napolitano de Veracruz* (Neapolitan *Flan* from Veracruz), page 171, and coffee.

HOME COOKING

Home-style meals can be as elaborate as restaurant fare. Bertha Delfín de Rodriguez, my friend in Veracruz, serves generous *comidas* to her family during the long mid-day break. One day we had a Oaxacan-style *mole* resembling *Mole Poblano* (*Mole* Puebla-Style), page 116, but sweeter. Served with it were *Arroz a la Veracruzana* (Rice Veracruz-Style), page 146, *Frijoles Negros* (Black Beans), page 151, a choice of *tortillas* or bread and *Agua de Naranja* (Orangeade), page 21. For dessert, we ate mangos from the tree that shades the patio and *Pan Tity* (Tity's Cake), page 180, made by Bertha's daughter.

Mexican cooks prefer fresh ingredients, although supermarkets stock instant refried beans, baking mixes, frozen *paella* and other convenience products. In general, the national taste for freshly prepared foods makes Mexican cuisine healthful and natural. Mexican cooks seem to know instinctively what is beneficial. Beans sprinkled with shredded cheese are rich in protein. And *tacos* are perfect little meals, combining meat, fresh vegetable garnishes and cheese in a neat tortilla package.

No matter how humble a dish, it is always fresh, tasty and prettily garnished, for Mexican cooks are artists at heart. They will add a slice of tomato, a bit of *cilantro*, a lime wedge here, a thin carrot curl there and a ruffle of lettuce before they feel the dish is fit to serve.

Fortunately, ingredients for Mexican cooking are becoming widely available in other parts of the world. Even unusual vegetables such as *chayotes*, *jícamas* and the little green tomatoes called *tomatillos* are finding their way into the world's markets. However, you need only a few basic foods to prepare a wide variety of dishes: *chiles*, which can be fresh or canned, cheese and instant *masa*. Many recipes in this book require no special ingredients at all. Nevertheless, they are authentically Mexican, acquired from good cooks on both sides of the border during many years of delightful dining. I know you will enjoy them.

BARBARA HANSEN

Barbara has always enjoyed Mexican cooking. She even taught herself Spanish so she could read original recipes and talk about food with Mexican cooks.

A staff writer for the food department of the *Los Angeles Times*, Barbara writes "Border Line," a column on Mexican food now appearing in many newspapers. *Mexican Cookery* is her third cookbook.

Barbara travels widely and frequently throughout Mexico, visiting markets, studying the produce and asking vendors how to prepare various foods. She discusses regional dishes with waiters and chefs in well-known restaurants as well as in neighborhood cafes.

When she returns to her home in Los Angeles, Barbara searches the markets for Mexican foods and their substitutes. Then, in her own kitchen, she tests and duplicates the recipes discovered in her travels.

Perhaps on your Mexican vacation, you'll enter a restaurant and recognize Barbara as one of the diners. If she is carefully sampling the food while a chef and waiter hover anxiously, you'll know she is on the track of a new recipe.

WHAT IS IT?

Achiote (ah-chee-OH-tay) — Dark red seeds from the annatto tree. *Achiote* is used for coloring and flavoring and is available in both seed and paste forms.

Biznaga (biz-NAH-ga) — Candied cactus. It is eaten as a sweet or chopped and used in desserts and other dishes. Citron may be substituted. Candied pineapple, although different in flavor, is close in texture.

Chayote (chy-OH-tay) — Delicately flavored, pear-shaped, light green squash. It may be large or small, spiny or smooth. The seed is flat and edible. The peel is not edible. Pattypan squash may be substituted.

Chorizo (chor-EE-so) — Spicy sausage. It may be made with either pork or beef. Chorizo labeled *Spanish-style* is milder than *Mexican-style.*

Cilantro (see-LAHN-tro) — Fresh coriander. It is commonly used in Mexico as a flavoring and garnish. You can grow your own. Buy the seeds (coriander) from the spice department in a supermarket. Plant them during warm weather after all danger of frost is past. *Cilantro* is also available in Oriental markets where it is called *Chinese parsley.*

Epazote (ay-pah-ZOH-tay) — A medicinal-tasting herb used in cooking black beans and often added to *quesadillas.* It grows wild in some areas. Its botanical name is *Chenopodium ambrosioides.*

Hojas (OH-hass) — Dried corn husks used as a wrapping for *tamales.* Rectangles of aluminum foil can be substituted.

Jamaica (ha-MIKE-ah) — Dried red hibiscus flowers. They are soaked in water to make a refreshing drink that has a light acid flavor. On the island of Jamaica, the flowers are called *roselle.* Another Caribbean name is *sorrel.* Their botanical name is *Hibiscus sabdariffa.*

Jícama (HEE-kah-mah) — A crisp, sweet, white root vegetable shaped somewhat like a turnip and covered with a brown skin. They range from small to very large. They are peeled, sliced and eaten raw.

Masa (MAH-sah) — Corn dough used for *tortillas, tamales* and other dishes. To make *masa,* dried corn kernels are cooked with calcium oxide, or lime, until the skins loosen. When the skins are removed, the corn is called *nixtamal* which is then ground to make masa. *Instant masa* is dried corn flour. It is mixed with water to make regular *masa.*

Mole (MOH-lay) — Highly flavored sauce made from a paste of *chiles,* chocolate and other ingredients. The paste is available in stores selling Mexican foods.

Nopales (noh-PAH-lays) or Nopalitos (noh-pah-LEE-tohs) — Small pads or leaves of the prickly pear cactus. They should be handled very carefully as the needles are painfully sharp and must be removed before using.

Pepitas (peh-PEE-tahs) — Hulled unsalted pumpkin seeds or squash seeds. They are salted and served as a snack, ground for sauces and sometimes used to make candy. Look for them in health food stores.

Piloncillo (pee-lon-SEE-yoh) — Unrefined brown sugar in the form of hard cones. The cones come in a variety of sizes. It is also called *panocha.* Dark brown sugar is a good substitute.

Plátanos (PLAH-tan-ohs) — Bananas. Mexico grows many varieties which differ in size, color and flavor.

Queso Fresco (KAY-soh FRES-coh) — Soft, white, crumbly cheese made from cow's milk. It is used in cooking or sprinkled over foods as a garnish. It is produced in Mexico as well as in areas that specialize in Mexican food. Other commonly used cheeses are Monterey Jack cheese and Cheddar cheese.

Rajas de Chiles (RAH-hass day CHEE-lays) — Strips of peeled roasted green chiles. Used in cooking.

Recado Colorado (ray-KAH-doh cohl-or-AH-doh) — A paste of *achiote,* see above, and seasonings such as pepper, cloves, cumin, garlic, oregano, salt and vinegar. Used extensively in Yucatan, it is also available in some Mexican markets outside the country. It may be called *adobo de achiote, achiote condimentado* or *recado rojo.*

Tamarindo (tah-mar-EEN-doh) — Fruit of the tamarind tree. It comes in brown pods with the pulp clinging to large seeds inside. It is also used in Indian and Southeast Asian cooking.

Tomatillos (toh-mah-TEE-yohs) — Small, firm green tomatoes. They are covered with a paper-like husk which is removed before they are cooked. *Tomatillos* may be as small as a marble or as large as a lime. Their distinctive acid flavor makes them excellent for sauces. They are available in many areas fresh or canned.

Tortillas (tor-TEE-yahs) — Flat bread made of corn flour or white flour. Considered the national bread of Mexico, they are used to make *enchiladas, tacos, burritos, totopos, quesadillas* and other Mexican foods.

Yerba Buena (YER-bah BWAY-nah) — Spearmint. It is widely used in Mexican cooking. Plain mint may be substituted but the flavor is slightly different.

CHILES

The most characteristic seasoning in Mexican cuisine is the *chile*. Fresh or dried, mild or hot, *chiles* appear in a multitude of dishes from the intricately spiced *Mole Poblano* (*Mole* Puebla-Style), page 116, to *Chile con Queso* (*Chile* with Cheese), page 24, a simple party dip.

The use of a particular *chile* in certain Mexican dishes is traditional. However, all *chiles* do not grow in any one region so cooks use whatever *chiles* are available in their area. A different *chile* may change the flavor of the dish only slightly. Most of us cannot detect these subtle flavor differences. As you become acquainted with *chiles* and the flavor and amount of heat each contributes, you will be able to substitute one *chile* for another, or one form of *chile* for another, depending on what you have available.

If you can't buy fresh *chiles*, use canned *chiles*. If poblano *chiles* are not available, use fresh or canned California *chiles*. Substitute *jalapeños* for *serranos* and vice versa. And if no hot *chiles* are available, use crushed dried *chiles*, ground red pepper or hot pepper sauce.

Substitute *chili* powder for whole dried *chiles* in dishes in which the *chiles* are pureed, allowing about one tablespoon of powder for each large *chile*. Use pure ground *chile*, if it's available, rather than the powders containing additional seasonings.

The following information will help you decide which available *chiles* are best for the dish you want to prepare.

California or Anaheim—Mild, long green *chiles* are named for the area near Los Angeles where they were once cultivated. You can buy them canned—whole or chopped. They are marketed fresh in some areas.

Jalapeño—Small, hot *jalapeño chiles* are named for Jalapa, the capital of Veracruz. They are widely distributed fresh, canned or pickled.

Serrano—Smaller and slimmer than *jalapeño chiles* and very hot, *serrano chiles* are available canned and sometimes fresh.

Poblano, Ancho or Pasilla—Fresh *chiles* include mild to medium hot, plump, dark green *poblano chiles*, also called *ancho* or *pasilla chiles*. They are ideal for stuffing with cheese or meat mixtures.

Güero—Not widely available, small hot *güero chiles* can be recognized by their pale yellow color. They are sometimes called *wax chiles*.

BEAT THE HEAT

A popular misconception about *chiles* is that the hottest part is the seeds. The heat actually comes from a substance called *capsaicin* in the veins. Anything touching *capsaicin*, such as your fingers, may be irritated.

CAUTION

After handling *chiles*, do not touch your face. *Capsaicin* stings sensitive areas such as eyes and lips If you're processing a large quantity of *chiles*, or if you have sensitive skin, wear rubber gloves, available at drug stores.

Chiles are unpredictable. A *chile* from a variety that is normally mild may possess extreme heat. As a precaution, sample mild California and *poblano chiles* before adding them to other foods. If they are hotter than you wish, reduce the quantity used. Some Mexican cooks reduce the heat in *chiles* by soaking peeled roasted *chiles* in salted water for several hours. Then they rinse the *chiles* thoroughly before using them. Another way to maintain the flavor and appearance of the *chile*, while reducing the heat, is to substitute sweet green pepper for half the amount of *chile* called for in the recipe.

KNOW YOUR CHILES

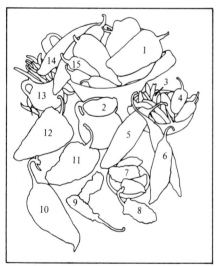

1 Fresh Poblano Chiles
2 Canned California Chile
3 Serrano Chiles
4 Jalapeño Chiles
5 New Mexico Chile
6 Guajillo Chiles
7 Canned Chipotle Chiles
8 Dried Chipotle Chile
9 Pasilla Negro Chile
10 Dried California Chile
11 Dried Ancho Chile
12 Mulato Chile
13 Dried Japonés Chiles
14 Fresh California Chiles
15 Güero Chiles

Blister fresh chiles in a broiler, turning as needed.

Or, toast them on a rack over a stove-top burner until blistered.

How To Roast & Peel Chiles

Or, deep-fry fresh chiles in hot oil until blistered.

Then place hot chiles in a plastic bag to steam. When cooled, pull off loosened peel.

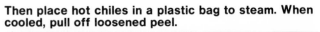

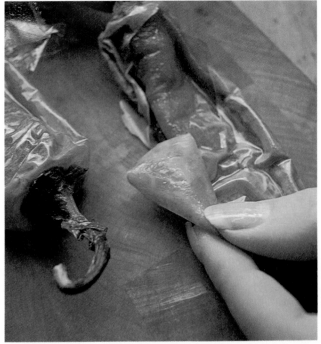

HOW TO PEEL FRESH CHILES

Before *chiles* can be peeled, their skins must be loosened. Do this by broiling, grilling or frying.

Broiling—Place *chiles* on a baking sheet in the broiler 3 to 4 inches from the heat. Broil until they are blistered on all sides, turning often with tongs. Remove *chiles* and place them in a plastic bag or brown paper bag. Let them steam in the bag for 10 to 15 minutes, then strip off the peel with your fingers or the tip of a knife.

Grilling—Place a wire rack over your stove burner. Place the *chiles* on the rack and cook until they are blistered all over, turning frequently. Place them in a plastic bag or brown paper bag to steam for 10 to 15 minutes before peeling.

Frying—Fry *chiles* in hot oil in a saucepan or skillet until pale blisters appear on all sides. Drain, cool them slightly and peel. **Use extreme caution because the spattering hot oil can cause severe burns.**

USE & STORAGE

To use a *chile* whole, cut a small slit in one side and carefully rinse it under running cold water to remove the seeds.

You can freeze peeled *chiles*. If you plan to use only one or two at a time, wrap them individually in plastic wrap, then place them in a plastic bag, seal and freeze. To use *chiles* in bulk, pack them unwrapped in freezer cartons. You can also freeze *chiles* that are blistered but unpeeled. They peel easily when thawed.

Dried Chiles

In Mexico, the most frequently used dried *chiles* are *ancho*, *mulato* and *pasilla chiles*. They are not markedly hot. If you're looking for a fiery dried *chile*, *pico de pájaro*, *arbol*, *tepín*, *serrano*, *cascabel*, *guajillos* and *japonés chiles* add more fire than most people can take! *Chipotle chiles* have a distinctive smoky flavor. They can be bought dried or canned in a marinade called *adobo*. Packages of dried California and New Mexico *chiles* look alike, but New Mexico *chiles* are hotter than the California variety.

HOW TO PREPARE DRIED CHILES

For most dishes, dried *chiles* must be soaked until they are soft and then pureed. To soften dried *chiles*, place them in a saucepan, cover with water and bring to a boil. Remove the saucepan from the heat and let the *chiles* soak in the hot water until softened. The papery peel may remain somewhat stiff, but the pulp will become tender. To puree, remove the stems and seeds. Process the *chiles* in a blender or food processor with just enough liquid to make a paste. Press the pureed *chiles* through a sieve to remove any bits of peel, then use the puree as directed.

How To Prepare Dried Chiles

Soak chiles in water until softened and pliable.

Puree soaked chiles in a blender. Press through a sieve.

9

Bebidas
Drinks

Mexico is a wonderful place to be thirsty. When the brilliant sun makes you long for a cooling drink, there's a multitude of choices. Markets and snack stands display huge jars filled with sparkling fruit drinks called *aguas frescas*, or cool waters. One of the most popular is orange juice made from Mexico's naturally sweet oranges. Try a *licuado*, made by blending bananas, papayas, strawberries or other fruits with milk, ice and sugar. The version here is *Licuado de Fresas* (Whipped Strawberry Drink).

Veracruz, Oaxaca and Chiapas are the important coffee-producing states, but wherever you are in Mexico, you must start the day with a cup of smooth, rich coffee. Many mornings I have awakened in my hotel room in Veracruz to the sounds from the nearby Gran Café de la Parroquia. Customers clink metal spoons against heavy glasses to summon an apron-clad man who carries a kettle in each hand. He pours a little coffee into a customer's glass from one kettle and fills it with hot milk from the other. Then the customer stirs in sugar and drinks unsurpassed coffee!

Mexican hot chocolate is traditionally made of chocolate blended with sugar, cinnamon and sometimes ground almonds. I have an old recipe describing how toasted cacao beans are ground with sugar and cinnamon on the slanted grinding stone, or *metate*. Fire under the *metate* melts the mixture to a paste that is molded into tablets, then dried. To make a substitute for Mexican chocolate tablets, see page 13. Hot chocolate is beaten with a *molinillo* until frothy. The *molinillo* is a carved wooden beater with loose rings that whirl through the chocolate as you spin the handle back and forth between your palms, page 19.

Atole is a hot, thick gruel of *masa*, or corn dough, diluted with water or milk. It may be plain or sweetened. When flavored with chocolate, it is called *champurrado*. *Atole de Francisco Morales* (Francisco Morales' *Atole*) and *Champurrado de María* (Maria's *Champurrado*) are included here.

Mexico has excellent beers, wines, brandies, rums and liqueurs. Kahlúa, the country's famous coffee liqueur, is delicious poured over ice cream or served as an after-dinner drink.

COCKTAIL BUFFET

Margarita Photo on page 11.
Margarita

Mexico's classic cocktail.

1 lime wedge
Salt
2 oz. tequila

3/4 oz. Triple Sec
1 tablespoon lime juice
Ice cubes

Rub rim of a glass with lime wedge, then swirl in salt to coat rim. Combine remaining ingredients in a cocktail shaker. Shake vigorously, then strain into prepared glass. Makes 1 serving.

Variations

Margarita de Granada (Pomegranate Margarita): Shake 1 teaspoon pomegranate seeds with mixture in cocktail shaker.
Margarita de Naranja (Orange Margarita): Omit Triple Sec. Add 2 tablespoons orange juice and 2 teaspoons Simple Syrup, page 21, to ingredients in cocktail shaker. Shake thoroughly.

Tijuana Tequila del Sol
Tequila Sunrise

This Tequila Sunrise has more flavor than most versions.

1-1/2 oz. tequila
2 teaspoons lime juice
2 teaspoons grenadine

1/4 cup strained orange juice (2 oz.)
Ice cubes

Combine tequila, lime juice, grenadine and orange juice in cocktail glass and stir. Add ice cubes. Makes 1 serving.

Tequila Daiquiri
Tequila Daiquiri

The variation is from Leon, Guanajuato.

1-1/2 oz. tequila
1-1/2 teaspoons lime juice

1 teaspoon sugar
Ice cubes

Combine tequila, lime juice and sugar with ice cubes in a cocktail shaker. Shake thoroughly and pour into a cocktail glass. Makes 1 serving.

Variation

Mulata (Tawny Daiquiri): Substitute gold rum for the tequila. Increase the lime juice to 1 tablespoon. Blend all ingredients thoroughly in a blender. Serve in a cocktail glass.

On the preceding page, from top to bottom: Margarita de Granada (Pomegranate Margarita), Margarita de Naranja (Orange Margarita), and a plain Margarita.

Ponche de Granada
Pomegranate Punch

A delightful aperitif to stimulate your appetite, or a soothing after-dinner drink.

4 large pomegranates
8 oz. gold tequila
1/2 cup sugar

1/4 cup water
1 cinnamon stick

Cut pomegranates in half. Peel back skins and remove seeds with your fingers or a spoon. Place seeds in food processor or blender. Grind until pulp is pureed and juice extracted. Turn into a sieve over a bowl. Press pulp with back of spoon to extract all juice. Discard seeds. Strain juice through a fine sieve, then through a fine cloth or paper coffee filter to remove bits of pulp. There should be about 2 cups juice. In a medium bowl, combine pomegranate juice and tequila. Place sugar and water in a saucepan and heat until sugar is dissolved and syrup is clear. Add syrup to juice mixture. Pour into a sterilized 1-quart jar. Add cinnamon stick. Seal and let stand in a dark place 1 month. To serve, strain mixture and serve as an aperitif or an after-dinner drink. Makes about 3-1/3 cups.

Sangrita Guadalajara
Sangrita Guadalajara-Style

Serve this sweet and spicy-hot fruit drink beside another liqueur glass of straight tequila.

1 cup orange juice
2 tablespoons plus 2 teaspoons lime
  juice
4 teaspoons grenadine

1/4 teaspoon freshly ground pepper
Salt
1/2 teaspoon hot pepper sauce, or to
  taste

In a small pitcher, combine orange juice, lime juice, grenadine, pepper, salt to taste and enough hot pepper sauce to give a decidedly spicy taste. Serve in shot glasses or liqueur glasses as an accompaniment to tequila. Makes 1-1/3 cups.

MEXICAN SPICED CHOCOLATE

Mexicans use tablets of spiced chocolate to make beverages and in cooking. For the equivalent of one 3-ounce tablet of Mexican chocolate, use 3 ounces of semisweet chocolate, 2 tablespoons of sugar, 1/4 teaspoon of vanilla extract and 1/2 teaspoon of cinnamon.

Sangrita de Tomate
Tomato Sangrita

To make a Bloody Mary, follow the instructions in the variation.

4 small tomatoes, peeled, seeded (1 lb.)
1/2 cup orange juice
3 tablespoons chopped onion
1 serrano chile or other small hot
  chile, seeded

1 tablespoon lime juice
2 teaspoons sugar
1/4 teaspoon salt

Combine tomatoes, orange juice, onion, chile, lime juice, sugar and salt in a blender. Blend until pureed. Add more salt if needed. Serve in shot or liqueur glasses as an accompaniment to tequila. Makes 2 cups.

Variation

Sangrita Maria (Bloody Mary): Pour 3 ounces Sangrita de Tomate into a cocktail glass. Stir in 1 ounce vodka. Add ice cubes. Squeeze juice from a lime wedge into sangrita mixture then drop lime wedge into mixture. Makes 1 serving.

Licór de Café
Coffee Liqueur

For a more authentic Kahlúa flavor, use Mexican instant coffee granules.

1/4 cup Mexican Nescafe or other
  instant coffee granules
2 cups sugar

1 cup boiling water
1-2/3 cups brandy
1 small vanilla bean

Sterilize a 1-quart canning jar and lid according to manufacturer's instructions. Place coffee granules and sugar in blender. Add boiling water and brandy. Blend at low to medium speed 5 to 10 minutes turning blender off occasionally. If blender begins to overflow, reduce speed. Pour into sterilized jar. Add vanilla bean. Cover tightly with sterilized lid. Let stand in a cool dark place 4 to 6 weeks. Remove vanilla bean. Makes 1 quart.

Cazuela
Casserole Cocktail

It takes a big thirst to handle this enormous drink.

1 orange, halved
1/2 small grapefruit
2 to 3 oz. vodka
1/2 cup Squirt

6 tablespoons strained orange juice
5 or 6 ice cubes
Few grains coarse salt

Squeeze juice from half of orange into a shallow 4 to 5-cup casserole or large brandy snifter. Cut 2 thin slices from remaining orange half; set aside. Reserve remaining orange for another use. Squeeze juice from grapefruit into casserole. Add vodka, Squirt, orange juice and ice cubes. Sprinkle with salt; stir. Float orange slices on top of mixture. Serve with a straw. Makes 1 serving.

Mexican Sling
Mexican Sling

If you're in the mood for a tall, cool, exotic drink, try this.

3/4 cup Agua de Jamaica, page 17
1-1/2 to 2 oz. vodka
1 tablespoon lime juice
1-1/2 teaspoons grenadine

3 or 4 ice cubes
1/2 orange slice
1 maraschino cherry
Mint sprigs

Prepare Agua de Jamaica. In a tall glass, combine vodka, lime juice, grenadine and Agua de Jamaica. Add ice cubes; stir. Spear orange slice and cherry on a long cocktail pick. Place pick in glass. Garnish glass with mint sprigs. Makes 1 serving.

Kahlúa Alejandro
Kahlúa Alexander

Smooth, cool and not too sweet. Besito, the dessert variation, is fun to watch.

1 oz. Kahlúa
1 oz. gin

2 tablespoons whipping cream
3 or 4 ice cubes

Combine Kahlúa, gin and cream in a cocktail shaker with ice cubes. Shake vigorously. Strain into a stemmed cocktail glass. Makes 1 serving.

Variation

Besito (Kiss): Fill a liqueur glass half full with Kahlúa. Spoon about 2 teaspoons evaporated milk on top. The Kahlua will boil up into the milk.

Café Mexicano
Mexican Coffee

A wonderful, warming drink for frosty weather.

1 oz. Kahlúa
1/2 oz. brandy
1 teaspoon chocolate syrup

Dash ground cinnamon
Hot coffee
Sweetened whipped cream

Place Kahlúa, brandy, chocolate syrup and cinnamon in a coffee cup or mug. Fill with hot coffee. Stir to blend. Top with sweetened whipped cream. Makes 1 serving.

Rompope
Rum Eggnog

Serve in liqueur glasses as an after-dinner drink or make Mousse de Rompope, page 182.

3 cups milk
1-1/2 cups sugar
6 egg yolks

1/4 teaspoon vanilla extract
6 oz. rum

Combine milk and sugar in a large saucepan. Stir constantly over medium heat until mixture boils. Continue stirring until mixture is reduced to 2-1/2 cups, about 30 minutes. Remove from heat; cool. In a small bowl, beat egg yolks until light and lemon-colored. Beat into cooled milk mixture. Return to heat. Stirring constantly, bring to boiling point. Do not boil. Remove from heat; stir in vanilla. Cool about 10 minutes. Beat in rum. Pour into a 1-quart jar. Cover and chill before serving or store in refrigerator. Makes about 3-1/3 cups.

How To Make Rompope

Boil milk and sugar until slightly thickened.

Add egg yolks, vanilla and rum, then chill and serve.

Sangría **Photo on page 25.**
Sangria

Mexico's wine cooler is the perfect beverage for spicy food and a hot climate.

1/3 cup Simple Syrup, page 21	1 orange, thinly sliced
1 fifth dry red wine, chilled	Juice of 1 orange
2 oz. brandy	1 cup club soda, chilled
1 lime, thinly sliced	Ice cubes
1 lemon, thinly sliced	

Prepare Simple Syrup. Combine wine, brandy, syrup, lime slices, lemon slices and orange slices and orange juice in a large pitcher. Refrigerate no longer than 1 hour or peels will make drink taste bitter. To serve, stir in club soda and pour over ice cubes in tall glasses or large wine glasses. Add a few of the fruit slices to each glass. Makes 6 servings.

Variations

Sangría con Jugos (Citrus Sangria): Stir 1 quart water and 1 cup sugar in a large pitcher until sugar is dissolved. Add 16 ounces dry red wine, 1 cup orange juice and 1/2 cup lime juice. Refrigerate 1 hour. Serve over ice cubes in tumblers or large wine glasses. Makes 8 to 10 servings.

Sangría Preparada (Sangria Collins): Stir 2 tablespoons lime juice, 1 ounce gin and 5 teaspoons sugar in a tall glass until sugar is dissolved. Stir in 3 ounces club soda. Add 3 or 4 ice cubes. Tilt glass and carefully pour in 2 ounces dry red wine to form a separate layer on top. Serve with a straw. Stir before drinking. Makes 1 serving.

Sangría de Jamaica (Jamaica Sangria): Combine 1/2 cup Agua de Jamaica, below, 4 ounces dry red wine and 1/4 cup orange juice in a tall glass. Add 3 or 4 ice cubes; stir. Makes 1 serving.

Agua de Jamaica
Jamaica Flower Water

You see big jars of this bright red drink, pronounced ha-MIKE-a, in Mexican marketplaces.

1/2 cup loosely packed dried red jamaica flowers	1/2 cup sugar
4 cups water	2 tablespoons lime juice

Rinse jamaica flowers; drain. Place in a saucepan with 2 cups water. Bring to a boil. Remove from heat and let stand until cooled and flowers are no longer red, 1 to 2 hours. Strain liquid into a pitcher. Discard flowers. Add remaining 2 cups water. Stir in sugar until dissolved. Stir in lime juice. Chill. Makes 4 servings.

Agua de Tamarindo
Tamarind Water

Fruit of the tamarind tree has an acidic flavor which is refreshing in hot weather.

8 tamarind pods
1 qt. water

5 to 6 tablespoons sugar
Ice cubes

Peel tamarind pods. Place peeled pods in a deep bowl; add water. Squeeze tamarind pods until water becomes amber-colored and flavor is extracted. Strain into a pitcher; discard seeds. Stir in sugar to taste. Add ice cubes. Makes 4 servings.

Licuado de Fresas
Whipped Strawberry Drink

This is typical of the frothy fruit drinks sold at juice shops in Mexico.

10 medium strawberries, washed, hulled
3/4 cup cold milk

2 tablespoons sugar

Combine strawberries, milk and sugar in blender. Process until strawberries are pureed and drink is frothy. Pour into a tall glass. Makes 1 serving.

Variation

Atole de Fresas (Strawberry Atole): Stir 1 tablespoon cornstarch into 1/4 cup cold water. Add to strawberry mixture in blender. Process until frothy. Pour into a small saucepan over medium heat. Cook and stir until mixture comes to a boil and thickens. Serve hot. Makes 2 servings.

If your supermarket doesn't have ingredients you need for a recipe, ask the manager to place an order. If no one asks for a product, the store manager doesn't know it's in demand.

Chocolate Mexicano

Mexican Chocolate

For the best flavor, use the special chocolate produced in Mexico.

1 circular tablet Mexican spiced
   chocolate (3 oz.) or 3 oz. semisweet
   chocolate, 2 tablespoons sugar,
   1/2 teaspoon cinnamon and
   1/4 teaspoon vanilla extract

3 cups milk

Place chocolate tablet or semisweet chocolate with flavorings and milk in a saucepan. Bring to a boil. When chocolate has softened, beat mixture with a molinillo or a rotary beater until blended and mixture stops boiling. Bring to a boil again and beat well over heat. Bring to a boil a third time and beat over heat to produce as much foam as possible. Pour into cups and serve immediately. Makes 4 servings.

Variation

Each circle of Mexican chocolate is divided into 8 triangles. For an individual serving of chocolate, melt 2 triangles with 3/4 cup milk and beat as directed.

How To Make
Chocolate Mexicano

Mexican chocolate comes in various shapes. The wooden *molinillo* is used to beat the chocolate.

Roll the molinillo between your palms beating the milk and chocolate until frothy.

Champurrado de María
Maria's Champurrado

Champurrado is similar to atole but it contains chocolate. See the variation below.

4 cups water
1 large cinnamon stick
1 cup instant masa
1-1/4 cups water
1/2 circular tablet Mexican spiced chocolate
  (1-1/2 oz.) or 1-1/2 oz. semisweet
  chocolate plus 1 tablespoon sugar,
  pinch of cinnamon and
  3 or 4 drops vanilla extract

1 cup firmly packed brown sugar
1 or 2 whole cloves
1 (13-oz.) can evaporated milk

Combine 4 cups water and cinnamon stick in a large saucepan over medium-high heat. Bring to a boil. Remove from heat. Cover and let stand 1 hour. Remove cinnamon stick. Gradually blend instant masa into 1-1/4 cups water until smooth. Strain masa through a sieve into cinnamon water. Add brown sugar, chocolate tablet or chocolate with flavorings, cloves and brown sugar. Bring to a boil over medium heat, stirring constantly. When mixture has thickened, add milk. Cook and stir until hot. Add water or milk for a thinner drink. Makes 6 to 8 servings.

Variations

To use fresh masa, omit 1/2 cup of the water added to instant masa. Blend fresh masa with 3/4 cup water until smooth. Proceed as directed above.

Atole de Francisco Morales (Francisco Morales' Atole): Combine 6 cups water and 2 cinnamon sticks in a large saucepan over medium-high heat. Bring to a boil. Remove from heat and let stand until water is a cinnamon-brown color, about 1 hour. Remove cinnamon sticks. Stir 1 cup instant masa into 1/2 cup water. Stir masa mixture and sugar into cinnamon-water until blended. Cook and stir over medium heat until mixture boils and thickens. Serve immediately. Makes 6 to 8 servings.

Café de Olla
Clay Pot Coffee

Spicy sweet coffee is traditionally served in a pottery mug.

6 cups water
1/4 lb. piloncillo or 1/2 cup firmly
  packed dark brown sugar

2 cinnamon sticks
4 whole cloves
1/2 cup ground coffee

In a large saucepan over high heat, bring water, piloncillo or brown sugar, cinnamon sticks and cloves to a boil; lower heat. Cover and simmer 15 minutes. Stir in coffee. Return to a boil for 1 minute. Remove from heat and let stand covered 1 minute. Strain and serve. Makes 6 servings.

Variation

Café al Instante (Instant Coffee): Omit coffee. Strain mixture and keep hot or prepare in advance and reheat. Place 1 heaping teaspoon instant coffee in each coffee cup or mug. Stir in hot spiced water.

Agua de Limón
Limeade

Fresh limeade is often served with Mexican meals.

3/4 cup lime juice
1/2 cup sugar

6 cups water
Ice

Combine lime juice and sugar in a large pitcher. Add water. Stir until sugar is dissolved. Serve with ice. Makes 6 servings.

Agua de Naranja
Orangeade

Orange juice becomes more thirst-quenching when diluted with water.

2 cups orange juice (7 to 10 oranges)
4-1/2 cups water

About 1/2 cup sugar
Ice

Combine orange juice and water in a large pitcher. Stir in sugar until dissolved, adjusting the amount according to the sweetness of the oranges. Serve with ice. Makes 6 servings.

SIMPLE SYRUP

Here's a simple syrup you can use to sweeten drinks such as Sangria, page 17.

Combine 1 cup sugar and 1 cup water in a small saucepan. Bring to a boil and cook until the sugar is dissolved and the mixture is clear. Pour the syrup into a container with a tight-fitting lid. Store it in the refrigerator up to 3 weeks.

Aperitivos y Botanas
Appetizers & Snacks

Appetizers in Mexico are called *entremeses,* *botanas, aperitivos* or *bocadillos.* They may be as simple as roasted peanuts or salted squash seeds, called *pepitas.* So many roasted peanuts are consumed in Mexico that great mounds of them are heaped for sale in some markets.

Miniature versions of Mexican snacks can be sensational appetizers. Serve *Taquitos* (Little *Tacos*) cut in half with *Guacamole* (Avocado Sauce), page 40, as a dip. Or bring out a big platter of *Tostaditas* (Cocktail *Tostadas*).

Corn chips, or *totopos,* are made by cutting corn *tortillas* into wedges and deep-frying them until crisp. The thinner the *tortillas,* the crisper the *totopos.* Serve them as scoops for *guacamole* and other dips. Or, top them with cheese and *chiles* and put them under the broiler to melt the cheese. *Totopos* can also be dipped into any of the salsas on pages 32 to 40. These are called *Nachos* (Cheese & *Chile* Corn Chips).

Jícama, a crisp, sweet vegetable is refreshing on a hot day. Street vendors sell it with carved cucumbers, mangos on sticks and other fruits and vegetables. When you buy them, the vendor sprinkles your purchase generously with lime juice and chili powder. If you want to avoid calories, use *jícama* sticks or other crisp vegetables instead of corn chips as dippers with *guacamole.*

Botana de Aguacate (Avocado Appetizer), page 56, is a refreshing salad you can also serve as an appetizer.

Ceviche de Alberto (Alberto's Marinated Fish), page 125, is a typical west coast appetizer of raw marinated fish. Don't dismiss *ceviche* until you've tried it. People who don't usually like fish go out of their way to eat in a restaurant serving *ceviche.*

MIDNIGHT SUPPER

Tostaditas   Photo on page 25.
Cocktail Tostadas

Use a 3-inch cookie cutter to cut small corn tortillas from larger ones, or make your own, page 74.

1-1/2 cups Guacamole, page 40
Oil for frying
20 (3-inch) corn tortillas
1/4 lb. chorizo
1/2 lb. ground beef
1 cup canned or homemade refried
  beans, heated

2 large tomatoes, diced (3/4 lb.)
Finely shredded lettuce
Grated Parmesan cheese
Sliced pickled jalapeño chiles,
  if desired

Prepare Guacamole; set aside. Pour oil 1 to 2 inches deep in a medium saucepan. Heat oil to 365°F (185°C). Fry tortillas in hot oil until crisp, turning once. Drain on paper towels. If not using immediately, store in an airtight container. Remove casing from chorizo. Fry in a large skillet until browned and crumbly. Push to one side and add beef. Cook and stir until beef is browned and crumbly. Mix meats in skillet. Spread each cooked tortilla with about 2 teaspoons refried beans, then about 1 tablespoon meat mixture. Add a few pieces of tomato, a layer of lettuce and a mound of guacamole. Sprinkle generously with cheese. Garnish with a jalapeño chile slice, if desired. Place a small piece of tomato in center. Makes 20 appetizers.

Quesadillas
Cheese Turnovers

Fill these golden brown turnovers with cheese, meat or beans.

1 cup instant masa
1/2 cup all-purpose flour
1/2 teaspoon baking powder
1/4 teaspoon salt
1/2 cup water
1/4 cup milk

8 oz. Monterey Jack cheese, finely
  shredded (2 cups)
Canned chopped green chiles or
  epazote to taste
Oil for frying

Combine instant masa, flour, baking powder and salt in a medium bowl. Blend in water. Add milk; stir well. Knead to make a smooth dough. Line bottom of tortilla press with plastic wrap. Divide dough into quarters. Divide each quarter into 4 equal parts, making 16 equal pieces in all. Work with 1 piece of dough at a time, keeping remainder covered in bowl. Shape each piece of dough into a ball. Place on tortilla press. Place another piece of plastic wrap on top of dough. Press with the palm of your hand to flatten ball slightly. Close tortilla press firmly and then open. Tortilla should be about 4-1/2 inches in diameter. Remove plastic wrap from both sides of tortilla. If necessary, loosen tortilla with a spatula. Place tortillas on a flat surface. Place a spoonful of cheese off-center on each tortilla. Press cheese down and top with chile or epazote to taste. Fold tortilla in half. Press edges together with your fingers. Turn edges and press to seal securely. Press edges with a fork or crimp to make a decorative edge. Keep uncooked quesadillas covered with a cloth towel to prevent them from drying out. Pour oil about 1 inch deep into a heavy skillet. Heat to 360°F (185°C). Fry a few quesadillas at a time in hot oil until browned on each side. Drain on paper towels. Serve hot. Makes 16 appetizers.

Chile con Queso

Chile with Cheese

A terrific party dip for tortilla chips. Keep it hot in a chafing dish or other warmer.

2 tablespoons vegetable oil
1 cup chopped onions
2 small garlic cloves, minced
4 fresh California chiles, roasted,
   peeled, chopped or 1 (4-oz.) can
   chopped green chiles
1 to 2 jalapeño, chiles or
   other small hot chiles, roasted,
   peeled, chopped

1 (8-oz.) can stewed tomatoes
8 oz. Monterey Jack cheese, shredded
   (2 cups)
8 oz. Longhorn cheese, shredded
   (2 cups)
1 cup dairy sour cream

Heat oil in a large saucepan. Add onions and garlic. Cook until tender, but not browned. Add chiles and tomatoes, breaking up tomatoes with a spoon. Lower heat. Add cheeses and cook until melted. Stir in sour cream. Cook just until heated; do not boil. Makes 4 cups of dip.

Botana de Frijol

Bean Dip

This spicy bean dip was created by Flor Silvestre, one of Mexico's leading singers.

1 cup dried pinto beans
Hot water for soaking
1/2 cup chopped onion
1 large garlic clove, pressed
1/2 teaspoon ground cumin
1-1/2 tablespoons bacon drippings
   or lard

1-1/2 tablespoons chili powder
1/2 teaspoon salt
1/4 cup butter, softened
2 oz. sharp Cheddar cheese, shredded
   (1/2 cup)
Dash hot pepper sauce, if desired

Cover beans with hot water and let soak overnight. The next day, drain and rinse beans. Cover with fresh hot water and bring to a boil. Add onion, garlic, cumin and bacon drippings or lard. Cover and simmer 2 hours. Add chili powder and 1/2 teaspoon salt. Cover and simmer 2 hours longer or until very tender. There should be only enough water left to keep beans from sticking. If too much water remains, uncover and boil down. Add butter and cheese; stir until melted. Turn into a blender or food processor and process until pureed. Taste and add salt as needed and hot pepper sauce, if desired. If chili powder is spicy, hot pepper sauce will not be needed. Serve hot. If mixture becomes too thick, add water 1 tablespoon at a time. Makes 3 cups of dip.

A tray of Mexican appetizers includes Chile con Queso (Chile with Cheese) surrounded by slices of jícama and Totopos (Corn Chips), page 30. Tostaditas (Cocktail Tostadas), page 23, are on the right of the tray and Sangria, page 17, is top left.

Botana de Chile

Chile Dip

Salt and garlic can be mashed on a piece of wax paper instead of in a bowl.

1 garlic clove
1/2 teaspoon salt
1 (1-lb.) can peeled whole tomatoes
3 slices bacon
2 medium onions, finely chopped
3 California chiles, roasted, peeled,
  chopped, or 6 tablespoons
  canned chopped green chiles

1/2 teaspoon sugar
Hot pepper sauce to taste
4 oz. sharp Cheddar cheese, shredded
  (1 cup)

In a small bowl, mash garlic and salt to a paste. Drain tomatoes, reserving liquid. Chop tomatoes. Slice bacon crosswise and brown in a large skillet over medium heat. Add garlic paste and onions. Cook until onions are golden. Add chopped tomatoes, reserved liquid, chiles and sugar. Stir over medium-low heat 15 minutes. Add hot pepper sauce to taste. Turn into a heated 1-quart casserole and top with cheese. Makes 2 cups of dip.

Botana de Salmón

Salmon Snack

Prepare these snacks ahead and serve them as a part of a cold buffet.

1 (15-1/2-oz.) can pink salmon
6 pimiento-stuffed green olives,
  chopped
2 teaspoons capers
3 green onions, chopped
1 pickled jalapeño chile,
  chopped

1/4 cup mayonnaise
1 tablespoon whipping cream
Freshly ground pepper
Salt
Crackers or toast rounds
Sliced stuffed olives, if desired

Drain and flake salmon. Place in a medium bowl. Add chopped olives, capers, onions and chile. Blend mayonnaise and cream in a small bowl. Stir into salmon mixture. Season with pepper to taste. Refrigerate at least 2 hours to let flavors blend. Taste and add salt if needed. Serve on crackers or toast rounds. Garnish with stuffed olive slices, if desired. Makes 2 cups of spread.

Canapés de Sardinas
Sardine Canapés

Sardines paired with jalapeño chiles make a snappy canapé.

1 tablespoon vegetable oil	1 tablespoon chopped fresh parsley
1/4 medium onion, finely chopped	15 salted crackers
1 garlic clove, minced	2 or 3 pickled jalapeño chiles,
1 (3-3/4-oz.) can sardines, drained	sliced
2 tablespoons dry white wine	

Heat oil in a small skillet. Add onion and garlic. Cook until tender but not browned. Add sardines, wine and parsley, stirring to break up sardines. Cook until heated through. Place teaspoonfuls of mixture on salted crackers. Top each canape with a slice of pickled jalapeño chile. Serve hot. Makes 15 small canapés.

Botana de Jícama
Jícama Snack

A refreshing and low-calorie appetizer or snack.

1 small jícama	Chili powder
Lime juice	Salt

Peel jícama. Using a fluted cutter, cut in 1/2-inch thick slices, then cut each slice into 1/2-inch thick sticks. Serve sticks plain or sprinkle with lime juice and chili powder, adding a little salt, if desired. Makes 2 to 3 servings.

Molletes
Broiled Bean Sandwiches

These open-face bean sandwiches are very popular in Mexico.

6 large French rolls or Bolillos, page 161	About 3/4 cup canned or homemade refried beans
3/4 cup Salsa Fresca, page 33, Salsa Mexicana, page 33, or other salsa	12 oz. Cheddar cheese, shredded (3 cups)

Prepare Bolillos and salsa, if used. For each sandwich, cut a roll or Bolillo in half. Spread each half with refried beans. Top with 1/4 cup cheese. Repeat with remaining rolls or Bolillos. Broil 4 to 5 inches from heat until cheese is melted and bubbly. Serve topped with salsa. Makes 12 servings.

Tostada de Queso
Cheese Crisp

These tortilla-based snacks resemble hot open-face sandwiches.

1 (12-inch) flour tortilla	**2 tablespoons canned or homemade salsa**
4 oz. Monterey Jack or Cheddar Cheese, shredded (1 cup)	

Preheat broiler. Place tortilla on a baking sheet. Sprinkle with cheese and dot with salsa. Broil until cheese is melted and bubbly. Serve at once. To serve, tear apart or cut in wedges with scissors or a sharp knife. Makes 4 servings.

Variations

Brush tortillas with butter. Brown lightly under broiler, then top with cheese and broil to melt cheese. Top with salsa before serving.

Top with chile strips and diced fresh tomatoes before broiling.

Top with Carnitas a la Casera, page 115, before broiling.

Tortas Mercado Central
Central Market Sandwiches

Shred your leftover Sunday roast to make the meat filling.

6 large French rolls or Bolillos, page 161	**Hot melted lard**
1-1/2 to 2 cups filling such as Machaca, page 88; Carnitas a la Casera, page 115; Carne Deshebrada, page 109; Chile Verde a la Fay, page 110; or Bistec Picado, page 105	**About 3/4 cup canned or homemade refried beans, heated**
	1-1/2 cups shredded lettuce
	1 medium tomato, chopped
	1/2 cup chopped onion
	Coarsely chopped fresh cilantro leaves
Canned or homemade salsa	**1 avocado, thinly sliced**
	Dairy sour cream

Prepare Bolillos, if used, desired filling and salsa. Preheat a griddle to 325°F (165°C). For each sandwich, cut a roll or Bolillo in half. Pull out a little of the soft center from each half; and discard. Dip cut surfaces in hot lard or brush with lard. Place cut sides down on preheated griddle and heat until cut sides are flecked with brown. Spread cut side of bottom of roll with refried beans. Top with a generous spoonful of filling, draining meat if there is too much sauce. Top meat with shredded lettuce, then add a little tomato, onion and cilantro. Add salsa to taste. Top with an avocado slice. Spread cut side of top of roll with sour cream and place over filling to make a sandwich. Repeat with remaining ingredients. Serve immediately. Makes 6 servings.

Nachos
Cheese & Chile Corn Chips

Use packaged tortilla or corn chips instead of Totopos if you don't have time to prepare your own.

Totopos, page 30
8 oz. Monterey Jack or Cheddar
cheese, shredded (2 cups)

1/2 cup sliced fresh or canned
jalapeño chiles or hot chile salsa

Prepare Totopos. Preheat broiler. Top each totopo with a mound of cheese and a chile slice or a little hot salsa. Place on a baking sheet and broil until cheese is just melted. Serve at once. Makes about 48 nachos.

Variations

Nachos con Salsa (Cheese & Chile Corn Chips with Sauce): Substitute Salsa Fresca, page 33, for jalapeño chiles or hot chile salsa. Top with a sprinkle of chopped green onions.
Nachos con Frijoles (Cheese & Chile Corn Chips with Beans): Place a spoonful of canned or homemade refried beans on each totopo before adding cheese.

How To Make Nachos

With a scissors or knife cut the tortillas into 8 triangles, then deep-fry until crisp.

Top deep-fried tortilla triangles with yellow cheese and salsa. Broil and top with chopped green onion.

Totopos **Photo on page 25.**
Corn Chips

Use these as dippers for salsas and guacamole or to garnish Frijoles Refritos, page 149.

6 corn tortillas
2 teaspoons salt dissolved in 1/4
cup water

Oil for deep-frying

Using kitchen scissors or a sharp knife, cut tortillas into eight triangles. Brush tortilla triangles on each side with salt water mixture. Tortillas may be cut in advance and let stand uncovered 3 hours or overnight to dry out slightly. The salt water wash may be omitted, if desired. Pour oil 2 to 3 inches deep in a medium saucepan. Heat oil to 365°F (185°C) over medium-high heat. Add tortilla chips a handful at a time and fry until lightly browned and crisp. Drain on paper towels. Store in an airtight container. Makes 48 corn chips.

Queso Fundido
Melted Cheese

Melt cheese in a pottery casserole, then fold it in a tortilla with salsa.

About 1/4 cup Salsa Fresca, page 33, or
other tomato salsa
About 1/4 cup Salsa Verde, page 36

6 corn tortillas cut in half
6 oz. Monterey Jack cheese, thinly sliced

Prepare salsas; set aside. Preheat oven to 400°F (205°C). Wrap tortilla halves in foil. Place cheese in a medium pottery casserole or other baking dish. Do not use a small casserole or cheese layer will be too thick. Bake 8 to 10 minutes, until cheese is melted and bubbly. Bake wrapped tortillas with cheese 5 to 7 minutes until heated through. Pour salsas into separate small bowls. Serve immediately. Spoon cheese from casserole onto a tortilla half. Tear tortilla half into 2 pieces, if desired. Add about 1 tablespoon of each salsa; fold and eat. Makes 4 appetizer servings.

Empanadas de Picadillo
Meat Turnovers

Make these tender meat pies in advance and reheat them for 5 to 10 minutes at 375°F (190°C).

1-1/2 cups Picadillo, page 108
2 cups all-purpose flour
2 teaspoons sugar
1/2 teaspoon salt
2/3 cup shortening

2 tablespoons butter
About 1/4 cup ice water
1 egg, separated
1 teaspoon water
2 teaspoons milk

Prepare Picadillo; set aside. Mix flour, sugar and salt in a medium bowl. Cut in shortening and butter with a pastry blender or 2 knives until mixture is thoroughly mixed with some pea-sized crumbs. Gradually add enough ice water to form a dough that will hold together. Preheat oven to 375°F (190°C). Lightly grease 2 baking sheets. Lightly beat egg white with 1 teaspoon water in a small bowl. Beat egg yolk with milk in another small bowl; set aside. On a lightly floured surface, roll out dough to slightly less than 1/8 inch thick. Cut in circles with a 3- to 3-1/2-inch cutter. Gather scraps together. Roll out and cut into more circles until all dough is used. Place a rounded teaspoonful of Picadillo on each pastry circle. Brush edges with egg white mixture. Fold circles in half and press edges with a fork to seal. Place on baking sheets. When all empanadas are prepared, brush with egg yolk mixture. Bake about 20 minutes or until browned. Place immediately on a rack to cool slightly. Serve warm. Makes about 26 empanadas.

Variation

Empanadas Dulces (Sweet Turnovers): Cut pastry dough into 4- to 5-inch circles. Fill with jam or preserves, guava paste, mincemeat or canned pumpkin pie filling. If desired, sprinkle empanadas with granulated sugar before baking.

Botana de Frutas
Fruit Cup

Spice this fruit cocktail to your taste at the table.

2 cups watermelon pieces
2 cups cantaloupe pieces
1 or 2 limes, cut in wedges

2 tablespoons crushed dried chiles or
  chili powder
Salt

Arrange watermelon and cantaloupe pieces on a platter or in a large bowl. Serve lime wedges and crushed dried chiles or chili powder in separate bowls. Take fruit as desired. Squeeze lime juice over fruit; sprinkle with dried chiles or chili powder and salt to taste. Makes 6 servings.

Salsas
Sauces

Most *salsas*, or sauces, in this section are to be spooned over meats, *tacos*, eggs and beans, spicing them to individual taste. They may also be served as a dip with *totopos*, or corn chips. *Salsa para Enchiladas* (*Enchilada* Sauce) and *Salsa de Chile en Polvo* (Chili Powder Sauce) are poured over *enchiladas* before baking. *Cebollas Yucatecas* (Onions Yucátan-Style) are a relish-like topping adding just the right touch to *Panuchos Mérida* (*Panuchos* Mérida-Style), page 100, and meat dishes.

Cilantro is an herb often used in Mexican cooking. It's the same as fresh coriander or Chinese parsley and is also common in Chinese and Southeast Asian dishes. Dried *cilantro* is sometimes available and may be substituted for fresh. When it is used as a garnish, you must have fresh sprigs or substitute fresh parsley, preferably the flat-leaf variety.

Salsas made with tomatoes are red and are called *salsas rojas*. *Salsas verdes*, or green sauces, acquire their color and distinctive acid flavor from green *tomatillos*. This little tomato-like vegetable, also called *miltomate* and *tomate de cáscara*, is covered with a parchment-like husk and contains many tiny seeds. Fresh *tomatillos* are available in some places but it may be easier to find them canned. One 13-ounce can equals about 3/4 pound of fresh *tomatillos*.

Salsas and *guacamoles* are traditionally ground in a *molcajete*, a bowl-shaped, rough stone mortar with a fat, tapered grinding stone. The broad end of the stone is used for grinding. *Molcajetes* grind easily and rapidly and give a chunky texture rather than the foamy puree made by a blender. If you bring home a *molcajete* from Mexico, be sure to grind some uncooked rice in it first to smooth off loose bits of stone. Otherwise your first *salsa* will be gritty!

To grind *salsa* in your blender, turn it rapidly on and off several times just to chop the ingredients. Don't puree them. An exception to this is American-style *taco* sauce, which is finely ground so it can be poured easily rather than spooned from a bowl.

Many *salsas* improve in flavor after they stand for a few hours. *Guacamole* is an exception. It may turn black in half an hour. Various methods are supposed to prevent blackening, including adding lime juice to the mixture, mashing the avocado with a plastic fork, placing the avocado pit in the mixture, and spreading a thin film of oil or mayonnaise over the surface of the *guacamole*. The only reliable way I have found to keep *guacamole* fresh and green is to make it just before serving.

LATE-NIGHT SNACK

Salsa Mexicana **Photo on page 35.**
Mexican Sauce

This basic sauce goes with many Mexican dishes.

**2 small tomatoes, peeled, chopped
  (1/2 lb.)**
**1 serrano chile, or other small hot
  chile, seeded, chopped**

1/4 cup cilantro leaves, chopped
1/3 cup chopped onion
1/4 teaspoon salt

In a medium bowl, combine tomatoes, chile, cilantro, onion and salt. Serve at room temperature. Makes 1-1/4 cups.

Variation

Omit cilantro leaves and add a dash of lime juice.

Salsa Fresca
Fresh Sauce

Tomatoes will peel easily if immersed in boiling water for 30 seconds, then dipped in cold water.

**4 small tomatoes, peeled, chopped
  (1 lb.)**
1/2 cup finely chopped onion
**1 jalapeño chile, seeded,
  finely chopped**
2 teaspoons olive oil

1 teaspoon vinegar
1 teaspoon lime juice
**1/2 teaspoon dried leaf oregano,
  crushed**
1/2 teaspoon salt

In a medium bowl, combine tomatoes, onion and chile. Add olive oil, vinegar, lime juice, oregano and salt. Mix well. Let sauce stand 2 hours to blend flavors. Serve at room temperature. Makes 2 cups.

Salsa de Chile y Jitomate
Chile & Tomato Sauce

Excellent flavor and not too hot.

**4 small tomatoes, peeled, finely
  chopped (1 lb.)**
**2 California chiles, peeled,
  finely chopped, or 1/3 cup canned
  chopped green chiles**

1/2 jalapeño chile, minced
1/2 medium onion, finely chopped
1/4 cup cilantro leaves, chopped
1 large garlic clove
1/2 teaspoon salt

Combine tomatoes, chiles, onion and cilantro in a medium bowl. Mash garlic with salt to make a paste. Stir garlic paste into tomato mixture. Let sauce stand 2 hours to blend flavors. Serve at room temperature. Makes about 2-1/2 cups.

Salsa Favorita
Favorite Sauce

Phil Villa, who raises chiles in California, says this is his favorite salsa.

6 güero chiles or other small
  hot chiles
1 large or 2 small green peppers
5 medium-large tomatoes, peeled
  (1-1/2 lbs.)

1/2 small onion, finely grated
1/2 garlic clove, pressed
1/2 teaspoon dried leaf oregano,
  crushed
1/4 to 1/2 teaspoon salt

Dice unpeeled chiles, green pepper and tomatoes into 1/4-inch pieces. Drain tomatoes. Combine diced chiles, green pepper and tomatoes with onion, garlic, oregano and salt. Cover and refrigerate overnight before serving. Makes about 4 cups.

Pico de Gallo
Rooster's Beak

This fresh vegetable salsa from Veracruz enhances meats.

2 small tomatoes, diced (1/2 lb.)
1 small onion, chopped
2/3 cup diced cucumber
6 small radishes, diced
1/2 cup loosely packed cilantro
  leaves, coarsely chopped

3 or 4 serrano chiles or other small
  hot chiles, seeded, finely chopped
Juice of 1/2 small lime
Salt

Mix tomatoes, onion, cucumber, radishes, cilantro and chiles. Squeeze lime juice over vegetables. Add salt to taste; stir. Serve immediately or refrigerate. Makes about 2-1/4 cups.

Salsa Picante
Hot Sauce

Make this sauce with pickled chiles—as many as you can take!

2 small tomatoes, peeled (1/2 lb.)
1/4 cup chopped onion
1 garlic clove
1/2 to 1 canned pickled
  jalapeño chile
1 teaspoon vegetable oil

1/2 teaspoon liquid from canned
  pickled jalapeño chiles
1/4 teaspoon dried leaf oregano,
  crushed
1/4 teaspoon salt

Combine tomatoes, onion, garlic and chile in blender or food processor. Blend until pureed. Heat oil in a small saucepan. Add tomato mixture, chile liquid, oregano and salt. Bring to a boil. Cook gently 10 minutes. Remove from heat. Let sauce stand 2 hours. Makes about 3/4 cup.

Garnish and flavor Mexican food with colorful sauces. Salsa Mexicana (Mexican Sauce), page 33, is at the top. Salsa Verde (Green Sauce), page 36, is on the left. Salsa Favorita (Favorite Sauce) is on the right.

34

Salsa Verde **Photo on page 35.**
Green Sauce

Tomatillos give special flavor to this make-ahead sauce.

2 or 4 jalapeño chiles or
  other small hot chiles, roasted,
  peeled
1 lb. fresh tomatillos or 1-3/4 cups
  canned tomatillos

5 cilantro sprigs
1 garlic clove
Salt

Remove stems from chiles; do not remove seeds. Set chiles aside. Remove papery husks from tomatillos. If using fresh tomatillos, place in a medium saucepan. Add cold water to cover. Bring to a boil; drain. If using canned tomatillos, drain. Place chiles, tomatillos, cilantro sprigs and garlic in blender or food processor. Blend until finely ground. Turn into a medium bowl. Cover and refrigerate overnight. Before serving, add salt to taste. Makes 2 cups.

Salsa Picante de Carmen
Carmen's Hot Sauce

For a milder salsa, use 1 or 2 chiles.

4 small tomatoes, peeled (1 lb.)
1 onion, coarsely chopped
1 garlic clove

4 jalapeño chiles, peeled, seeded
2 tablespoons vegetable oil
1/2 teaspoon salt

Cut tomatoes in half and cut out stems. Place in blender or food processor with onion and garlic. Blend just until tomatoes are chopped but not pureed. Add chiles. Blend a few seconds or until chopped. Heat oil in a medium saucepan. Add chile mixture and salt. Bring to a boil; reduce heat. Simmer uncovered 10 minutes. Cool and serve at room temperature. Makes 2 cups.

Salsa de los Machos
Extra-Hot Chile Sauce

Grind the chiles with a mortar and pestle or molcajete. Serve the sauce with Carne Asada, page 106.

9 jalapeño chiles or other
  small hot chiles (about 1/4 lb.)
1 garlic clove

1/4 teaspoon salt
1 tablespoon lime juice

Roast chiles on an ungreased griddle over medium heat until blistered on all sides. Cut off stems but do not peel. Grind chiles with garlic and salt in a mortar or molcajete. Add lime juice and continue grinding until pulverized. Makes about 1/4 cup blazingly hot salsa.

Salsa para Enchiladas

Enchilada Sauce

If dried chiles aren't available, try Salsa de Chile en Polvo, page 39.

8 dried California chiles	1 teaspoon vinegar
Water	3/4 teaspoon salt
1-1/2 tablespoons lard or	1/4 teaspoon dried leaf oregano,
vegetable oil	crushed
1 garlic clove	1/4 teaspoon ground cumin
1 tablespoon all-purpose flour	1/8 teaspoon garlic powder

Wash chiles thoroughly. Place in a large saucepan and cover generously with water. Cover and bring to a boil. Remove from heat and let stand 45 minutes or until softened. Drain chiles, reserving soaking liquid. Pull off stems, slit chiles open and rinse off seeds. Place chiles and 1 cup soaking liquid in blender or food processor. Process until pureed. Turn into a sieve and rub through sieve into bowl to eliminate small bits of peel. Rinse blender with an additional 1 cup soaking liquid and pour over remaining pulp in sieve. Heat lard or oil and garlic in a medium saucepan. When lard or oil is fragrant with garlic, discard garlic clove. Stir in flour until mixture is smooth. Cook about 1 minute. Add pureed chile mixture and remaining ingredients. Bring to a boil; reduce heat. Cook and stir until slightly thickened. Taste and add more salt if needed. Makes about 2-1/3 cups.

Variations

For a hotter sauce, substitute 2 or 3 dried New Mexico chiles for 2 or 3 of the California chiles.

Substitute 1/2 to 1 cup broth for an equal amount of chile soaking liquid.

Substitute 1/2 cup tomato juice or tomato sauce for 1/2 cup of the soaking liquid.

When you have leftover salsas, be sure to store them in the refrigerator. Most sauces improve in flavor after 24 hours.

Salsa de Chile Güero
Güero Chile Sauce

If you do not have a molcajete, use your blender to grind the ingredients.

2 güero chiles or other small
  hot chiles
Boiling water
1 large garlic clove
1/4 teaspoon salt
2 small tomatoes, peeled, cored
  (1/2 lb.)

1/2 cup canned tomato sauce
1/2 cup water
1/2 teaspoon dried leaf oregano,
  crushed

Boil chiles in water to cover 15 minutes. Drain and cool slightly. Remove peel. Discard peel and stems but retain seeds. Place garlic and salt in molcajete and grind until pureed. Add chiles; grind. Add tomatoes one at a time, grinding after each addition. If molcajete becomes too full, scrape contents into a bowl and set aside until all ingredients are ground, then mix well. Stir tomato sauce and 1/2 cup water into ground mixture. Stir in oregano. Let sauce stand 2 hours to blend flavors. Makes 1-1/2 cups.

How To Make
Salsa de Chile Güero

Peel cooked güero chiles. Carefully remove stems but not seeds.

Grind chiles and tomatoes with garlic and salt in a *molcajete* or blender.

Salsa de Jitomate de Elva
Elva's Tomato Sauce

The perfect sauce for those who don't like hot chile.

1 (15-oz.) can tomato sauce
1/2 cup water
1/2 small onion

3/4 teaspoon garlic salt
1/2 teaspoon dried leaf oregano,
   crushed

Pour tomato sauce into a medium saucepan. Pour water into tomato sauce can to dissolve all bits of sauce. Pour water into blender or food processor. Add onion; blend until pureed. Add to tomato sauce. Stir in garlic salt and oregano. Bring to a boil; reduce heat. Simmer gently 15 minutes. Makes 2 cups.

Salsa de Chile en Polvo
Chili Powder Sauce

An easy and mild enchilada sauce.

3 tablespoons vegetable oil
2 tablespoons all-purpose flour
1/4 cup mild, or California red
   chili powder
2 cups beef broth
2 (10-1/2-oz.) cans tomato puree

1/2 teaspoon dried leaf oregano,
   crushed
1/4 teaspoon ground cumin
1/4 teaspoon garlic powder
Salt

Heat oil in a large saucepan. Stir in flour and cook 1 minute. Stir in chili powder. Add beef broth, tomato puree, oregano, cumin and garlic powder. Taste and add salt if needed. Simmer 15 minutes. Makes about 4-2/3 cups of sauce, enough for 12 enchiladas.

Cebollas Yucatecas
Onions Yucatan-Style

Pickled red onions garnish meats and other dishes in Yucatán.

1 medium, red onion
Boiling water
2 tablespoons white vinegar
1 small garlic clove, crushed

1/8 teaspoon dried leaf oregano,
   crushed
4 peppercorns
1/8 teaspoon salt

Peel onion. Cut in half through stem end, then slice thinly. Place in a small saucepan. Pour boiling water over onions and immediately turn into a colander to drain. Return drained onion slices to saucepan. Add vinegar, garlic, oregano, peppercorns and salt. Bring to a boil. Immediately turn into a serving bowl and let stand until cooled, stirring occasionally. Makes about 1-1/2 cups.

Guacamole
Avocado Sauce

Delicious as a dip or as a garnish for other dishes.

2 medium avocados
1 small tomato, chopped
2 tablespoons minced onion

1 teaspoon lime or lemon juice
1/2 teaspoon garlic powder
1/2 teaspoon salt

Peel avocados. Mash with a fork in a medium bowl. Stir in tomato, onion, lime or lemon juice, garlic powder and salt. Serve at once. Makes 6 servings.

Variations

Substitute 1 small garlic clove for garlic powder. Mash garlic with salt to make a paste, then stir into avocado mixture.

Guacamole de María Elena (Maria Elena's Avocado Sauce): Stir together 2 peeled mashed avocados, 1 peeled finely chopped tomato, 1 seeded minced serrano chile or other small hot chile and 1/2 teaspoon salt. Makes about 2 cups.

Guacamole a la Veracruzana (Avocado Sauce Veracruz-Style): Beat together 2 peeled mashed avocados, 1 tablespoon olive oil, 2 teaspoons lime juice and 1/2 teaspoon salt. Stir in 2 tablespoons minced onion and 1 teaspoon minced jalapeño chile or other small hot chile. Makes about 2 cups.

Guacamole del Conquistador (Conquistador Hotel's Avocado Sauce): Stir together 2 peeled mashed avocados, 2 chopped small tomatoes, 4 minced small green onions, 2 seeded minced serrano chiles or other small hot chiles, 2 tablespoons chopped cilantro leaves, 1/2 teaspoon salt and pepper to taste. Makes 2 to 3 cups.

Guacamole con Tomatillos (Avocado Sauce with Tomatillos): Simmer 6 husked tomatillos in 1-inch deep water for 10 minutes. Drain, cool and finely chop. If using canned tomatillos, drain and finely chop. Combine finely chopped tomatillos, 2 peeled mashed large avocados, 2 garlic cloves mashed with 1/2 teaspoon salt, 1/4 cup finely chopped onion, 2 tablespoons chopped cilantro leaves, 1/4 to 1/2 minced small jalapeño chile or other small hot chile and freshly ground pepper to taste. Makes about 3 cups.

Chile powder or Chili powder: The Spanish word is chile (CHEE-lay). In English-speaking countries, chili (CHILL-ee) is the most common usage.

Sopas
Soups

Mexico is justly famous for its soups. They are rich in variety and flavor—a delight to weary travelers in need of a restorative.

Two types of soups are responsible for some confusion among Mexico's visitors: *Sopas aguadas* are *wet soups*, the type covered in these recipes. *Sopas secas* are *dry soups* made with rice, pasta or *tortillas*. *Sopa Seca de Arroz* (Dry Rice Soup) is on page 143. Restaurant menus do not always make this distinction, much to the chagrin of the tourist who asks for a bowl of soothing rice soup and receives a plate of dry rice.

Hearty soups like *Cocido* (Vegetable-Beef Soup), *Pozole Blanco* (White Hominy Soup) and *Menudo* (Tripe Soup) are meals in themselves with *Bolillos* (French Rolls), page 161, or *tortillas* and a salad on the side. *Cocido* is a soup-stew loaded with vegetables, meat and always sporting a chunk or two of corn-on-the-cob.

Pozole can be red with *chile* or clear, as in *Pozole Blanco* (Golden Hominy Soup), a recipe from Guadalajara. This simply seasoned pork, chicken and hominy soup is topped with a bright array of garnishes to give considerable dash and fresh flavor.

Menudo (Tripe Soup) is famous as a hangover remedy. And it really works, says Vivian Flores, who keeps her restaurant in East Los Angeles open after hours on weekends to dispense gallons of this nourishing soup. Its effectiveness is credited to its high protein content.

Caldo de Queso (Cheese Soup) is an extraordinary soup flavored with tomatoes and *chiles*. *Gazpacho a la Guadalajara* (Cold Soup Guadalajara-Style) is a novel version of *gazpacho* including both corn and avocado.

One Mexican soup theme with many variations is shredded chicken in broth. Add lime juice and *tortilla* croutons and you have *Sopa de Lima* (Lime & *Tortilla* Soup). Add vermicelli to make *Sopa de Pollo y Fideos* (Chicken & Vermicelli Soup). Put in herbs and vegetables such as *cilantro*, green onions, avocado and green *chile* for *Caldo Xochitl* (*Xochitl* Chicken Soup). *Xochitl* is a girl's name and an Indian word for flower. *Caldo Tlalpeño* (Chicken Soup from Tlalpan) has many variations. My version is from Tijuana on the Mexico-California border. It contains garbanzo beans, rice and the smoke-flavored *chipotle chile*. Chopped fresh *jalapeño chiles* can be served on the side if the *chipotle chile* doesn't supply enough heat!

Caldo Largo de Veracruz (Fish Soup Veracruz-Style) also contains *chile*. However, most Mexican soups are mildly seasoned and easy on the palate. You season them to taste with hot *salsa* from the table and a squeeze of lime juice.

CINCO DE MAYO PARTY

Cocido
Vegetable-Beef Soup

If you can't find cilantro sprigs to garnish this colorful dish, use parsley sprigs.

3 lbs. beef chuck neck bones
9 cups water
Salt
Arroz Rojo, page 142
1 large potato, peeled, cut in 1-inch
  cubes
1 large carrot, cut in 1/2-inch pieces
2 ears corn, cut in 8 pieces

2 zucchini, cut in thick slices
1 large celery stalk, cut in half
  lengthwise, then in 2-inch
  lengths
Chopped onion
Cilantro sprigs
Lime wedges
Canned or homemade salsa

Place beef bones in a large pot or Dutch oven. Add water and salt to taste. Bring to a boil. Skim foam from surface. Cover loosely and simmer 2 to 2-1/2 hours or until meat is very tender. Let meat cool in broth. Prepare Arroz Rojo; set aside. Remove meat from bones and cut in large chunks; discard bones. Strain broth through a fine sieve. Return meat and broth to pot. Bring to a boil; reduce heat. Add potato and carrot. Cover and simmer about 25 minutes. Add corn and zucchini. Cover and simmer 15 minutes. Add celery. Cover and continue to simmer 5 to 10 minutes or until celery is tender. Taste and add salt if needed. To serve, ladle broth, meat and some of each vegetable into large soup bowls. Top each serving with a generous spoonful of Arroz Rojo, 1 or 2 tablespoons chopped onion and 2 or 3 cilantro sprigs. Serve with lime wedges and salsa. Makes 8 servings.

How To Make Cocido

Remove corn husks. Cut each corn cob into quarters.

Mound Arroz Rojo in center of soup and top with onions and a cilantro sprig.

Caldo de Albóndigas
Meatball Soup

A popular dish at Antonio's Restaurant in Los Angeles.

1 lb. extra-lean ground beef
2 eggs, beaten
1/2 canned pimiento, chopped
1/3 cup loosely packed cilantro
   leaves, chopped
2 garlic cloves, minced
1/2 teaspoon ground cumin
1/2 teaspoon salt

Dash pepper
2 qts. beef broth
1 medium onion, chopped
2 medium carrots, diced
2 medium zucchini, diced
1/3 head cabbage, sliced
Salt

Mix beef, eggs, pimiento, cilantro, garlic, cumin, salt and pepper in a large bowl. Mixture will be very soft. Form into balls about 1 inch in diameter. Heat broth in a large pot or Dutch oven until boiling. Lower meatballs gently into broth a few at a time. Bring to a boil again. Skim foam from surface. Add onion, carrots and zucchini. Bring to a boil; reduce heat. Simmer uncovered 25 minutes. Add cabbage. Cook 5 minutes longer or until all vegetables are tender. Taste and add salt if needed. Makes 8 servings.

Caldo de Queso
Cheese Soup

A prize recipe from Ernesto Navarro of El Nuevo México Cafe in Los Angeles.

2 tablespoons vegetable oil
1 onion, finely chopped
4 green onions, finely chopped
1 garlic clove, minced
4 medium tomatoes peeled, chopped
   (1-1/4 lbs.)
6 peeled fresh California chiles or
   canned chiles, cut in thin strips
1/2 cup loosely packed cilantro
   leaves, coarsely chopped

1 cup water
1 teaspoon salt
Pepper to taste
1 qt. milk
8 oz. Monterey Jack cheese, shredded
   (2 cups)
4 oz. Longhorn cheese, shredded
   (1 cup)
1/4 lb. butter

Heat oil in a large saucepan. Add onion, green onions and garlic. Cook until tender but not browned. Add tomatoes. Cook gently about 15 minutes. Stir in chile strips and cilantro. Add water, salt and pepper to taste. Keep warm. In another large saucepan, combine milk, Monterey Jack and Longhorn cheeses and butter. Stir over medium heat just until cheeses and butter are melted. Add tomato mixture. Stir over medium heat just until mixture comes to boiling point. Do not boil or cheese may curdle. Serve at once. Makes 8 servings.

Sopa de Tortilla Mazatlán

Tortilla Soup Mazatlán-Style

Crumbled toasted chiles add distinctive flavor to this soup.

2 lbs. meaty beef soup bones	1 tablespoon vegetable oil
1 qt. water	1 small onion, cut in half lengthwise,
6 peppercorns	thinly sliced
1 bay leaf	1 garlic clove, minced
1/4 small onion	2 tomatoes, peeled, finely chopped (1/2 lb.)
1/2 teaspoon salt	Freshly ground pepper
2 dried pasilla chiles	Salt
4 corn tortillas	1/4 cup finely diced celery
Oil for frying	1/4 cup finely diced carrot

Place bones in a large pot or Dutch oven. Add water, peppercorns, bay leaf, 1/4 onion and 1/2 teaspoon salt. Bring to a boil. Skim foam from surface. Cover and simmer 2 hours, skimming again if necessary. Strain broth and let cool. Spoon off fat. Toast pasilla chiles in an ungreased medium skillet over medium heat 3 or 4 minutes, turning frequently. Do not scorch. Let cool. Break in half and remove seeds. Crumble chiles and place in a small dish. Cut tortillas in 2"x1/2" strips. Pour oil for frying 1-inch deep into a small saucepan. Heat to 365°F (185°C). Fry tortilla strips in hot oil until lightly browned and crisp. Drain on paper towels. Heat 1 tablespoon vegetable oil in a large saucepan. Add sliced onion and garlic. Cook slowly until onion is very tender but not browned. Stir in tomatoes and pepper to taste. Cook slowly 10 to 15 minutes. Add reserved strained broth and salt to taste. Simmer gently 15 minutes. Add celery and carrot. Simmer 15 minutes longer. To serve, place a handful of fried tortilla strips in each bowl; add soup. Top with crumbled chiles as desired. Makes 4 servings.

Caldo Tlalpeño

Chicken Soup from Tlalpan

If you like the smoky flavor of the chipotle chile, float a whole chile in each bowl.

1 whole chicken breast or 2 half	8 peppercorns
chicken breasts	2 dried or canned chipotle chiles
6 cups water or chicken broth	Water
1/4 medium onion	1 (8-3/4-oz.) can garbanzo beans,
1 bay leaf	drained
1 garlic clove	1/3 cup uncooked long-grain rice
Salt	4 large green onions, chopped

Place chicken breast in a large saucepan. Add water or broth, 1/4 medium onion, bay leaf, garlic, salt to taste and peppercorns. Bring to a boil; reduce heat. Cover and simmer 45 minutes. If using dried chipotle chiles, place in a small saucepan. Add water to cover and bring to a boil. Remove from heat. Let stand until softened, 45 minutes to 1 hour. Drain and slice. If using canned chipotle chiles, drain and slice. Remove chicken from broth; shred, discarding skin and bones. Strain broth; return strained broth to saucepan. Add shredded chicken; bring to a boil. Add garbanzo beans and rice. Cover and simmer 20 minutes or until rice is tender. Place a few chile slices in each soup bowl, add soup and sprinkle with green onions. Makes 6 servings.

Sopa de Lima **Photo on pages 122 and 123.**
Lime & Tortilla Soup

A famous soup of Yucatán. This version is from the Casa del Balam in Mérida.

2 corn tortillas	4 cups chicken broth
Oil for frying	1 cup shredded cooked chicken
2 teaspoons vegetable oil	Salt
1/3 cup chopped onion	1 tomato, chopped
1 California chile, roasted, peeled,	1 tablespoon lime juice
chopped, or 1/4 cup canned	4 large lime slices
chopped green chiles	

Cut tortillas in 2"x1/2" strips. Pour oil for frying 1/2 inch deep into a small saucepan or skillet. Heat to 365°F (185°C). Fry tortilla strips in hot oil until browned and crisp. Drain on paper towels. Heat 2 teaspoons vegetable oil in a large saucepan. Add onion and chile. Saute until onion is tender but not browned. Add broth, chicken and salt to taste. Cover and simmer 20 minutes. Add tomato; simmer 5 minutes longer. Stir in lime juice. Taste and add more lime juice if desired. To serve, ladle soup into bowls and add some fried tortilla strips. Float a lime slice in the center of each serving. Makes 4 servings.

Sopa de Pollo y Fideo
Chicken & Vermicelli Soup

If you have an 8-ounce package of vermicelli, use about 1/8 of it for this recipe.

1 large chicken breast	2 teaspoons vegetable oil
6 cups water	1 large tomato, peeled, seeded, chopped
1/4 small onion	2 California chiles, roasted, peeled,
1 garlic clove	seeded, chopped, or 1/3 cup canned
Salt	chopped chiles
8 peppercorns	6 cilantro sprigs or parsley sprigs
1/2 small onion, thinly sliced	1 oz. vermicelli

Place chicken breast in a large saucepan. Add water, 1/4 onion, garlic, salt to taste and peppercorns. Bring to a boil; reduce heat. Cover and simmer 45 minutes. Let cool slightly. Remove chicken. Shred chicken meat discarding skin and bones. Strain broth; return chicken to broth. Cook sliced onion in oil in a small skillet until tender but not browned. Add to soup. Bring to a boil. Add tomato, chiles, cilantro sprigs or parsley sprigs and vermicelli. Cook 15 minutes. Taste and add salt if needed. Makes 6 servings.

Pozole Blanco

Golden Hominy Soup

Pozole isn't complete until you garnish it lavishly.

1 lb. boneless lean pork	12 peppercorns
6 chicken thighs	6 cups water
1/2 medium onion	Garnishes, see below
2 garlic cloves	1 (1-lb., 13-oz.) can golden hominy
2 teaspoons salt	

Garnishes:

Salsa Fresca, page 33,	1/2 head lettuce, shredded
Salsa Mexicana, page 33 or	1 avocado, sliced
or other salsa	2 tablespoons dried leaf oregano,
1/2 medium onion, chopped	crushed
6 to 8 radishes, sliced	6 small limes, halved

Cut pork in 1-inch cubes and place in a large saucepan. Place chicken thighs in another large saucepan. Cut onion half into 2 pieces. In each saucepan, place 1 piece of onion, 1 garlic clove, 1 teaspoon salt, 6 peppercorns and 3 cups water. Bring each to a boil. Skim foam from surface. Cover pork and simmer 1 hour. Cover chicken and simmer 45 minutes. Prepare salsa and vegetables for Garnishes. Remove cooked pork and chicken from broths with a slotted spoon and place in a large pot or Dutch oven. Strain broths and add to meat. Drain and rinse hominy and add to meat. Bring to a boil; reduce heat. Cover and simmer 30 minutes. Taste pozole and add more salt if needed. Serve pozole in large soup bowls. Add garnishes to soup as desired. Makes 6 servings.

Garnishes:

Arrange salsa, onion, radishes, lettuce, avocado, oregano and limes in separate bowls.

Caldo Xochitl

Xochitl Chicken Soup

Chile slices make the soup quite hot and can be omitted.

4 cups strong chicken broth	12 to 16 cilantro sprigs
1-1/2 cups shredded cooked chicken	1 serrano chile or other small hot
Salt	chile, thinly sliced, if desired
1 small avocado, peeled, sliced	3 green onions, chopped

Combine broth and chicken in a large saucepan. Season with salt to taste and bring to a boil. In each of 4 broad shallow soup bowls, place one-fourth of the avocado slices, 3 or 4 cilantro sprigs and a few chile slices, if desired. Add hot broth and chicken. Sprinkle each serving with chopped green onion. Makes 4 servings.

Gazpacho a la Guadalajara
Cold Soup Guadalajara-Style

Be sure the tomatoes you use are ripe and juicy.

2 large ears corn or 2 cups frozen
    whole-kernel corn, thawed
Boiling salted water
2 medium cucumbers
2 avocados, peeled, cut in small
    pieces

5 medium tomatoes, seeded,
    finely chopped (1-1/2 lbs.)
1 teaspoon salt
1/2 teaspoon freshly ground pepper
Canned or homemade hot chile salsa

Cook ears of corn or thawed frozen corn in boiling salted water 5 minutes; drain. If using fresh corn, slice kernels from cobs. Scrape cobs with a sharp spoon; discard cobs. Place corn in a tureen or serving bowl. Peel cucumbers. Cut in half lengthwise and scrape out seeds. Cut cucumbers into small pieces. Add cucumber pieces, avocado pieces and tomato to corn. Add salt and pepper; mix well. Taste and add more seasoning if needed. Add chile salsa to taste or serve salsa separately in a small bowl. Refrigerate 1 hour. Serve cold. Makes 10 to 12 servings.

Sopa de Elote y Chayote
Corn & Squash Soup

Chayote is rare in many areas. You might substitute zucchini or pattypan squash.

Salsa Mexicana, page 33, or
    other hot salsa
2 large ears corn or 2 cups frozen
    whole-kernel corn, thawed
2 tablespoons butter
1 large celery stalk, chopped
1 garlic clove minced

2 large green onions, white part only,
    chopped
1/4 to 1/3 cup diced carrot
3 cups chicken broth
Salt
1 cup cubed cooked chayote

Prepare salsa; set aside. If using fresh corn, cut kernels from cobs, then scrape cobs with a sharp spoon. Discard cobs. Heat butter in a large saucepan. Add corn, celery, garlic and onions. Saute 10 minutes. Add carrot, broth and salt to taste. Bring to a boil; reduce heat. Cover and simmer gently 45 minutes. Add chayote. Cook until heated through. Serve in soup bowls. Serve salsa separately. Makes 6 servings.

Sopa de Coliflor y Champiñones

Cauliflower & Mushroom Soup

Make a different cauliflower soup by adding chile.

2 cups cauliflowerets	1/2 teaspoon salt
Boiling salted water	1/8 teaspoon white pepper
3 tablespoons butter	2 beef bouillon cubes
1 slice onion, minced	3 cups milk
1 cup sliced mushrooms	Canned chipotle chiles, sliced,
2 tablespoons all-purpose flour	if desired

Wash and drain cauliflowerets. Slice larger flowerets. Cook in boiling salted water 8 minutes or until barely tender. Drain. Melt butter in a large saucepan. Add onion and mushrooms. Cook until onion is tender but not browned. Stir in flour; cook 1 minute. Add salt, white pepper, bouillon cubes and milk. Cook and stir until hot and slightly thickened. Add cauliflowerets. Cook until heated through. To serve, spoon into individual soup bowls. Float a slice of chipotle chile on top of each serving if desired. Serve at once. If soup is allowed to stand and becomes too thick, thin with a little milk or broth. Makes 4 servings.

Crema de Calabacitas

Cream of Zucchini Soup

This creamy, pale green soup is especially good served cold.

4 medium zucchini (1 lb.)	2 tablespoons finely chopped onion
2 cups water	1 tablespoon all-purpose flour
Salt	1 (13-oz.) can evaporated milk
2 tablespoons cilantro leaves or	1 cup chicken broth
parsley leaves	Cilantro leaves or parsley leaves for
2 tablespoons butter	garnish

Wash zucchini. Cut off stem ends, then cut in large pieces. Place in a large saucepan. Add water and a pinch of salt. Bring to a boil. Cover and cook until tender, about 20 minutes. Cool zucchini in cooking liquid. Place zucchini, 1 cup cooking liquid and 2 tablespoons cilantro or parsley in blender; process until pureed. Heat butter in a medium saucepan. Add onion. Cook until tender but not browned. Stir in flour. Cook and stir 1 minute. Add pureed zucchini mixture, evaporated milk and chicken broth. Stir to blend. Season with salt if needed. Stir over medium heat until soup comes to a boil. Serve at once or chill and serve cold. Garnish each serving with a few whole cilantro leaves or parsley leaves. Makes 6 servings.

Crema de Champiñones
Cream of Mushroom Soup

Clean mushrooms by immersing them briefly in cold water then patting dry in a cloth towel.

1 lb. mushrooms (2 to 3 cups)	**2 tablespoons butter**
Water	**1/2 small onion, finely chopped**
4 cups milk	**1 teaspoon salt**

Clean mushrooms and cut off ends of stems. Pour water 1/4 inch deep in a medium saucepan. Add mushrooms. Bring to a boil; reduce heat. Cover and simmer until tender, 7 to 10 minutes. Drain, discarding cooking liquid. Place half the cooked mushrooms in blender with 2 cups milk. Blend until pureed. Slice or chop remaining mushrooms. Melt butter in a medium saucepan. Add onion. Cook until tender but not browned. Add pureed mushroom mixture, sliced or chopped mushrooms, remaining 2 cups milk and salt. Bring to a boil. Cover and simmer 20 minutes. Makes 6 servings.

Sopa de Frijol Maya
Mayan Bean Soup

Serve this simple soup from Yucatán with fried tortilla strips as croutons.

1 cup dried black beans	**1/2 medium onion, chopped**
Hot water for soaking	**1 tablespoon vegetable oil**
5 cups hot water	**2 small tomatoes, peeled, chopped**
1/4 medium onion	**(1/2 lb.)**
1 garlic clove	**1/2 teaspoon salt**
1/2 teaspoon salt	

Place beans in a large saucepan. Pour hot water for soaking over beans to cover generously. Let beans soak overnight. Drain and rinse beans. Add 5 cups hot water, 1/4 onion, and garlic. Bring to a boil. Cover and simmer 2 hours. Add 1/2 teaspoon salt. Simmer 2 hours longer or until very tender. Cool beans in their liquid, then puree a cup at a time with liquid in blender. Press through a sieve to remove skins. Return to large saucepan. In a medium saucepan, cook chopped onion in oil until tender but not browned. Add tomatoes. Cook until softened. Puree tomato mixture in blender or food processor. Add to beans with 1/2 teaspoon salt. Simmer 15 minutes longer. Soup should not be too thick. If necessary, thin with a little water. Makes 6 servings.

Sopa de Elote
Corn Soup

Ground corn adds to the creamy appearance of this delicious soup.

3 small ears corn or 1-1/2 cups
  frozen whole-kernel corn, thawed
1 garlic clove
1/2 teaspoon salt
1 tablespoon butter
1 small onion, chopped
3 small tomatoes, peeled, chopped
  (3/4 lb.)

1 qt. beef broth
1/2 teaspoon dried leaf oregano,
  crushed
1/4 cup whipping cream
Cilantro leaves or parsley leaves

If using fresh corn, cut kernels from cobs. Scrape cobs with a sharp spoon; discard cobs. Measure corn. You should have about 1-1/2 cups. Reserve excess corn for another use. Puree 3/4 cup corn in blender or food processor; set aside. Mash garlic with salt to make a paste. Melt butter in a large saucepan. Add onion and garlic paste. Cook until onion is tender but not browned. Add tomatoes. Cook slowly 10 minutes, mashing tomatoes with a spoon. Add broth, oregano, pureed corn and whole corn kernels. Taste and add salt if needed. Bring to a boil; reduce heat. Cover and simmer 30 minutes. Stir in cream. Cook until heated through. To serve, pour into soup bowls and garnish with cilantro or parsley. Makes 6 servings.

Variation

Add 1 chopped, peeled, roasted California chile or 2 tablespoons canned chopped green chiles to the soup with the broth.

How To Make Sopa de Elote

After cutting corn from cob, scrape cob with a spoon to remove milky residue.

Stir cream into cooked soup base. Heat without boiling until hot.

Potaje de Habas
Fava Bean Soup

Fava beans are also called broad beans.

1-1/2 cups dried fava beans (8 oz.)
5-1/2 cups water
1/2 onion, cut in 2 pieces
2 garlic cloves
1 tomato
1/4 medium onion
2 slices thick sliced bacon or 3
   slices regular bacon, diced

1 Spanish-style chorizo link, thinly
   sliced
2 tablespoons olive oil
1 teaspoon salt
1 spearmint or mint sprig, if desired

Wash beans and place in a large saucepan. Add water and bring to a boil. Add onion pieces and garlic. Cover and simmer until beans are tender, about 1 hour. Remove onion from beans; discard. Puree beans in blender, adding enough cooking liquid to blend smoothly. Press through a sieve to remove skins. Return to saucepan. Roast tomato and 1/4 medium onion on an ungreased griddle until tomato is blistered all over and onion is flecked with brown. Puree roasted tomato and onion in blender. In a medium skillet, brown bacon and chorizo in olive oil. Add pureed tomato mixture. Cook 2 to 3 minutes. Add bacon mixture, salt and spearmint or mint if desired to beans. Bring to a boil and simmer uncovered until thickened as desired, 30 to 45 minutes. Taste and add more salt if needed. Makes 6 servings.

Sopa de Aguacate
Avocado Soup

An elegant first course for a dinner party.

1 large avocado, peeled, cut in half
1/2 cup whipping cream
1/2 cup milk
1 cup chicken broth
1 teaspoon lime juice

1/2 teaspoon Maggi seasoning
Dash white pepper
Salt
Dairy sour cream
Chopped fresh chives

Place avocado in blender or food processor. Add whipping cream, milk, broth, lime juice, Maggi seasoning, white pepper and salt to taste. Blend until smooth. Chill. Serve in small bowls. Top with a spoonful of sour cream. Sprinkle with chives. Makes 6 to 8 servings.

Menudo
Tripe Soup

It's traditional to recover from a night on the town with a bracing bowl of menudo.

2-1/2 lbs. tripe
1/2 calf's foot
1/3 cup vinegar
Cold water
2 garlic cloves
1/2 small onion
About 3 qts. water
Salt

1-1/2 cups hominy
Red Chile Puree, see below, or 1 cup
   canned red chile sauce
Finely chopped green onions
Chopped cilantro leaves
Lemon wedges
Corn tortillas, heated

Red Chile Puree:
8 California chiles (1/4 lb.)
2/3 cup water

Scrape off any fat from tripe. Cut tripe into 1-inch squares. Place tripe and calf's foot in a large bowl. Add vinegar and cold water to cover generously. Let stand 3 hours. Drain. Rinse tripe and calf's foot thoroughly. Place in a large pot. Add garlic and onion. Pour in water to cover ingredients plus 1 to 1-1/2 inches, about 3 quarts. Add salt to taste. Bring to a boil; reduce heat. Cover and simmer about 6 hours or until tripe is tender. After 1 hour, skim foam from surface of soup. Skim again as needed. Add more water if liquid evaporates. Prepare Red Chile Puree. Add hominy and Red Chile Puree during last hour of cooking. Ladle into large bowls. Serve chopped green onions, cilantro, lemon wedges and hot corn tortillas separately. Makes 10 to 15 servings.

Red Chile Puree:
Remove stems from chiles. Break chiles open and rinse out seeds. Place in a saucepan with water to cover. Bring to a boil. Continue to boil until chiles are softened, about 5 minutes. Drain; discard water. Place chiles in blender; puree. Add enough water to make puree the consistency of tomato sauce. Press pureed chiles through a sieve to remove bits of peel. Makes about 1 cup.

Variation
Substitute 1-1/2 cups nixtamal (cooked dried corn) for canned hominy. Combine with soaked tripe and calf's foot, garlic, onion and water. Cook as directed above.

Caldo Largo de Veracruz
Fish Soup Veracruz-Style

If epazote is not available, top each serving with a sprig of cilantro or parsley.

1 fish head or 1/2 lb. fish scraps
5 cups water
1 teaspooon salt
4 small tomatoes (1 lb.)
1 small onion
3 garlic cloves, unpeeled

1 dried small hot chile
3 tablespoons olive oil
1 or 2 epazote sprigs
1-1/2 lbs. red snapper or other white
   fish fillets

Wash fish head or scraps. Place in a large pot or Dutch oven. Add water and salt. Bring to a boil; reduce heat. Simmer uncovered 30 minutes. Remove fish head or scraps; discard. Strain broth and return to pot. Heat a large heavy skillet over medium heat. Place tomatoes, onion, garlic cloves and chile in skillet. Toast lightly. If chile begins to burn, remove from skillet. Remove garlic cloves as soon as peel starts to brown. Toast tomatoes and onion until scorched on all sides. Peel toasted garlic and scorched tomatoes. Combine with scorched onion and toasted chile in blender or food processor; puree. Heat olive oil in skillet. Add tomato puree. Cook 5 minutes over medium heat. Add cooked tomato puree and epazote to fish broth. Rinse fish fillets. Cut into chunks. Bring fish broth mixture to a boil. Add fish. Bring to a boil again; reduce heat. Simmer uncovered 10 minutes. Taste and add more salt if needed. Serve soup in large bowls. Makes 4 to 6 servings.

Sopa de Nuez de Nogal
Walnut Soup

Soaking the walnuts in hot water helps loosen any thick, tough skins.

1 cup walnuts
Boiling water
1/2 medium onion, coarsely chopped
3 cups chicken broth
2 tablespoons butter
2 tablespoons all-purpose flour

1-1/2 cups half-and-half
1 bay leaf
1/8 teaspoon white pepper
Salt
Parsley leaves or chopped fresh chives

Cover walnuts with boiling water and let stand 5 minutes; drain. Pull off any dark loose skins. Combine drained walnuts, onion and 1 cup broth in blender or food processor; puree. Melt butter in a large saucepan. Stir in flour. Cook and stir 1 minute. Stir in half-and-half. Add bay leaf. Cook and stir until mixture comes to a boil and thickens. Add walnut mixture and remaining chicken broth. Add white pepper and salt to taste. Stir frequently over medium heat until soup is slightly thickened, 30 to 45 minutes. Remove bay leaf. Serve hot or chilled, garnished with parsley or chives. Makes 4 to 6 servings.

Ensaladas y Verduras
Salads & Vegetables

Mexican markets fairly bloom with produce that makes you long for a salad bowl. But salads and cooked vegetables are likely to be piled on top of or around your main course—not in a salad bowl. The sautéed fish fillets I had in Yucatán came sprinkled with peas, topped with potatoes and garnished with lime halves, a tomato slice, a long slice of cooked carrot, another of crisp cucumber and a lettuce leaf. Even a *taco* boasts a salad in the form of lettuce, onions and tomatoes stuffed inside.

More formal salads do exist. For the spectacular *Ensalada de Nochebuena* (Christmas Eve Salad), beets, lettuce and an assortment of fruits and nuts are arranged on a platter. The ingredients may be tossed with cooking liquid from the beets to make them a deep pink. Sometimes pomegranate seeds or little colored candies called *colaciones* are sprinkled over the salad.

Mexican salads are not always served with dressing. There may be a lime cut in half on the side so you can squeeze lime juice to taste over your salad.

Mexican corn is tougher and chewier than corn in some other parts of the world. If corn is one of your favorite vegetables, be sure to try *Tamal de Elote en Cazuela* (Green Corn Tamale Casserole) in this section and *Soufflé de Elote* (Corn Soufflé), page 136.

Although corn is basic to Mexico's cuisine, tomatoes, onion and garlic are just as important, for they are sautéed as a beginning to many dishes. You may see Indian women in Oaxacan markets wearing garlic wreaths on their heads!

Squash is also popular. Varieties include pear-shaped *chayotes* with a delicate but distinctive flavor. They are available in some areas outside Mexico. If you can't locate *chayote*, substitute scalloped pattypan squash.

Several recipes for *chiles rellenos*, or stuffed *chiles*, appear in this section. *Chiles* can be stuffed with meat and potatoes, with tuna or shrimp salad, with vegetables, beans or cheese, or with *Picadillo* (Minced Meat), page 108. Large dried *chiles* may be soaked until they're softened, then stuffed with a typical filling. Stuffed *chiles* may be batter-coated and fried or served plain. If fresh *chiles* are not available, use canned whole green *chiles* or bell peppers. However, bell peppers must be boiled or steamed until they are tender so they will have a texture similar to a roasted *chile*.

PATIO BARBECUE

Ensalada de Aguacate Uxmal
Uxmal Avocado Salad

A hotel near the ruins of Uxmal in Yucatán serves this salad.

2 tablespoons white vinegar	**1/2 cup olive oil**
2 teaspoons prepared mustard	**3 small avocados**
1/4 teaspoon salt	**Lettuce leaves**

Combine vinegar, mustard and salt in a small bowl. Slowly beat in olive oil with a whisk until dressing is blended and thickened. Do not peel avocados. Just before serving, cut avocados in half and remove pits. Place an avocado half on a lettuce leaf on each salad plate. Fill centers with dressing. Makes 6 servings.

Ensalada Mixta Uxmal   Photo on pages 122 and 123.
Uxmal Mixed Salad

Mounds of brightly colored vegetables are linked with an avocado slice.

3 tablespoons white vinegar	**Lettuce leaves**
1 tablespoon prepared mustard	**2 medium carrots, peeled, grated**
1/4 teaspoon salt, heaping	**1 (1-lb.) can julienned beets, drained**
3/4 cup olive oil	**1 small avocado, sliced**

Combine vinegar, mustard and salt in a medium bowl. Gradually beat in olive oil with a whisk until dressing is blended and thickened. Line 6 salad plates with lettuce leaves. Place a mound of carrots on lettuce. Place a mound of beets beside carrot mound. Place an avocado slice across the top. Serve dressing separately to be spooned over salad as desired. Makes 6 servings.

Botana de Aguacate
Avocado Snack

An avocado cocktail with unusual flavor.

1/2 cup diced, seeded, peeled cucumber	**2 teaspoons Maggi seasoning**
2 green onions with tops, chopped	**2 teaspoons olive oil**
1 tablespoon chopped fresh parsley	**1 teaspoon cider vinegar**
1 tomato, chopped, drained	**1 teaspoon lime juice**
1 medium avocado, peeled, diced	**Lettuce leaves**

Combine cucumber, green onions and parsley in a medium bowl; chill. Place tomato in a small bowl; chill. Just before serving, add tomato and avocado to cucumber mixture. Combine Maggi seasoning, olive oil, vinegar and lime juice in a small bowl. Mix well and pour over salad. Toss gently. Line stemmed glasses or small dishes with a portion of lettuce leaf. Spoon salad into lettuce leaf. Serve as a first course. Makes 4 servings.

Ensalada Guanajuato
Five-Bean Salad Guanajuato-Style

According to the cooks in the colonial town of Guanajuato, the more kinds of beans, the better.

**1 cup drained or canned cooked pinto
  beans**
1 cup drained cooked black beans
**1 (8-3/4-oz.) can garbanzo beans,
  drained**
1 (8-oz.) can cut green beans, drained
1 cup drained canned wax beans
1/2 green pepper, cut in thin strips
1/4 red onion, thinly sliced

6 tablespoons vegetable oil
3 tablespoons vinegar
1/2 teaspoon salt
1/4 teaspoon dried leaf oregano, crushed
1/8 teaspoon garlic powder
Freshly ground black pepper
1 tomato, chopped, drained
3 tablespoons mayonnaise

If cooking your own pinto and black beans, cook until firm-tender and not mushy. Combine pinto beans, black beans, garbanzo beans, green beans and wax beans in a large bowl. Add green pepper and red onion. In a small bowl, mix oil, vinegar, salt, oregano, garlic powder and black pepper to taste. Pour over salad and toss gently but thoroughly. Cover and refrigerate overnight. Just before serving, add tomato and mayonnaise. Toss until blended. Makes 6 to 8 servings.

Ensalada de Ejotes
Green Bean Salad

If you have fresh oregano, use it to give this salad a special touch.

1 lb. fresh green beans
Boiling salted water
1/3 cup olive oil
2 tablespoons white wine vinegar

Salt and freshly ground pepper
1 cup water
1/2 medium red onion, thinly sliced
1/2 teaspoon dried leaf oregano, crushed

Wash green beans and snap off tips. Cut beans in thin diagonal slices. Cook sliced beans in 1 quart or more boiling salted water 8 to 10 minutes, until tender. Turn into a sieve. Rinse well with cold water. Drain thoroughly. Beat olive oil and vinegar together in a small bowl. Pour over beans. Add salt and pepper to taste; toss. Bring 2 cups water to a boil in a small saucepan. Drop in onion. Stir; drain immediately. Arrange onion slices over beans. Sprinkle oregano over salad. Chill. Makes 4 to 6 servings.

Ensalada de Nochebuena
Christmas Eve Salad

A spectacular combination of fruits and nuts topped with ruby pomegranate seeds.

4 small beets
Water
2 tablespoons sugar
1/4 lb. jícama or 1 additional
    red apple
1 orange
2 to 3 tablespoons lime juice or
    lemon juice
1 red apple

2 small bananas
6 large romaine lettuce leaves, finely
    shredded
3 tablespoons roasted unsalted peanuts
2 tablespoons pine nuts
1/4 cup pomegranate seeds
2 tablespoons sugar
1/4 teaspoon salt
3 tablespoons white vinegar

Cut off beet tops, leaving about 1 inch of stems. Do not remove root. Scrub beets and place in a small saucepan. Add water to cover and 2 tablespoons sugar. Bring to a boil; reduce heat. Cover and simmer 45 minutes or until beets are tender. Drain and rinse with cold water. Rub off skins under cold running water. Refrigerate beets until serving time. Before serving, peel jícama and cut in thin small wedges. If using apple, leave unpeeled. Peel orange and cut in thin slices. Cut each slice in half. Place lime juice or lemon juice in a small bowl. Cut unpeeled apple into thin wedges. Dip each wedge in juice to prevent discoloration. Peel banana and cut into thin slices. Dip into juice. Cut cooked and peeled beets into thin slices. Line a broad shallow salad bowl with shredded romaine lettuce. Arrange jícama, orange, beet, apple and banana slices in alternating circles or other pattern on lettuce. Sprinkle with peanuts and pine nuts. Top with pomegranate seeds. In a small bowl; blend 2 tablespoons sugar, salt and vinegar until sugar is dissolved. Drizzle over salad just before serving. Makes 6 servings.

Variation

Reserve cooking liquid from beets. Cut jícama, apple, orange, bananas and beets into small chunks. Combine with nuts and pomegranate seeds. Add dressing and enough beet liquid to color mixture a bright pink. Toss gently and arrange on romaine leaves. Serve immediately.

Gelatina de Sangrita
Sangrita Salad Mold

A spicy Mexican version of tomato aspic.

2 cups Sangrita de Tomate, page 14
1 (6-oz.) pkg. lemon flavored gelatin
2 cups boiling water

Mayonnaise
Lime slices

Prepare Sangrita de Tomate. Mix gelatin and boiling water in a medium bowl. Refrigerate until gelatin starts to set, then stir in Sangrita Tomate. Turn into a 5 or 6-cup mold. Refrigerate until firm. To unmold, dip bottom of mold in warm water about 10 seconds. Invert mold onto a platter. Remove mold. Garnish salad with mayonnaise and lime slices. Makes 8 servings.

Ensalada de Coliflor
Cauliflower Salad

Colors of the Mexican flag appear in this pretty salad from Zihuatanejo.

1 medium cauliflower (about 1-1/2
  lbs.)
Boiling salted water
1/3 cup vegetable oil
White vinegar

1/2 teaspoon salt
1 tablespoon chopped fresh parsley
1 tablespoon chopped canned pimiento
2 tablespoons finely diced hard-cooked
  egg white

Separate cauliflower into cauliflowerets. Wash and drain. Generously cover with boiling salted water. Cook until crisp-tender, 6 to 7 minutes longer. Drain and rinse with cold water. Drain well. Pour 1/3 cup oil into a measuring cup. Add enough vinegar to measure 1/2 cup. Add salt, parsley, pimiento and egg white. Stir dressing well. Pour over cauliflowerets; toss to mix. Chill. Toss again before serving. Makes 4 servings.

Ensalada de Berenjenas
Eggplant Salad

A different salad with Middle East origins.

1 (1-lb.) eggplant
1 garlic clove
1/2 teaspoon salt
2 tablespoons finely diced, peeled,
  roasted California chile or
  canned chopped green chiles
1/2 cup finely diced green pepper

1 tablespoon chopped fresh parsley
2 tomatoes, peeled, chopped (1/2 lb.)
2 tablespoons lime juice
2 tablespoons vegetable oil
Freshly ground black pepper
Salt
Lettuce leaves

Preheat oven to 450°F (230°C). Pierce eggplant several times with a fork. Bake eggplant in an 8-inch square baking dish 30 minutes; cool. Peel and chop very fine. Mash garlic with salt to make a paste. Combine garlic paste, chile, green pepper, parsley and tomatoes in a medium bowl. Add chopped eggplant. Toss to mix. Add lime juice, oil, black pepper to taste and additional salt, if needed. Toss to mix. Cover and refrigerate several hours. Serve on lettuce. Makes 4 servings.

Aderezo de Hierbas
Herb Dressing

This salad dressing is delicious on most tossed salads.

1/2 cup vegetable oil
2 tablespoons cider vinegar
1 tablespoon lime juice
1/2 teaspoon dried leaf oregano,
  crushed

1 small piece bay leaf, crumbled
1/4 teaspoon minced garlic
1/2 teaspoon salt
1/8 teaspoon freshly ground pepper

Combine all ingredients in a jar with a tight-fitting lid. Cover and shake thoroughly. Let stand several hours or overnight to blend flavors. Shake well before using. Makes about 2/3 cup.

Ensalada Tropical
Tropical Salad

Street vendors in Mexico sell fruits and vegetables seasoned this way.

1/2 lb. jícama	2 tablespoons lime juice
2 cups thinly sliced fresh pineapple	1/4 teaspoon salt
1 medium cucumber	3/4 teaspoon chili powder

Peel jícama and cut into thin slices. Peel cucumber and slice crosswise in thin circles. On a large platter, arrange cucumber, jícama and pineapple slices in circles. Drizzle lime juice over salad. Sprinkle with salt and chili powder. Makes 8 servings.

Ensalada de Frutas
Fruit Salad

A health-food restaurant in Mérida serves this breakfast-in-a-dish.

1 small papaya, peeled, seeded	2 cups plain yogurt
1 red apple, unpeeled	1-1/2 cups granola
1 or 2 bananas	1/2 cup chopped walnuts
1 small pineapple, peeled, cored	6 to 8 tablespoons honey
1 cup coarsely diced fresh coconut	

Cut papaya, apple and banana in bite-size pieces. Cut pineapple in wedges. For each serving, place some of the papaya, apple, banana, pineapple and coconut in layers on a platter. Pour yogurt over fruit. Top with a generous layer of granola. Sprinkle with nuts. Drizzle with honey. Makes 6 to 8 servings.

Calabacitas con Crema
Zucchini with Cream

Cream gives a rich flavor to this vegetable casserole.

8 medium zucchini (2 lbs.)	3/4 cup whipping cream
Boiling salted water	1/4 cup fine dry breadcrumbs
4 oz. Monterey Jack cheese, shredded	Salt
(1 cup)	2 tablespoons butter

Cook zucchini in boiling salted water until crisp-tender, about 10 minutes. Drain and rinse with cold water. Preheat oven to 350°F (175°C). Butter an 8-inch square baking dish. Cut zucchini in diagonal slices. Layer half the slices in buttered baking dish. Top with half of the cheese, half of the cream, and half of the breadcrumbs. Sprinkle with salt to taste. Layer remaining zucchini slices. Top with remaining cheese, cream, breadcrumbs and salt to taste. Dot with butter. Bake uncovered 30 minutes or until cheese is melted and begins to brown. Makes 6 servings.

Calabacitas con Elote
Zucchini With Corn

Combining squash and corn is popular in Mexican cooking.

3 large ears corn or 3 cups thawed
    frozen whole-kernel corn
6 medium zucchini (1-1/2 lbs.)
2 poblano or California chiles,
    roasted, peeled, or 2 canned whole
    green chiles

3 small tomatoes, peeled (3/4 lb.)
1/4 medium onion
1-1/2 tablespoons butter
1/4 teaspoon dried leaf oregano, crushed
3/4 teaspoon salt
Pepper

If using fresh corn, slice kernels off cobs, then scrape cobs with a sharp spoon. Discard cobs. Cut zucchini into 1/2- to 3/4-inch cubes. Cut chiles into short thin strips. Puree tomatoes with onion in blender or food processor. Melt butter in a large saucepan or Dutch oven. Add corn kernels and zucchini cubes. Cook over medium-low heat until zucchini is crisp-tender, about 3 minutes. Add chile strips, tomato mixture, oregano, salt and pepper to taste; stir. Cover and cook over medium heat 5 to 10 minutes until zucchini is tender. Makes 6 to 8 servings.

Variation

For a spicy flavor, substitute 2 pickled jalapeño chiles, sliced, for the peeled or canned chiles.

Tamal de Elote en Cazuela
Green Corn Tamale Casserole

Green corn means fresh corn, but you can use frozen kernels too.

1 (4-oz.) can whole green chiles
3 cups fresh corn kernels or
    frozen whole-kernel corn
1/3 cup yellow cornmeal
2 tablespoons butter, melted

2 teaspoons sugar
1/2 to 1 teaspoon salt
4 oz. Cheddar cheese, shredded (1 cup)
1 (1-lb.) can stewed tomatoes
1/2 teaspoon dried leaf oregano, crushed

Preheat oven to 350°F (175°C). Butter a 1-quart baking dish; set aside. Rinse chiles and cut in wide strips. Combine corn kernels, cornmeal, butter, sugar and salt in blender or food processor. Grind until corn is fine. If using a blender, you may have to grind 1/4 to 1/2 cup at a time. Layer half the corn mixture in buttered baking dish. Top evenly with all the chile strips. Cover with cheese. Top with remaining corn mixture. Cover with foil; bake 1 hour. Heat stewed tomatoes and oregano in a small saucepan. Serve as a sauce with the casserole. Makes 4 servings.

Buñuelos de Coliflor
Cauliflower Fritters

Oil will stay hot if you cook only 3 or 4 pieces of food at a time.

1 (1-lb.) cauliflower, broken into
   medium flowerets
Oil for frying
1 egg
3/4 cup milk

3/4 cup all-purpose flour
1 teaspoon sugar
3/4 teaspoon baking powder
1/4 teaspoon salt
Pinch nutmeg

Cook cauliflowerets in boiling salted water 6 to 7 minutes or until just tender; drain. Pour oil 1 inch deep into a medium saucepan. Heat oil to 365°F (185°C). Beat egg with milk in a small bowl. Combine flour, sugar, baking powder, salt and nutmeg in a medium bowl. Gradually stir milk mixture into flour mixture. Beat until smooth. Dip cauliflowerets into batter. Fry in hot oil until golden brown on each side. Drain on paper towels. Serve immediately. Makes 6 servings.

How To Make
Buñuelos de Coliflor

Dip cooked cauliflowerets in batter. Drain slightly.   **Deep-fry them in hot oil until golden brown.**

Chiles en Nogada
Chiles in Nut Sauce

To make this famous red, white and green dish from Puebla, cook the chiles several hours ahead.

**8 poblano chiles or California
  chiles, roasted, peeled**
4 cups water
1 tablespoon salt
1 small garlic clove
1/2 teaspoon salt
1 tablespoon vegetable oil
3/4 lb. ground pork
1/2 medium onion, finely chopped
1 small pear, peeled, diced
1 small tart apple, peeled, diced

**1/4 cup raisins, plumped in hot water,
  drained**
**2 small tomatoes, peeled, diced
  (1/2 lb.)**
1/4 cup slivered almonds, diced
**1/4 cup finely diced candied cactus
  (biznaga), citron, or candied
  pineapple**
Nogada, see below
Seeds of 1 large pomegranate

Nogada (Nut Sauce):
1-1/2 cups chopped walnuts
1 (3-oz.) pkg. cream cheese, softened
1 tablespoon sugar

3 tablespoons brandy
3/4 cup milk

Cut as small a slit as possible in one side of each chile to remove seeds. Leave stems on. Place chiles in a large saucepan. Add water and 1 tablespoon salt. Bring to a boil and boil 1 minute. Remove from heat and let stand several hours or refrigerate overnight. Drain chiles; rinse and drain again. Mash garlic with 1/2 teaspoon salt to make a paste. Heat oil in a large skillet. Add pork. Cook until browned, stirring to crumble. Add garlic paste and onion. Cook until onion is tender. Add pear, apple, raisins, tomatoes, almonds and candied cactus, citron, or pineapple. Simmer 15 minutes, stirring occasionally. Prepare Nogada. Taste meat mixture and add more salt if needed. Let cool slightly. Spoon meat mixture into chiles. To serve, top chiles with Nogada and sprinkle with pomegranate seeds. Serve warm or at room temperature. Makes 8 servings.

Nogada (Nut Sauce):
Combine all ingredients in blender or food processor. Process until smooth.

Zanahorias con Tequila
Carrots Flamed with Tequila

Ignite the tequila at a side table to avoid any accidents.

3 medium carrots (1 lb.)
Boiling salted water
3 tablespoons butter

1/4 teaspoon dried dill weed, crushed
Salt and pepper
1/4 cup tequila (2 oz.)

Peel carrots and cut in thin diagonal slices. Cook in boiling salted water 10 minutes; drain. Melt butter in a large stovetop casserole, a large skillet, or a presentation pan. Add carrot slices. Saute 2 to 3 minutes, sprinkling with dill and salt and pepper to taste. Add tequila; ignite. When flames die down, stir and serve. Makes 4 servings.

Ensalada de Papas con Chile Poblano
Potato Salad with Poblano Sauce

Chiles add new flavor to potato salad.

6 medium boiling potatoes (2 lbs.)
Boiling salted water
1-1/3 cups mayonnaise
3 tablespoons milk
4 poblano chiles, roasted, peeled, or
  4 canned whole green chiles

1/2 medium onion, finely chopped
6 oz. Monterey Jack cheese, shredded
  (1-1/2 cups)
2 teaspoons lemon juice
Salt and pepper

Peel potatoes. Cook in boiling salted water to cover until tender, about 30 minutes. Drain and cool. Cut potatoes in 1/2-inch cubes. Blend mayonnaise and milk in a small bowl; set aside. Cut chiles in thin strips about 1-1/2 inches long. Combine cubed cooked potatoes, chile strips, onion and 2/3 of the cheese in a large bowl. Sprinkle with lemon juice. Add salt and pepper to taste. Pour mayonnaise mixture over salad. Toss gently but thoroughly. Turn into a serving bowl and sprinkle top with remaining cheese. Makes 10 servings.

Ensalada de Papas con Camarones
Potato Salad with Shrimp

A delicate and different potato salad.

2 (4-1/4-oz.) cans tiny shrimp
2 tablespoons lime or lemon juice
1 garlic clove
4 cups diced, cooked boiling potatoes
  (about 3 potatoes)
1/2 cup diced celery
1/4 cup chopped green onion

1/2 cup dairy sour cream
1/2 cup mayonnaise
1 teaspoon salt
1/2 teaspoon dry mustard
1/4 teaspoon dried leaf tarragon,
  crushed
1/4 teaspoon white pepper

Drain shrimp; rinse and drain again. Mix with lime juice in a small bowl; chill. Rub the inside of a large salad bowl with cut side of garlic clove. Discard garlic. Combine potatoes, celery and onion in bowl. Add shrimp. In a small bowl, combine sour cream, mayonnaise, salt, dry mustard, tarragon and white pepper. Mix well. Add to potato mixture and stir gently. Refrigerate several hours. Taste and add more salt if needed. Makes 8 servings.

Ensalada de Macarrón y Queso
Macaroni & Cheese Salad

For directions on roasting and peeling chiles, see pages 7 to 9.

1 cup small elbow macaroni, uncooked
Boiling salted water
1 teaspoon vegetable oil
1/2 cup drained canned or cooked
   fresh peas
2 tablespoons finely chopped red onion
1 cup small-curd cottage cheese
1/2 cup mayonnaise

1/2 cup diced cooked carrot,
   drained
1/4 cup diced peeled, roasted,
   poblano chiles or canned
   chopped green chiles
1/2 teaspoon salt
Lettuce leaves
Tomato wedges

Cook macaroni in boiling salted water until tender, 8 to 10 minutes. Drain and cool. Place in a medium bowl. Toss with oil. Add peas, onion, cottage cheese, mayonnaise, carrot, chile, and salt. Toss gently but thoroughly. Chill. Line 6 salad plates with lettuce leaves. Spoon macaroni mixture onto lettuce leaves. Garnish with tomato wedges. Makes 6 servings.

Chiles Rellenos de Queso
Cheese-Stuffed Chiles

By leaving on the stems, Mexican cooks show they used fresh chiles.

Tomato Sauce, see below
6 California chiles, roasted, peeled,
   or 6 canned whole green chiles
4 oz. Monterey Jack cheese

Oil for frying
3 eggs, separated
About 1/2 cup all-purpose flour

Tomato Sauce:
4 small tomatoes, peeled (1 lb.)
1/2 medium onion or 1 small onion
1 garlic clove
1 tablespoon vegetable oil
1/2 cup chicken broth
1/2 teaspoon salt

2 small California chiles, peeled,
   seeded, chopped, or 1/4 cup canned
   chopped green chiles
Pinch ground cloves
Pinch ground cinnamon

Prepare Tomato Sauce; keep warm. Cut as small a slit as possible in one side of each chile to remove seeds. Leave on stems. Pat chiles dry with paper towels. Cut cheese into 6 long thin sticks. Place 1 stick in each chile. Use more cheese if chiles are large. If chiles are loose and open, wrap around cheese and fasten with wooden picks. Pour oil 1/4 inch deep into a large skillet. Heat oil to 365°F (185°C). Beat egg whites in a medium bowl until stiff. Slightly beat egg yolks in a small bowl. Add all at once to beaten egg whites. Fold in lightly but thoroughly. Roll chiles in flour, then dip in egg mixture to coat. Fry in hot oil until golden brown, turning with a spatula. Drain on paper towels. Serve immediately topped with Tomato Sauce. Makes 6 servings.

Tomato Sauce:
Combine tomatoes, onion and garlic in blender or food processor; puree. Heat oil in a medium saucepan. Add tomato mixture. Cook 10 minutes, stirring occasionally. Add broth, salt, chiles, cloves and cinnamon. Simmer gently 15 minutes. Makes about 2 cups.

Chayotes con Queso
Chayotes with Cheese

Supermarkets that carry Latin American foods may have queso fresco, Mexico's white cheese.

1-1/2 lb. chayotes
Water
2 tablespoons butter
1 small onion, finely chopped
1/2 to 1 serrano chile or other small
  chile, finely chopped, if desired

Salt and freshly ground pepper
4 oz. Monterey Jack cheese, shredded or
  crumbled queso fresco (1 cup)

Cut chayotes in quarters. Place in a large saucepan with water to cover. Bring to a boil; reduce heat. Cover and boil gently 30 minutes or until tender. Drain and cool. Remove seeds. Peel chayotes and cut in large dice. Melt butter in a large skillet. Add onion and chile, if desired. Cook until onion is tender but not browned. Add diced, cooked chayotes. Toss to coat with onion mixture. Season with salt and freshly ground pepper to taste. Cook until heated through. Top with cheese. Cover and cook until cheese is melted, about 5 minutes. Uncover and stir gently. Makes 4 to 5 servings.

How To Make
Chiles Rellenos de Queso

Cut small slits in 1 side of roasted, peeled chiles. Remove seeds.

Stuff chiles with cheese strips before coating with flour and batter.

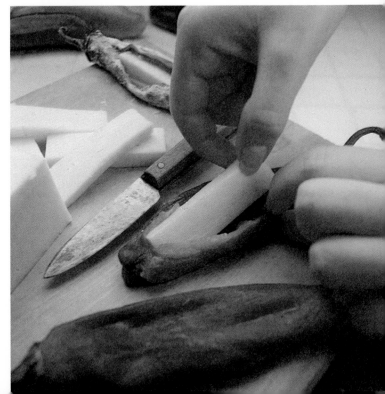

Chiles Rellenos de Elote

Chiles Stuffed with Corn

To show you the variety of Mexican-style stuffed chiles, here's a baked version.

**6 poblano chiles, roasted, peeled,
 or 6 canned whole green chiles**
Salted water
**3 ears corn or 3 cups thawed frozen
 whole-kernel corn**
1 garlic clove
1/2 teaspoon salt
1 tablespoon vegetable oil
1 tablespoon butter

1 onion, chopped
1 large tomato, peeled, chopped
Freshly ground black pepper
1/4 teaspoon dried leaf oregano, crushed
**8 oz. Monterey Jack cheese, shredded
 (2 cups)**
Cheese Sauce, see below
1/4 cup grated Parmesan cheese

Cheese Sauce:
2 tablespoons butter
2 tablespoons all-purpose flour
1-1/2 cups milk
1/4 teaspoon salt

Dash white pepper
**1/2 cup reserved shredded Monterey
 Jack cheese**

Cut as small a slit as possible in one side of each chile to remove seeds. Leave on stems. Soak poblano chiles in salted water for 1 hour or longer. Do not soak canned chiles. If using fresh corn, cut kernels from corn cobs and set aside. Mash garlic with salt to make a paste. Heat oil and butter in a large skillet. Add garlic paste and onion. Cook until onion is tender but not browned. Add tomato, corn kernels, black pepper and oregano. Cook over medium heat 10 to 15 minutes, until corn is almost tender. Remove from heat. Reserve 1/2 cup of shredded Monterey Jack cheese for Cheese Sauce. Stir remaining cheese into corn mixture; set aside. Prepare Cheese Sauce. Preheat oven to 350°F (175°C). Drain poblano chiles; rinse and drain again. If using canned whole green chiles, drain; rinse and drain again. Stuff chiles with corn mixture and place in a large, shallow baking dish. Pour Cheese Sauce over stuffed chiles. Sprinkle with Parmesan cheese. Bake 20 to 30 minutes until hot and lightly browned on top. Makes 6 servings.

Cheese Sauce:
Melt butter in a medium saucepan. Stir in flour. Gradually add milk, stirring until smooth. Cook and stir until sauce boils and thickens. Stir in salt, pepper and reserved cheese. Cook and stir until cheese is melted.

Chayotes Rellenos
Stuffed Chayotes

Sometimes called vegetable pears, chayotes belong to the squash family.

2 large chayotes	2 small tomatoes, peeled, chopped,
Water	drained (1/2 lb.)
1 garlic clove	1 tablespoon chopped fresh parsley
1/2 teaspoon salt	2 oz. Cheddar cheese, shredded,
1 tablespoon butter	(1/2 cup)
1 small onion, chopped	Fresh parsley

Cut chayotes in half lengthwise. Place in a large saucepan with water to cover. Bring to a boil; reduce heat. Cover and simmer until chayotes are tender when pierced with a fork, 30 to 45 minutes. Drain and cool. Scoop out pulp with a sharp spoon, being careful not to tear shells. Reserve shells. Dice pulp and set aside. Preheat oven to 350°F (175°C). Mash garlic with salt to make a paste. Melt butter in a large skillet. Add garlic paste and onion. Cook until onion is tender but not browned. Add tomatoes, chayote pulp and 1 tablespoon parsley. Simmer 15 minutes or until tomatoes are cooked and liquid is evaporated. Spoon mixture into reserved chayote shells. Sprinkle with cheese and top with additional chopped parsley. Bake 20 minutes or until cheese is melted and vegetables are heated through. Makes 4 servings.

How To Make
Chayotes Rellenos

Cook chayotes until tender. Scoop pulp from cooked chayotes without tearing shell.

Spoon filling into shells, top with cheese and a parsley sprig. Bake until hot.

Chiles Rellenos de Atún
Chiles Stuffed with Tuna

A new approach for tuna salad—serve it in a chile.

4 poblano chiles or California
  chiles, roasted, peeled
Salted water
Tuna Salad, see below
1 medium carrot, peeled, thinly
  sliced
Boiling salted water
2 tablespoons olive oil
1 small onion, sliced

1 garlic clove, thinly sliced
1 bay leaf, crumbled
1/4 teaspoon dried leaf oregano,
  crushed
Pinch dried leaf thyme
Salt and freshly ground pepper
2 tablespoons white vinegar
Parsley sprigs

Tuna Salad:
1 (6-1/2-oz.) can tuna, drained,
  flaked
1 medium celery stalk, chopped
1-1/2 tablespoons chopped onion

1-1/2 teaspoons lemon juice
Salt and pepper
1/4 cup mayonnaise
1 tablespoon whipping cream

Cut as small a slit as possible in one side of each chile to remove seeds. Leave on stems. Cover poblano chiles with salted water and let stand 1 hour or longer. Do not soak canned chiles. Prepare Tuna Salad; chill. Cover and cook carrot in boiling salted water 5 minutes; drain. Heat olive oil in a large skillet. Add onion and garlic. Cook until onion is tender but not browned. Add cooked carrot, bay leaf, oregano, thyme and salt and pepper to taste. Cook a few minutes longer, but do not let vegetables brown. Stir in vinegar; remove from heat. Drain chiles. Rinse well and drain again. Stuff chiles with chilled Tuna Salad. Place on a platter. Top with vegetable mixture and garnish with parsley sprigs. Serve chilled. Makes 4 servings.

Tuna Salad:
In a medium bowl, combine tuna, celery, onion, lemon juice and salt and pepper to taste. Blend mayonnaise and cream in a small bowl. Add to tuna mixture. Toss with a fork.

Camarones para Chiles Rellenos
Shrimp Stuffing for Chiles

Use any chiles rellenos recipe to prepare chiles. Then stuff with this delectable shrimp.

2 tablespoons vegetable oil
2 green onions, chopped
6 oz. shrimp, cooked chopped
2 tomatoes, peeled, seeded, chopped

2 tablespoons capers
1 tablespoon chopped pimiento-stuffed
  olives
1/2 teaspoon dried leaf oregano, crushed

Heat oil in a medium skillet. Saute onions until tender. Add remaining ingredients. Cook over medium heat until thickened, 7 to 10 minutes. Makes enough filling for 8 to 10 chiles.

Jalapeños y Verduras en Escabeche
Pickled Jalapeño Chiles & Vegetables

Refrigerate these easy-to-make pickles and serve as a sauce or as a side dish.

Water
Salt
1/4 cup sliced celery
1/4 cup sliced carrot
1/2 cup small cauliflowerets
1/4 cup vegetable oil
1/4 medium onion, slivered
2 garlic cloves
1 cup white vinegar

1 small bay leaf
1/4 teaspoon dried leaf oregano,
 crushed
Pinch dried leaf thyme, crushed
8 peppercorns
1/2 teaspoon salt
1 (6-1/2-oz.) can jalapeño
 chiles (not pickled)

Bring 1 to 2 cups salted water to a boil in a small saucepan. Drop in celery and immediately remove with a slotted spoon. Drop in carrots and boil 4 minutes. Drain and rinse with cold water. Bring another 1 to 2 cups salted water to a boil. Add cauliflowerets. Boil 4 minutes. Drain and rinse with cold water. Heat oil in a medium saucepan. Add onion and garlic. Cook until onion is crisp-tender but not browned. Add vinegar, bay leaf, oregano, thyme, peppercorns and salt. Simmer 5 minutes. Add jalapeño chiles with liquid, celery, carrot and cauliflowerets. Bring to a boil and remove from heat. Spoon vegetables carefully into a clean hot jar. Cover with the hot cooking liquid. Let cool; cover with a tight fitting lid. Refrigerate 1 or 2 days before using to blend flavors. Oil in pickles will become cloudy in refrigerator. Let pickles stand at room temperature a few minutes before serving and cloudiness will disappear. Makes about 3 cups.

How To Make
Jalapeños y Verduras en Escabeche

Cook celery, carrots and cauliflowerets. Drain and rinse; drain again.

Spoon hot cooked vegetables into a jar. Cover with hot cooking liquid.

Chiles Rellenos de Guacamole
Guacamole Stuffed Chiles

Cooks in Mexico use limes more than they use lemons.

**6 small poblano chiles or 4
  fresh California chiles,
  roasted, peeled**
Salted water
Vinaigrette Dressing, see below
2 medium avocados
1 small tomato, chopped

1/2 small onion, finely chopped
1/2 teaspoon lime juice or lemon juice
1/2 teaspoon salt
1/8 teaspoon ground cumin
Lettuce leaves
Tomato wedges

Vinaigrette Dressing:
6 tablespoons olive oil
2 tablespoons white vinegar
1/2 teapoon salt
1/4 teaspoon paprika

1/8 teaspoon freshly ground pepper
1 teaspoon chopped fresh parsley
1/2 teaspoon chopped fresh chives

Cut as small a slit as possible in one side of each chile or pepper to remove seeds. Leave on stems. Soak in salted water 1 hour. Drain; rinse well and drain again. Cover and refrigerate until serving time. Prepare Vinaigrette Dressing. Let stand to blend flavors. At serving time, peel avocados and slice into a medium bowl. Mash with a fork. Stir in tomato, onion, lime juice or lemon juice, salt and cumin. Line a platter with lettuce leaves. Place a spoonful of avocado mixture in each chile. Place stuffed chiles on lettuce leaves; garnish with tomato wedges. Shake dressing and pour over chiles. Makes 4 to 6 servings.

Vinaigrette Dressing:
Combine all ingredients in a jar with a tight-fitting lid. Shake well. Shake again before using.

Ensalada Verde de Vivián
Vivian's Green Salad

A hearty green salad good with anything from carne asada to enchiladas.

1 medium head butter lettuce
**1/2 medium green pepper, cut in thin
  slivers**
1/4 cup cilantro leaves

1/4 cup sliced pitted ripe olives
1/4 cup drained canned garbanzo beans
1/4 cup sliced green onions
1/4 to 1/3 cup Italian dressing

Rinse and drain lettuce. Tear into bite-size pieces. Place in a salad bowl. Add green pepper, cilantro, olives and garbanzo beans. Toss with enough Italian dressing to coat lightly. Makes 6 servings.

Platos de Tortillas
Tortilla Dishes

Corn has always been important in the Mexican kitchen. The Mayans believed man was created from corn dough, or *masa*. The Aztecs worshipped corn gods. Many foods eaten today, including *tortillas*, *tamales* and the corn beverage *atole*, were enjoyed by Mexican Indians long before the Spanish conquerors arrived.

Although corn is no longer worshipped, it is still bad form to throw away a *tortilla*. Leftover *tortillas* are cut up and fried to make *Totopos* (Corn Chips), page 30, or they are cut into strips or squares, deep-fried and mixed with sauce for *Chilaquiles con Salsa Verde* (Tortilla Strips with Green Sauce). Sometimes *tortillas* are ground and used to thicken or flavor a dish such as *Mole Poblano* (Mole Puebla-Style), page 116. The most novel use of *tortillas* I've seen was at a beachfront restaurant in Zihuatanejo. *Tortillas* that appeared

to shingle the roof were being dried for burro feed!

Tacos, enchiladas and *tamales*, as most of us know them, are often made quite differently in Mexico. In addition to crisp fried *tacos*, you'll find soft *tacos*—made by wrapping filling in steamed tortillas. *Enchiladas* are usually rolled and served at once without baking. And they are frequently topped with crumbly Mexican-style cheese rather than melted cheese. Although they are eaten all year, *tamales* are traditional for Christmas. Families gather to share in the preparation of dozens of *tamales* to serve to visiting family and friends during the holidays.

My recipes are only a sampling of *tortilla* foods. It is impossible to catalog all these dishes or to account for regional customs and the variations of different cooks.

COMPANY DINNER

Tortillas de Maíz
Corn Tortillas

Versatile tortillas can be folded, stacked, rolled or cut into chips and fried.

1 cup instant masa
1/2 cup water

Place instant masa in a medium bowl. Work in water with your fingers to make a soft dough. If dough is crumbly or dry, blend in a little more water. Shape dough into a ball. Cover with a damp towel; let stand 20 minutes. Preheat an ungreased griddle or large heavy skillet over medium heat. Line the bottom of a tortilla press with plastic wrap. If you're not using a tortilla press, place plastic wrap on a flat surface. Divide dough into equal pieces according to the number and size tortillas desired. Shape each piece of dough into a ball and place on the lined tortilla press or flat surface. Place another piece of plastic wrap on top of dough. Press with the palm of your hand to flatten ball slightly. Close tortilla press firmly and then open. Or flatten dough by pressing with the bottom of a small heavy skillet. If necessary, press plastic with your fingers to flatten further. Peel plastic from top and bottom of tortilla. If tortilla sticks, dough is too wet; work in 1 teaspoon instant masa. Add more masa, a little at a time, if necessary. If tortilla crumbles, dough is too dry; work in 1 teaspoon water. Add more water, a little at a time, if necessary. To bake tortillas, cook on preheated griddle or skillet until lightly spotted with brown on each side, turning once. Stack cooked tortillas and cover with a dry cloth towel. Tortillas may feel stiff as they come from the griddle but will soften as they stand. Makes six 6-inch tortillas.

How Much to Make How Many?

Mix 1 cup of instant masa with 1/2 cup of water as directed above.

Divide Masa Into:	To Make:
6 pieces	six 6-inch tortillas
8 pieces	eight 5-inch tortillas
12 pieces	twelve 4-inch tortillas
20 pieces	twenty 3-inch tortillas

CORN TORTILLAS

In Mexico you buy hot fresh *tortillas* from the neighborhood *tortilleria*. You can also buy dough for *tortillas*, called *masa*. In other countries, dried corn flour called *instant masa* is often available. It is mixed with water to make *masa* for *tortillas*. One brand is Masa Harina, produced by the Quaker Oats Company. Mexican-style corn *tortillas* and other corn products should be made with this flour—not with cornmeal.

Shaping *tortillas* takes practice. Skilled *tortilla* makers pat the dough into a thin circle between their hands. Some use a metal or wooden *tortilla* press. If you don't have a *tortilla* press, use a heavy, flat object such as an iron skillet to press the dough. Press the dough between pieces of plastic wrap to prevent sticking.

Work warm water into masa with your fingers to make a soft dough. Then shape dough into balls.

Flatten balls and place on tortilla press between pieces of plastic wrap.

How To Make
Tortillas de Maíz

Close tortilla press firmly; open press.

Peel plastic from top of tortilla. Invert onto a flat surface and remove bottom plastic.

Tortillas de Harina
Flour Tortillas

Popular in Northern Mexico, flour tortillas are eaten like bread and used to make burritos.

2 cups all-purpose flour
1/2 teaspoon salt
1/4 cup lard

About 1/2 cup warm water
Additional lard
Additional flour

Combine 2 cups flour and salt in a medium bowl. Rub in 1/4 cup lard with your fingers until evenly mixed. Gradually stir in enough water to make a soft dough. Divide dough into quarters. Divide each quarter into 3 equal pieces, making 12 pieces of dough in all. Shape each piece into a smooth ball. With your hands, smooth additional lard over each ball to coat generously. Place balls in a medium bowl; cover with a dry cloth towel. Let stand at least 15 minutes. Preheat an ungreased griddle or large heavy skillet over medium heat. Shape each ball into a flat round patty. Sprinkle both sides of patties with flour. On a lightly floured surface, roll out each patty to an 8-inch circle. Place each tortilla on preheated griddle. Cook until bubbles form on top and underside is flecked with brown. Turn tortilla and press down bubbles with towel. Cook until bottom is flecked with brown. Stack cooked tortillas and cover with a dry cloth towel. Serve immediately or wrap in foil and reheat briefly in oven before serving. Makes twelve 8-inch tortillas.

FLOUR TORTILLAS

Only flour, shortening and water are used to make flour *tortillas* and they are rolled out with a rolling pin. However, as in making corn *tortillas*, practice will improve the product.

Flour *tortillas* can be bought in several sizes: 4-inch and 6-inch or snack-size, 8-inch or table-size, and 12-inch or 15-inch *tortillas* for *burritos*. When you make your own, you can make any size, but *tortillas* should be evenly shaped and evenly cooked so the edges are not ragged or thin and dry.

Mexican cooks want their *tortillas* eaten at the height of perfection so they serve them directly from the griddle. Cold *tortillas* can be warmed on a griddle or wrapped in foil and heated in the oven at 350°F (175°C) for 15 minutes. Experts warm them over an open flame, but if you're a novice, you may end up with a charred *tortilla!*

ENCHILADAS

An *enchilada* is a corn *tortilla* rolled around a filling, baked in a sauce and served with a variety of garnishes. The filling and sauce are prepared and cooked in advance. When the *enchiladas* are assembled, they are baked to melt the cheese and to heat thoroughly.

How to Soften Tortillas—Begin by using tongs to place *tortillas* one at a time in hot oil or hot melted lard for just a few seconds on each side. This will soften them so they can be rolled without cracking and breaking. Drain the *tortillas* over the skillet or on paper towels. Some recipes call for dipping the *tortillas* in sauce either before or after softening. This is not necessary but may add flavor to the *tortillas.*

Filling & Rolling—Place a softened *tortilla* on a plate or flat surface. Spread a spoonful of filling in a strip just below the center. Roll up tightly and place the *enchilada* seam-side down in a baking dish. The baking dish is not greased, but spooning a little sauce over the bottom of the dish may prevent the *enchiladas* from sticking. When all the *enchiladas* are filled and rolled, cover them with the sauce so they won't become dry while baking. Be sure the *enchilada* ends are covered or they will be dry and tough.

Preparing in Advance—If you fill and roll up *enchiladas* in advance, don't cover them with sauce. *Enchiladas* soaked in sauce will be mushy. Instead, spread a little sauce on the edges and tops to keep them moist. Cover and refrigerate the prepared *enchiladas* until you're ready to bake them. Pour the rest of the sauce over the *enchiladas* and top with shredded cheese just before baking.

Freezing—Leftover *enchiladas* freeze well wrapped in foil. Thaw *enchiladas* 2 to 4 hours at room temperature and reheat them at 350°F (175°C).

Enchiladas de Leche

Enchiladas in Milk Sauce

To keep assembled enchiladas warm, cover them with foil and place them in a 200°F (95°C) oven.

1-1/4 cups Salsa para Enchiladas, page 37
8 oz. queso fresco or farmer cheese, room temperature, crumbled (2 cups)
1 medium onion, chopped

1 cup milk
2 eggs, beaten
Salt
1/2 cup lard
12 corn tortillas

Prepare Salsa para Enchiladas. Set aside about 1/2 cup cheese and a third of the onion for topping. Combine enchilada sauce and milk in a shallow saucepan. Bring to a boil. Gradually stir some of the hot sauce into beaten eggs. Pour egg mixture into saucepan. Add salt to taste. Heat until steaming but do not boil or sauce will curdle. Heat lard in a medium skillet. Use tongs to dip 1 tortilla at a time in sauce then in hot lard. Hold in lard 3 to 5 seconds. Quickly turn tortilla and fry other side, 3 to 5 seconds. Place tortilla on a plate. Add about 2 tablespoons of the cheese and about 1 teaspoon of the onion. Roll up and place seam-side down on a warm platter; keep warm. When all enchiladas are prepared, top with remaining sauce, then reserved cheese and onion. Serve at once. Makes 12 enchiladas.

Enchiladas de Pollo en Mole
Chicken Mole Enchiladas

Mole paste can be bought in gourmet shops or Mexican food stores.

1/2 cup mole paste
2 cups chicken broth
2 tablespoons toasted slivered almonds
1/2 oz. semisweet chocolate
1/4 teaspoon Maggi seasoning

1/3 cup plus 1 tablespoon vegetable oil
8 corn tortillas
2 cups shredded cooked chicken
1 teaspoon sesame seeds

Combine mole paste, chicken broth, almonds, chocolate and Maggi seasoning in blender or food processor. Process until smooth. Heat 1 tablespoon oil in a medium saucepan. Add mole paste mixture. Bring to a boil; reduce heat. Simmer uncovered until slightly thickened, 5 to 10 minutes. Heat 1/3 cup oil in a medium skillet. With tongs, carefully place 1 tortilla at a time in hot oil. Hold in oil 3 to 5 seconds until softened. Quickly turn tortilla and soften other side, 3 to 5 seconds, then dip in mole sauce to coat. Lay coated tortilla on a plate and top with a spoonful of the chicken. Roll up tightly and place seam-side down on a warm platter. Repeat with remaining tortillas. Top enchiladas with remaining sauce; sprinkle with sesame seeds. Serve immediately. Makes 8 enchiladas.

Variation
Substitute leftover sauce from Mole Poblano, page 116, for the mole paste.

Enchiladas de Queso
Cheese Enchiladas

You'll be proud to serve enchiladas with your own homemade sauce.

2-1/3 cups Salsa para Enchiladas,
  page 37, or Salsa de Chile
  en Polvo, page 39
8 oz. cheese such as Cheddar or
  a combination of Cheddar and
  Monterey Jack, shredded (2 cups)

1/4 cup vegetable oil
6 corn tortillas
1 small onion, chopped
4 green onions, chopped

Prepare salsa; heat in a medium saucepan. Reserve about a third of the cheese for topping enchiladas. Heat oil in a medium skillet. With tongs, carefully place 1 tortilla at a time in hot oil. Hold in oil 3 to 5 seconds until softened. Quickly turn tortilla and soften other side, 3 to 5 seconds. Drain over skillet or on paper towels. Immediately dip tortilla in hot enchilada sauce; remove at once. Do not soak tortilla or it may tear. Place tortilla on a plate and arrange some of the cheese in a strip just below the center. Sprinkle cheese with chopped onion. Roll up tightly and place seam-side down in an 8-inch square or other shallow, medium baking dish. Preheat oven to 350°F (175°C). When all enchiladas are prepared, cover with remaining sauce. Sprinkle with reserved cheese. Bake 15 to 20 minutes, until cheese is melted and enchiladas are heated through. Garnish with green onions and serve at once. Makes 6 enchiladas.

Carefully dip tortillas into hot oil 3 to 5 seconds on each side.

How To Make
Enchiladas de Queso

Then dip tortilla into sauce and remove at once.

Place cheese and onion in a strip just below the center. Roll up tightly. Place seam-side down in baking dish.

Enchiladas de Pollo **Photo on cover.**
Deluxe Chicken Enchiladas

Company coming? These enchiladas are plumper than most and perfect banquet food.

2 whole chicken breasts	1/4 cup cilantro leaves
Water	3/4 cup whipping cream
1/2 small onion	1 egg
1 bay leaf	Salt
8 peppercorns	1/4 cup lard
Salt	8 corn tortillas
1/2 medium onion, chopped	4 oz. Cheddar or Monterey Jack cheese,
3 tablespoons grated Parmesan cheese	shredded (1 cup)
4 oz. Monterey Jack cheese, shredded	Guacamole, page 40
(1 cup)	1 cup dairy sour cream
1 (4-oz.) can green chiles	3 or 4 radishes, sliced
1 (13-oz.) can tomatillos, drained or	2 cups shredded lettuce
1-3/4 cups drained canned tomatoes	12 ripe olives

Place chicken breasts in a large pot or Dutch oven. Add water to cover, onion, bay leaf, peppercorns and salt to taste. Bring to a boil; reduce heat. Cover and simmer 45 minutes or until tender. Cool chicken in broth. Drain, reserving broth for another use. Shred chicken with 2 forks or with your fingers. Mix shredded chicken, chopped onion, Parmesan cheese and 1 cup shredded Monterey Jack cheese. Taste and add salt if needed. Set aside. In blender or food processor, combine green chiles, tomatillos or tomatoes, cilantro, whipping cream and egg. Blend until smooth. Add salt to taste. Set aside. Preheat oven to 350°F (175°C). Heat lard in a small skillet. With tongs, carefully place 1 tortilla at a time in hot lard. Hold in lard 3 to 5 seconds until softened. Quickly turn tortilla and soften other side, 3 to 5 seconds. Drain over skillet or on paper towels. Place 1/8 of the chicken mixture on each tortilla, pressing the mixture to make it compact. Roll tightly and place seam-side down in a 12'' x 7-1/2'' baking dish. Pour chile-cream mixture over enchiladas and sprinkle evenly with 1 cup shredded Cheddar or Monterey Jack cheese. Bake 20 minutes, or until heated through and bubbly. Prepare Guacamole. For each serving, place 2 enchiladas on a plate and top with about 3 tablespoons sour cream. Place a mound of Guacamole over sour cream. Garnish with radish slices. Place 1/2 cup shredded lettuce next to enchiladas, if desired. Place a mound of Guacamole on lettuce. Top Guacamole with 1 tablespoon sour cream and 2 ripe olives if desired. Makes 8 enchiladas.

Enchiladas Verdes
Green Enchiladas

These enchiladas from Guadalajara are folded rather than rolled.

1 whole chicken breast	**1/2 medium onion**
Water	**1 large garlic clove**
1/4 medium onion	**1 tablespoon lard**
Salt	**1/2 teaspoon salt**
3 peppercorns	**1/4 cup lard**
1 lb. fresh tomatillos or 1 cup	**6 corn tortillas**
drained canned tomatillos	**Crumbled queso fresco or shredded**
Water	**Monterey Jack cheese**

Place chicken breast in a large saucepan. Add water to cover. Add onion quarter, salt to taste and peppercorns. Bring to a boil; reduce heat. Cover and simmer 45 minutes. Cool chicken breast in broth. Drain, reserving 1/4 cup broth. Reserve remaining broth for another use. Remove meat from bones and shred with 2 forks or your fingers. If using fresh tomatillos, remove papery husks. Wash husked tomatillos and place in a medium saucepan. Add 1/2 inch water. Bring to a boil; reduce heat. Cover and simmer 10 minutes or until tender; drain. Cool slightly. Do not cook canned tomatillos. Place cooked or canned tomatillos in blender or food processor with 1/2 onion and garlic. Process until pureed. Heat 1 tablespoon lard in a medium saucepan. Add pureed tomatillo mixture, reserved broth and 1/2 teaspoon salt. Bring to a boil; reduce heat. Cover and simmer sauce 15 minutes. When ready to prepare enchiladas, warm shredded chicken and bring sauce to a simmer. Heat 1/4 cup lard in a medium skillet. With tongs, carefully place 1 tortilla at a time in hot lard. Hold in lard 3 to 5 seconds until softened. Quickly turn tortilla and soften other side, 3 to 5 seconds. Drain over skillet or on paper towels. Place a spoonful of the shredded chicken on each tortilla. Sprinkle with salt and add a spoonful of sauce. Fold tortilla in half over filling. Place on a warm plate. Top with more sauce and sprinkle with crumbled queso fresco or Monterey Jack cheese. Serve immediately. Makes 6 enchiladas.

Papadzules
Egg-Filled Enchiladas

Enchiladas filled with hard-cooked eggs are popular in Yucatán.

4 hard-cooked eggs	**Salt and pepper**
Tomato Sauce for Enchiladas Jaiba,	**1/3 cup vegetable oil**
page 83	**8 corn tortillas**

Prepare eggs; keep warm. Prepare Tomato Sauce; keep warm. Just before serving, peel and chop eggs. Add salt and pepper to taste. Heat oil in a medium skillet. With tongs, carefully place 1 tortilla at a time in hot oil. Hold in oil 3 to 5 seconds until softened. Quickly turn tortilla and soften other side, 3 to 5 seconds. Drain over skillet or on paper towels. Place a spoonful of the chopped egg on each tortilla and roll up. Place 2 papadzules seam-side down on each plate and top with about 1/2 cup Tomato Sauce. Serve immediately. Makes 8 enchiladas.

Enchiladas Suizas
Swiss Enchiladas

Suiza means the dish includes a dairy product.

1 whole chicken breast	**1 tablespoon packed fresh cilantro**
Water	**leaves**
1/4 small onion	**1 serrano chile or other small hot**
1 bay leaf	**chile, seeded**
4 peppercorns	**2 tablespoons vegetable oil**
Salt and pepper	**1/2 teaspoon salt**
1 lb. fresh tomatillos or 1 cup	**1/4 cup vegetable oil**
drained canned tomatillos	**6 corn tortillas**
Water	**6 oz. Monterey Jack cheese, coarsely**
1/2 small onion	**shredded (1-1/2 cups)**
1 large garlic clove	**Dairy sour cream**

Place chicken breast in a large saucepan with water to cover. Add 1/4 onion, bay leaf, pepper-corns and salt to taste. Bring to a boil; reduce heat. Cover and simmer 45 minutes. Cool chicken breast in broth. Drain, reserving 1 cup broth. Remove meat from bones and shred chicken with 2 forks or with your fingers. Add salt and pepper to taste. If using fresh tomatillos, remove papery husks. Wash husked tomatillos and place in a medium saucepan. Add 1/2 inch water. Bring to a boil; reduce heat. Cover and simmer 10 minutes or until tender; drain. Cool slightly. Do not cook canned tomatillos. Place cooked or canned tomatillos in blender or food processor with 1/2 onion, garlic, cilantro and chile. Process until pureed. Heat 2 tablespoons oil in a medium saucepan. Add pureed tomatillo mixture. Cook 2 to 3 minutes. Add reserved chicken broth and 1/2 teaspoon salt. Bring to a boil; reduce heat. Cover and simmer sauce 15 minutes. Preheat oven to 350°F (175°C). Heat 1/4 cup oil in a medium skillet. With tongs, carefully place 1 tortilla at a time in hot oil. Hold in oil 3 to 5 seconds until softened. Quickly turn tortilla and soften other side, 3 to 5 seconds. Drain over skillet or on paper towels. Place a spoonful of the shredded chicken on tortilla. Roll up and place seam-side down in a shallow baking dish. When all enchiladas are assembled, cover with sauce and top with cheese. Bake 15 to 20 minutes, until cheese is melted and bubbling. To serve, top each enchilada with a spoonful of sour cream. Makes 6 enchiladas.

Enchiladas de Jaiba
Crab Enchiladas

For something really different, try these enchiladas from Veracruz.

Tomato Sauce, see below
Crab Filling, see below
1/4 cup vegetable oil
6 corn tortillas

Dairy sour cream
1 tablespoon chopped fresh parsley
1 tablespoon chopped almonds

Tomato Sauce:
4 small tomatoes, peeled (1 lb.)
1/2 medium onion
1 garlic clove
1/4 to 1/2 jalapeño chile or
  other small hot chile

1 tablespoon vegetable oil
1/2 teaspoon salt

Crab Filling:
1 tablespoon vegetable oil
1/2 medium onion, chopped
1 small garlic clove, minced
6 oz. cooked or canned crab, drained,
  flaked
3 Spanish-style green olives, pitted,
  chopped

1 tablespoon raisins, plumped in hot
  water, drained
1 tablespoon chopped almonds
1 tablespoon chopped parsley
1 teaspoon capers
Salt to taste

Prepare Tomato Sauce and keep warm. Prepare Crab Filling. Preheat oven to 350°F (175°C). Heat oil in a medium skillet. With tongs, carefully place 1 tortilla at a time in hot oil. Hold in oil 3 to 5 seconds until softened. Quickly turn tortilla and soften other side, 3 to 5 seconds. Drain over skillet or on paper towels. Place a generous spoonful of Crab Filling on each tortilla. Roll up and place in a baking dish. When all enchiladas are prepared, cover with Tomato Sauce. Cover baking dish with foil. Bake 15 minutes or until heated through. Garnish enchiladas with a generous spoonful of sour cream. Sprinkle with parsley and almonds. Makes 6 enchiladas.

Tomato Sauce:
Combine tomatoes, onion, garlic and chile in blender or food processor and process until pureed. Heat oil in a medium saucepan. Add tomato mixture and salt. Bring to a boil; reduce heat. Simmer gently uncovered 10 minutes. Makes about 2 cups.

Crab Filling:
Heat oil in a medium skillet. Add onion and garlic. Cook until tender. Stir in remaining ingredients. Cook over medium heat 3 to 5 minutes.

Enchiladas Chatas de Nuevo México
New Mexican Flat Enchiladas

In New Mexico, each stack of tortillas, meat and beans would be topped with a fried egg.

1/2 cup dried pinto beans
Hot water for soaking
1 medium onion
2 garlic cloves
Water for cooking
1/2 teaspoon salt
2 tablespoons vegetable oil
1 (1-lb. 3-oz.) can enchilada sauce or
  2-1/4 cups Salsa para Enchiladas,
  page 37
1 lb. ground beef
1/2 teaspoon dried leaf oregano,
  crushed

1/2 teaspoon ground cumin
Salt
8 oz. Longhorn or mild Cheddar cheese,
  shredded (2 cups)
1/2 cup vegetable oil
12 corn tortillas
1 avocado, cut in 16 thin slices
3/4 cup dairy sour cream
4 cups finely shredded lettuce
12 pitted ripe olives
2 small tomatoes (1/2 lb.), cut in 12
  wedges

Sort beans to remove small stones and other foreign matter. Place beans with hot water to cover in a medium saucepan. Cover and let stand overnight or at least 8 hours. Drain beans and rinse well. Place soaked beans, 1/8 of the onion and 1 garlic clove in a 2-quart saucepan. Add fresh hot water to cover generously. Bring to a boil; reduce heat. Cover with lid ajar and simmer 2 hours. Add 1/2 teaspoon salt. Simmer 2 hours longer, until beans are tender but not mushy. Heat canned sauce or prepare Salsa para Enchiladas. Chop remaining onion. Mince remaining garlic clove. Heat 2 tablespoons oil in a large, heavy skillet. Add beef. Cook until no longer pink, stirring to crumble. Add chopped onion and minced garlic. Cook until onion is almost tender. Add 1-1/4 cups enchilada sauce or salsa, oregano and cumin. Add drained beans. Simmer 5 minutes. Taste and add salt if needed. Divide cheese into four 1/2-cup portions, one for each enchilada. Prepare each enchilada in a 9-inch pie plate or other ovenproof plate. Heat 1/2 cup oil in a medium skillet. For each enchilada, use tongs to lower tortilla gently into hot oil. Hold in oil 3 to 5 seconds until softened. Quickly turn tortilla and soften other side, 3 to 5 seconds. Drain over skillet or on paper towels. Place in pie plate. Cover evenly with 1/3 cup meat mixture and a little cheese. Soften another tortilla in hot oil; drain and place on top of cheese. Add another 1/3 cup meat mixture and a little cheese. Soften a third tortilla; drain and place on stack. Add another 1/3 cup meat mixture and remaining portion of cheese. Cover evenly with 1/4 cup remaining enchilada sauce. Prepare 3 more enchiladas. While preparing last enchilada, preheat oven to 350°F (175°C). Bake enchiladas 10 to 15 minutes, or until cheese is melted. Top each stack with 4 avocado slices arranged like spokes of a wheel. Place a mound of sour cream in the center. Arrange shredded lettuce around each enchilada. Garnish with olives and tomato wedges. Makes 4 large servings.

Variation
Substitute 1-1/2 cups drained canned pinto beans for cooked dried beans.

TACO PARTY

Entertaining with *tacos* is fun and economical. Arrange the food buffet-style on colorful painted trays and in wooden bowls. Glazed pottery and baskets of various sizes and shapes make marvelous and authentic serving containers and decorations. Set a festive mood with brightly colored napkins, large paper flowers and candles.

In this section you'll find recipes for *Tacos de Pollo* (Chicken Tacos), *Tacos de Manuel* (Manuel's Tacos) and *Tacos de Machaca* (Shredded Beef Tacos). Or choose from fillings such as *Frijoles Refritos* (Refried Beans), page 149; *Carnitas a la Casera* (Home-Style Meats), page 115; *Carne Deshebrada* (Shredded Meat), page 109; and *Mole de Puerco* (Pork *Mole*), page 114.

Buy packages of shaped *taco* shells or shape your own, page 90. If you want to serve soft *tacos*, buy corn *tortillas*, wrap them in foil and heat them in a preheated 350°F (175°C) oven for about 15 minutes. Spoon whatever fillings you want along one end of a warm *tortilla*, roll it up and eat it immediately.

Refried beans are expected at a Mexican meal, so if you don't serve them as a *taco* filling, be sure they appear as a side dish. Any of the rice recipes on pages 139 to 147 will round out your traditional menu.

Tacos are usually garnished with shredded lettuce, chopped green onions, chopped tomatoes and canned or homemade *salsa*. See *Salsas* (Sauces), pages 32 to 40. Sour cream and shredded Cheddar or Monterey Jack cheese add to the intriguing flavor and texture contrasts. If avocados are in season, top your tacos with *Guacamole* (Avocado Sauce), page 40. Many supermarkets carry *guacamole* or avocado dip in the frozen food section. Arrange the garnishes in separate bowls or in a sectioned platter.

Greet each guest with a *Margarita*, page 12, or a glass of *Sangria*, page 17. *Sangria* can be poured from a large iced pitcher or ladled from an elegant punch bowl. Ice cream topped with *Kahlúa* provides an easy but satisfying dessert.

MENU
Margaritas, page 12
Tacos de Pollo (Chicken Tacos), page 91
Shredded Lettuce
Chopped Green Onions
Chopped Tomatoes
Salsa Fresca (Fresh Sauce), page 33
Sour Cream
Shredded Cheddar Cheese
Guacamole (Avocado Sauce), page 40
Frijoles Refritos (Refried Beans), page 149
Arroz a la Mexicana (Rice Mexican-Style), page 140
Ice Cream with Kahlúa

The Taco Party on the following pages shows from bottom left: Tacos de Pollo (Chicken Tacos), taco shells, Margaritas, filling for Tacos de Pollo, Frijoles Refritos (Refried Beans) and Carne Deshebrada (Shredded Meat). On the tray are bowls of chopped onion, shredded cheese, shredded lettuce, chopped tomato and Guacamole (Avocado Sauce).

Tacos de Machaca
Shredded Beef Tacos

Machaca is spiced shredded beef. It is often served by itself as a main dish.

Machaca, see below
6 to 8 corn tortillas

Garnishes, see below

Machaca:
1 lb. boneless beef chuck
1 cup water
6 peppercorns
1/4 medium onion
Salt
1 garlic clove
1/4 teaspoon salt
1 tablespoon vegetable oil

1/2 medium onion, chopped
1 California chile or 1 poblano chile,
  roasted, peeled or 1 canned whole
  green chile
2 small tomatoes, peeled, chopped
  (1/2 lb.)
1/4 teaspoon ground cumin
Freshly ground pepper

Garnishes:
Salsa Fresca, page 33, Salsa Mexicana,
  page 33, or other salsa
1 avocado
Juice of 1/2 lime

Salt
1 onion, chopped
Cilantro leaves, chopped

Prepare Machaca. Preheat oven to 350°F (175°C). Wrap tortillas in foil and place in oven until softened, about 15 minutes. Prepare Garnishes. For each taco, place a spoonful of Machaca on a warm tortilla. Top with avocado mixture, onion, cilantro and salsa to taste. Fold tortilla around filling. Repeat with remaining ingredients. Serve immediately. Makes 6 to 8 tacos.

Machaca (Shredded Beef):
Place meat in a large saucepan. Add water, peppercorns, 1/4 onion and salt to taste. Bring to a boil; reduce heat. Cover and simmer until meat is very tender, about 1-1/2 hours. Cool meat in broth. Drain, reserving 1/3 cup broth. Shred meat with 2 forks. Mash garlic with 1/4 teaspoon salt to make a paste. Heat oil in a large skillet. Add chopped onion and garlic paste. Cook until onion is tender. Cut chile into short strips. Add chile strips and tomatoes to cooked onion. Cook 3 to 4 minutes. Add meat, cumin and freshly ground pepper to taste. Cook and stir until meat is heated through. Stir in reserved broth. Taste and add salt if needed. Keep warm.

Garnishes:
Prepare salsa. Mash avocado in a small bowl. Stir in lime juice and salt to taste. Beat until smooth. Place avocado mixture, onion, cilantro and salsa in separate bowls.

Tacos de Manuel
Manuel's Tacos

These tacos are cooked with the filling inside. Freeze extra filling for another use.

Steak & Chorizo Filling, see below
16 to 20 corn tortillas
Oil for frying
1 small head lettuce, shredded
8 oz. Longhorn cheese, shredded
  (2 cups)

3 large tomatoes, chopped (1 lb.)
1 (6-oz.) can pickled jalapeño chiles,
  drained, sliced

Steak & Chorizo Filling:
1 lb. flank steak
Water
Salt
1 potato (about 8 oz.)
Boiling salted water

2 tablespoons vegetable oil
2 oz. chorizo
1/4 medium onion, chopped
1 (8-oz.) can tomato sauce
Pepper

Prepare Steak & Chorizo Filling. Preheat oven to 350°F (175°C). Wrap tortillas in foil, making 2 packets and place in oven until warmed and softened, about 15 minutes. Place about 2 tablespoons filling in center of each warmed tortilla. Fold in half and fasten with wooden picks. Pour oil 1/2 inch deep into a large skillet. Heat to 365°F (185°C). Fry filled tacos in hot oil until crisp. Drain over skillet or on paper towels. Remove wooden picks. Serve lettuce, cheese, tomatoes and chiles in separate bowls to add to tacos as desired. Makes 16 to 20 tacos.

Steak & Chorizo Filling:
Place steak in a large saucepan. Cover with water; add salt to taste. Bring to a boil; reduce heat. Cover and simmer until tender, about 1 hour. Let cool in broth; drain. Cut meat across the grain into 1-1/2-inch long pieces. Shred with 2 forks. Peel potato. Cook in boiling salted water until tender but not mushy, about 20 minutes. Drain and cool. Grate cold potato on a coarse grater. Heat 2 tablespoons oil in a large skillet. Add shredded cooked meat. Cook and stir 3 minutes. Remove meat from skillet. Remove chorizo from casing. Cook in skillet until crumbly. Add onion to chorizo. Cook until onion is tender, stirring occasionally. Add cooked steak. Stir to blend with chorizo mixture. Stir in grated potato and tomato sauce. Season with pepper to taste. Simmer 5 minutes, stirring occasionally. Makes about 3 cups.

Taquitos
Little Tacos

Taquitos cut in half and served with guacamole for dipping make delightful appetizers.

**About 1-1/4 cups Steak & Chorizo Filling
  for Tacos de Manuel, page 89
16 to 20 corn tortillas**

**Oil for frying
Guacamole, page 40**

Prepare Steak & Chorizo Filling. Preheat oven to 350°F (175°C). Wrap tortillas in foil, making 2 packets. Place in oven until softened, about 15 minutes. Place 1 tablespoon filling in a narrow strip at one end of each tortilla. Roll up tightly; fasten in center with a wooden pick. Pour oil 1/2 inch deep into a medium skillet. Heat to 365°F (185°C). Fry several taquitos at a time until crisp. Drain over skillet or on paper towels. Remove wooden picks. To freeze, refrigerate taquitos about 1 hour immediately after frying. Wrap 10 chilled taquitos at a time in heavy foil or freezer wrap; store in freezer. Use within 2 months. To serve frozen taquitos, remove from freezer, unwrap and place in a baking dish. Cover lightly with foil and bake in a preheated 350°F (175°C) oven 20 to 30 minutes until heated through. Prepare Guacamole. Serve taquitos topped with Guacamole. Makes 16 to 20 taquitos.

HOW TO MAKE & FILL TACO SHELLS

No special equipment is needed to make *taco* shells. You can buy devices to hold *tortillas* in shape while being fried and racks to hold them while being stuffed, but they are not necessary.

To make *taco* shells, heat 1/2 cup of lard or vegetable oil in a large skillet to 365°F (185°C). Dip a flat corn *tortilla* in the hot lard or oil on both sides to soften it. Holding it with tongs, fold the softened *tortilla* in half and fry it until crisp, turning once. Drain *taco* shells on paper towels.

To fill a *taco* shell, gently pull it open without breaking it so you can drop in a large spoonful of meat, beans or other filling. Top the filling with garnishes such as onion, lettuce and tomato.

You can fry *tacos* after they are filled. Heat each *tortilla* on a griddle until softened or wrap a stack of *tortillas* in foil and place them in an oven preheated to 350°F (175°C) for about 15 minutes. Place a spoonful of filling on each warmed *tortilla* and fold in half. Fasten securely with wooden picks. Fry a few *tacos* at a time in hot oil until they are crisp, turning as necessary. Drain *tacos* on paper towels. Before serving, remove the wooden picks and add garnishes.

Tacos de Pollo   **Photo on pages 86 and 87.**
Chicken Tacos

Try these after the holidays with leftover turkey.

1 garlic clove
1/2 teaspoon salt
1 tablespoon vegetable oil
1 onion, chopped
1 or 2 tomatoes, peeled, chopped
1 or 2 California chiles, roasted,
   peeled, chopped, or 2 to 4
   tablespoons canned chopped
   green chiles

Pinch pepper
1/8 teaspoon ground cumin
3-1/2 to 4 cups shredded cooked chicken
12 to 15 homemade or packaged taco
   shells
1/2 small head lettuce, shredded
5 oz. Longhorn cheese, shredded
   (1-1/4 cups)
Dairy sour cream

Mash garlic with salt to make a paste. Heat oil in a large skillet. Add onion and garlic paste. Cook until onion is tender. Add tomatoes, chiles, pepper and cumin. Stir in chicken. Cook and stir until mixture is fairly dry. Taste and add more salt and cumin, if desired. Fill taco shells with chicken mixture. Serve lettuce, cheese and sour cream in separate bowls to add to tacos as desired. Makes 12 to 15 tacos.

HOW TO MAKE TAMALES

Tamales are surprisingly easy to make. With a simple basic dough such as *Masa Para Tamales* (Tamale Dough), page 94, you can make any type of tamale, large or small, flavored or plain, sweet or savory. Plain unflavored *tamales* are often served as a bread substitute.

You may be able to buy *masa* especially prepared for *tamales* in your area, but the recipes in this book call for dried instant *masa* which is widely available. Although tamale dough is traditionally made with lard, you can use vegetable shortening if you prefer.

Corn Husks—Place the *hojas*, or dried corn husks, in a dishpan, sink or bucket and cover them with hot water. Let them stand 1 hour or longer until they are softened. Just before using, rinse each corn husk separately and remove any silk. Drain them well and pat with paper towels to remove excess water. If the husks are too wide for the size tamale you want, tear off 1 side. If the husks are too narrow, overlap 2 husks to make a wide one. If dried corn husks aren't available, use a 9'' x 7'' piece of foil for each tamale, see How To Prepare *Tamales* in Foil, page 94.

Filling & Folding—To fill *tamales*, place a soaked, drained and dried corn husk in the palm of your hand, point toward you. Place a spoonful of dough in the center and spread it slightly. Leave a 1/2-inch margin around the edge of the dough to allow for folding the husk. Place a little filling on the dough and spread it slightly with your fingers. Fold the sides of the husk to the center, enclosing the filling completely. Some cooks like to spread a little more dough over the filling before folding in the sides of the corn husk. After you have folded in the sides of the corn husk, fold the pointed end under, keeping the seam on the outside. At this point, you can stand the *tamales* on their folded ends in the steamer with the open ends up.

Another method of closing the *tamales* is to fold the wide end over the pointed end and tie each tamale with string around the center to secure the ends. For a primitive effect, tear a soaked corn husk into thin strips and use the strips as ties.

A third method is to tie both ends of the *tamales* instead of folding them, leaving some space in each tamale for the dough to expand as it steams.

Cooking Tamales—You'll need a large pot with a rack high enough to keep the *tamales* above water. Racks for steaming vegetables work well. If you improvise a rack, you may have to pad it with extra corn husks or crumpled foil so the *tamales* will be well above the water level. After you pour water into the pot, stand the *tamales* upright on the rack. If they are open at one end, cover them with more husks or foil to prevent water from dripping in. Bring the water to a boil, cover the pot and steam 1 hour or until the tamale dough pulls away easily from the husk. To test, remove 1 tamale with tongs and open it carefully. **Keep in mind that the steam from the tamale will be extremely hot!** Be sure the water does not boil away while the *tamales* are cooking. Add more water as needed.

Storing & Reheating—Wrap leftover *tamales* in foil and store them in the refrigerator for no longer than 3 or 4 days. If they are wrapped securely, they can be frozen. Thaw frozen *tamales* at room temperature before reheating. Wrap them in foil and warm in an oven preheated to 350°F (175°C). You can also steam them again, following the method discussed above.

To reheat *tamales* in a microwave oven, wrap them in waxed paper and microwave until they feel soft and hot. If they overcook, the dough will be tough.

Beat lard or shortening into dough until light and fluffy.

Spread masa on softened corn husk. Top with filling.

How To Make Tamales

Top filling with more masa, if desired. Fold sides over filling, turn end under, keeping seam on outside.

Stand tamales on a rack in a steamer. Stand on folded ends with open ends up.

Masa para Tamales
Tamale Dough

With this dough and the recipes on the following pages, you can make a variety of tamales.

2 cups instant masa
1 teaspoon baking powder
1/2 teaspoon salt

1-1/4 cups lukewarm broth or water
2/3 cup lard or vegetable shortening

Combine instant masa, baking powder and salt in a medium bowl. Work in broth or water with your fingers to make a soft moist dough. In a small bowl, beat lard or shortening until fluffy. Add to masa and beat until dough has a spongy texture. Place a cupful of water nearby. Continue to beat dough until a small piece placed on the surface of water in the cup floats. Prepare tamales with desired filling. Makes enough dough for about 16 small tamales.

Masa Fresca Para Tamales
Fresh Tamale Dough

This version is closest to the fresh masa purchased in Mexican markets.

2 (1-lb. 13-oz.) cans white hominy
(6 cups)
1 cup frozen whole-kernel corn, thawed

1/4 lb. lard
1 teaspoon salt
1 teaspoon baking powder

Grind hominy and corn a little at a time in a food grinder or food processor. Whip lard, salt and baking powder until fluffy. Beat lard mixture into hominy mixture. Use to make tamales. Makes enough dough for 16 small tamales.

HOW TO PREPARE TAMALES IN FOIL

Place *masa* and filling just above the center of a 9" x 7" piece of foil. Fold foil in half, enclosing *masa* and filling completely. Fold edges twice to make a secure seal. Stand tamale folded-edge down on a rack over water in a large pot. Cover the pot and steam for 1 hour or until the dough pulls away easily from the foil.

Tamales de Puerco
Pork Tamales

Prepare the filling a day in advance for these mildly seasoned tamales.

1 lb. pork butt	8 peppercorns
2-1/2 cups water	2/3 cup Salsa para Enchiladas, page 37
1/4 medium onion	Corn husks or foil wrapping for
1 garlic clove	16 tamales
1 bay leaf	Masa para Tamales prepared with warm
Salt	pork broth, page 94

A day in advance, trim fat from meat. Cut meat in chunks and place in a large saucepan. Add water, onion, garlic, bay leaf, salt to taste and peppercorns. Bring to a boil. Skim foam from surface; reduce heat. Cover and simmer 1 hour. Prepare Salsa para Enchiladas. Drain meat, reserving 1-1/4 cups broth for tamale dough. With 2 forks, shred meat and mix with salsa. Refrigerate meat mixture and reserved broth overnight. Prepare foil wrapping or soak corn husks 1 hour in hot water. Soak a few additional husks to cover tamales. Rinse and pat dry with paper towels. Prepare Masa para Tamales with warm pork broth. Hold each corn husk with point toward you. Place a rounded tablespoonful of dough at large end of husk. Spread with fingers. Place 1 tablespoon pork filling on dough. Top with another tablespoon of dough; spread to cover filling. Fold sides of husk over tamale. Fold pointed end of corn husk under with seam on outside. Stand tamales on folded ends on a rack over water in a large pot. Cover with additional husks or foil. Bring water to a boil; reduce heat. Cover and steam 1 hour or until dough pulls away easily from husk. Makes 16 tamales.

Tamales de Queso y Chile
Cheese & Chile Tamales

Savory tamales can take the place of rice or bread.

Corn husks or foil wrapping for	4 California chiles, roasted, peeled,
16 tamales	cut in strips, or 1 (4-oz.) can
Masa para Tamales prepared with warm	chopped green chiles
chicken broth, page 94	
6 oz. Monterey Jack cheese, cut in	
16 cubes	

Prepare foil wrapping or soak corn husks 1 hour in hot water. Soak a few additional husks to cover tamales. Rinse and pat dry with paper towels. Prepare Masa para Tamales with warm chicken broth. Hold each corn husk with point toward you. Place 1 tablespoon dough at large end of husk. Spread with fingers. Place 1 cheese cube and a few chile strips or chopped chiles in center of dough. Top with another tablespoon dough; spread to cover filling. Fold sides of husk over tamale. Fold pointed end of corn husk under with seam on outside. Stand tamales on folded ends on rack over water in a large pot. Cover with additional husks or foil. Bring water to a boil; reduce heat. Cover and steam 1 hour or until dough pulls away easily from husk. Makes 16 tamales.

Tamales de Piña
Pineapple Tamales

Sweet fruit tamales are a breakfast treat as well as a dessert.

**Corn husks or foil wrapping for
18 tamales
1 (8-3/4-oz.) can crushed pineapple
in unsweetened pineapple juice
Water
Masa para Tamales, page 94, prepared
with warmed reserved pineapple
juice and water**

**1/2 cup packed dark brown sugar
1 cup diced candied pineapple, cut in
small pieces**

Prepare foil wrapping or soak corn husks 1 hour in hot water. Soak a few additional husks to cover tamales. Rinse and pat dry with paper towels. Drain pineapple thoroughly, reserving juice. Add water to juice to make 1-1/4 cups. Prepare Masa para Tamales, using warm juice mixture as liquid. When dough floats in water, beat in brown sugar, then drained pineapple. Hold each corn husk with point toward you. Place a rounded tablespoonful of dough at large end of husk. Spread with fingers. Add several pieces of candied pineapple and top with another tablespoon dough; spread to cover filling. Fold sides of husk over tamale. Fold pointed end of corn husk under with seam on outside. Stand tamales on folded ends on a rack over water in a large pot. Cover with additional husks or foil. Bring water to a boil; reduce heat. Cover and steam 1 hour or until dough pulls away easily from husk. Makes 18 tamales.

Tamales Dulces
Sweet Tamales

These tamales don't have to be covered with corn husks while they are steaming.

**Corn husks or foil wrapping for
16 or 17 tamales
1/2 cup lard or vegetable shortening
1/4 cup sugar
1-1/2 cups instant masa
1/4 teaspoon salt**

**1 cup water
1/2 teaspoon baking powder
1/2 cup finely diced citron
1/2 cup raisins
1/2 cup slivered almonds**

Prepare foil wrapping or soak corn husks 1 hour in hot water. Beat lard or shortening in a medium bowl until fluffy. Beat in sugar until smooth and creamy. In another medium bowl, combine instant masa, salt and water. Stir until blended into a very soft dough. Place a cupful of water nearby. Add masa mixture to lard mixture. Beat dough until a small piece placed on the surface of the water in the cup floats. Beat in baking powder. Hold each corn husk with point toward you. Place a tablespoonful of dough in center of each corn husk. Spread with your fingers. Top with a few pieces of citron, a few raisins and a few almonds. Fold sides of husk over filling. Fold pointed end of husk to center; fold top end over point. Tie each tamale around the center to hold ends in place. Stand tamales on folded ends on a rack over water in a large pot. Bring water to a boil; reduce heat. Cover and steam 1 hour or until dough pulls away easily from husk or foil. Makes 16 or 17 tamales.

BURRITOS

Burritos are made by wrapping a filling such as refried beans or a beef and bean mixture in a large flour *tortilla*. They are usually held like a sandwich and eaten plain, but are occasionally topped with sauce. Usually 12-inch flour *tortillas* are used but smaller 8-inch *tortillas* may also be used with less filling. Appetizer *burritos* require very little filling in 6-inch *tortillas*.

Dessert *burritos* are filled with canned or fresh fruit—strawberries are especially popular—and deep-fried until crisp, then sprinkled with powdered sugar or topped with whipped cream.

Deep-fried *burritos* called *chimichangas* are a specialty of southern Arizona. They are made with paper-thin flour *tortillas* and filled with beans or a chicken or meat mixture. Delightfully crisp and flaky, they are served plain or topped with *salsa*, *guacamole* or sour cream.

Burritos
Burritos

Chile Verde a la Fay, page 110, or Machaca, page 88, can be substituted for Carnitas a la Casera.

Carnitas a la Casera, page 115
1/2 cup Guacamole, page 40, or 1
   avocado, sliced
4 (12-inch) flour tortillas

3/4 cup canned or homemade refried
   beans, heated
1 cup shredded lettuce
1/4 cup homemade or canned salsa

Prepare Carnitas a la Casera and Guacamole. For each burrito, heat a tortilla on a large ungreased griddle until hot and pliable but not dry. Place about 1/2 cup meat filling a little below center. Add about 3 tablespoons refried beans, a little shredded lettuce and about 2 tablespoons Guacamole or an avocado slice. Top with about 1 tablespoon salsa. Fold sides of tortilla over filling to center. Fold bottom over filling and roll up, enclosing filling completely. Repeat with remaining ingredients. Serve immediately or burritos will be soggy. Makes 4 servings.

Variation

Dessert Burritos: Substitute frozen strawberries or apple pie filling for filling listed above. Heat 1/2 inch oil in a large skillet to 365°F (185°C). Fry burritos until golden brown.

Burritos de Chiles Rellenos
Stuffed Chile Burritos

Reheat stuffed chiles in foil in a 350°F (175°C) oven for 15 minutes.

4 Chiles Rellenos de Queso, page 66
4 large (12-inch) flour tortillas

1/2 cup canned or homemade refried
   beans, heated

Prepare Chiles Rellenos de Queso. Remove stems if made with whole fresh chiles. Heat each tortilla on an ungreased griddle until softened. Spread 2 tablespoons refried beans across tortilla about halfway between center and bottom. Place 1 stuffed chile on top of beans. Fold sides of tortilla over filling to center. Fold bottom over filling; roll up. Top each burrito with hot tomato sauce. Makes 4 servings.

Tostadas de Carne
Meat Tostadas

My friend Dave eats these after dinner and considers them dessert.

2 cups Carnitas a la Casera,
  page 115
Salsa Jitomate de Elva, page 39
Oil for frying

4 corn tortillas
4 oz. finely shredded Monterey Jack
  cheese (1 cup)

Prepare Carnitas a la Casera and Salsa Jitomate de Elva. Heat oil in a medium skillet. Fry tortillas in hot oil until crisp and lightly browned. Drain over skillet or on paper towels. Top each with 1/2 cup meat mixture, 1/4 cup cheese and a large spoonful of salsa. Makes 4 servings.

Chilaquiles con Salsa Verde
Tortilla Strips with Green Chile Sauce

Do not mix chicken, sauce and tortilla chips in advance or chips will become too soft.

1 whole chicken breast
2-1/2 cups water
1/4 small onion
1 bay leaf
Salt
4 peppercorns
1 lb. fresh tomatillos or 1-3/4 cups
  drained canned tomatillos
1 jalapeño chile or other
  small hot chile
Water
1 small onion, coarsely chopped

1 garlic clove
1/4 cup fresh cilantro leaves, loosely
  packed
1/2 teaspoon salt
Oil for frying
8 corn tortillas
1/2 cup dairy sour cream, room
  temperature
4 oz. Monterey Jack cheese, shredded
  (1 cup)
Cilantro sprigs

Place chicken breast in a medium saucepan. Add 2-1/2 cups water, 1/4 onion, bay leaf, salt to taste and peppercorns. Bring to a boil; reduce heat. Cover and simmer until chicken is tender, about 45 minutes. Cool chicken in broth. Drain, reserving broth. Shred meat with 2 forks or with your fingers; set aside. Remove papery husks from tomatillos. Remove stem and seeds of chile. Wash fresh tomatillos and chile and place in a medium saucepan. Add water almost to cover. Bring to a boil; reduce heat. Cover and simmer 10 minutes; drain. Do not cook canned tomatillos. Place cooked or canned tomatillos, chile, chopped onion, garlic and cilantro in blender or food processor and process until pureed. Pour into same saucepan. Add 2 cups reserved chicken broth and 1/2 teaspoon salt. Bring to a boil; reduce heat. Simmer gently uncovered 30 minutes. Keep sauce hot. Pour oil 1/4 inch deep into a medium skillet. Heat to 365°F (185°C). With kitchen scissors, cut tortillas into 1-1/2" x 1" strips. Fry tortilla strips in hot oil until crisp and lightly browned. Drain on paper towels. Arrange fried tortilla strips in a large shallow baking dish. Add shredded chicken at room temperature; mix. Pour sauce over tortilla strips and chicken. Place sour cream in a flat mound in center of mixture. Cover with shredded cheese. Place baking dish under broiler until cheese is melted and bubbly and ingredients are heated through. Garnish with cilantro sprigs; serve immediately. Makes 6 servings.

Tostadas
Tostadas

To make tostadas, stack beans, meat and garnishes on a crisp fried tortilla.

2 cups finely shredded Carnitas a la Casera, page 115	**Oil for frying**
	6 corn tortillas
1/3 to 1/2 cup Salsa Jitomate de Elva, page 39	**3/4 cup canned or homemade refried beans**
	2 cups finely shredded lettuce
3/4 cup Guacamole, page 40	**1/2 cup dairy sour cream**

Prepare Carnitas a la Casera, Salsa Jitomate de Elva and Guacamole. Pour oil 1/4 inch deep into a medium skillet. Heat to 365°F (185°C). Fry each tortilla on both sides until browned and crisp. Drain over skillet or on paper towels. Spread each tortilla with refried beans; top with about 1/3 cup Carnitas a la Casera. Add a layer of lettuce, a large spoonful of Guacamole and a spoonful of sour cream. Top with Salsa Jitomate de Elva. Makes 6 servings.

Variation

Substitute shredded chicken or beef for Carnitas a la Casera.

How To Make
Chilaquiles con Salsa Verde

Remove outer husk from tomatillos before using.

Cut corn tortillas into 1-1/2" x 1" strips before frying in hot oil.

Panuchos Mérida
Panuchos Mérida-Style

Photo on pages 122 and 123.

Mérida Internacional Café makes this version of Yucatán bean-stuffed tortillas.

1 cup shredded cooked chicken
2/3 cup Frijoles Refritos made with
   black beans, page 149, heated
1/3 cup Cebollas Yucatecas, page 39
1 cup instant masa

1/2 cup water
Oil for frying
1 tomato, chopped
3 or 4 canned pickled jalapeño
   chiles, cut in slivers

Prepare chicken, Frijoles Refritos and Cebollas Yucatecas. Mix instant masa and water with your fingers in a small bowl. Add a little more water if needed to make a smooth dough. Line bottom of tortilla press with plastic wrap. Divide dough into thirds. Divide each third into 4 equal parts, making 12 small pieces in all. Preheat an ungreased griddle over medium-high heat. Shape each piece of dough into a ball. Place on tortilla press. Place another piece of plastic wrap on top of dough. Press with the palm of your hand to flatten slightly. Close tortilla press firmly, then open. Tortilla should be about 4 inches in diameter. Remove plastic from both sides of tortilla. Bake tortillas on hot griddle until each side is lightly spotted with brown but tortilla is still pliable. Do not overbake. Stack and cover cooked tortillas with a dry cloth towel to prevent them from drying. Just before serving, pour oil 1/4 inch deep into a medium skillet. Heat to 365°F (185°C). Fry tortillas in hot oil until lightly browned and crisp. Drain over skillet or on paper towels. To serve, spread each tortilla with hot beans and top with shredded chicken, tomato, chile slivers and Cebollas Yucatecas. Serve immediately. Makes 12 panuchos.

Panuchos Campeche
Panuchos Campeche-Style

Sandwich-style panuchos are made in the market of Campeche.

1/4 cup Frijoles Refritos made with
   black beans, page 149
Cebollas Yucatecas, page 39
1 cup instant masa
1/2 cup water

1/2 cup finely shredded cooked chicken
Oil for frying
1 tomato, chopped
2 or 3 pickled jalapeño chiles,
   cut in slivers

Prepare Frijoles Refritos and Cebollas Yucatecas. Mix instant masa and water with your fingers in a small bowl. Add a little more water if needed to make a smooth dough. Line bottom of tortilla press with plastic wrap. Divide dough into quarters; divide each quarter into 5 equal parts, making 20 pieces in all. Shape each piece into a ball. Place on tortilla press. Place another piece of plastic wrap on top of dough. Press with the palm of your hand to flatten ball slightly. Close tortilla press firmly, then open. Tortilla should be about 3 inches in diameter. Remove plastic from both sides of tortilla. Place tortillas on a flat surface. Spread 1 teaspoon beans on the middle of each tortilla. Top with 1 or 2 tiny shreds of chicken. Cover with another tortilla and press edges with your fingers or a fork to seal. Keep uncooked panuchos covered with a dry cloth towel to prevent them from drying. If dough becomes dry and crumbly, add a few drops of water. Pour oil 1/4 inch deep into a medium skillet. Heat to 365°F (185°C). Fry panuchos in hot oil on both sides until crisp. Drain on paper towels. To serve, top with tomato, chile slivers and Cebollas Yucatecas. Serve immediately. Makes 10 panuchos.

Sopes de María Elena
Mary Ellen's Sopes

Sopes, also called gorditas, are little fried masa cups filled with beans and garnishes.

Frijoles con Chorizo, page 152, heated
Salsa Mexicana, page 33
Guacamole, page 40
1-1/2 cups instant masa
3/4 cup water
Oil for frying

8 oz. Cheddar cheese, shredded
  (2 cups)
1/2 head iceberg lettuce,
  finely shredded
6 radishes, thinly sliced
Dairy sour cream

Prepare Frijoles con Chorizo, Salsa Mexicana and Guacamole. Mix instant masa and water with your fingers in a small bowl. Add a little more water if needed to make a smooth dough. Line bottom of tortilla press with plastic wrap. Preheat an ungreased griddle over medium-high heat. Shape dough into 16 to 18 balls about 1 inch in diameter or slightly larger. Place 1 ball at a time on tortilla press. Place another piece of plastic wrap on top of dough. Press with the palm of your hand to flatten slightly. Close tortilla press firmly and then open. Tortilla should be about 3-1/2 inches in diameter. Peel plastic from top and bottom of tortilla. Bake tortillas one at a time on hot griddle 10 seconds on each side; do not overbake. Remove from griddle and immediately fold up edges, pressing and pinching to form a firm rim 1/3 to 1/2 inch high. Use a cloth towel if tortilla is too hot. Return to griddle and bake on bottom 1 minute. Just before serving, pour oil 1/4 inch deep into a medium skillet. Heat to 365°F (185°C). Fry each sope base on both sides until lightly browned and crisp. Drain on paper towels. Fill with a spoonful of hot Frijoles con Chorizo. Add some of the cheese, lettuce and radish slices. Top with a spoonful of Salsa Mexicana, a spoonful of Guacamole and a little sour cream. Serve immediately. Makes 16 to 18 sopes.

Quesadilla con Guacamole
Cheese Crisp with Avocado Sauce

Flour tortillas folded over a cheese filling are especially popular with youngsters.

Guacamole, page 40
1 (8-inch) flour tortilla
2 oz. Cheddar or Longhorn cheese,
  shredded (1/2 cup)
2 tablespoons chopped tomato

1 tablespoon chopped green onion
1-1/2 teaspoons chopped cilantro leaves
Homemade or canned hot salsa, if desired
2 or 3 tomato wedges
1 ripe olive

Prepare Guacamole. Preheat oven to 350°F (175°C). Sprinkle one half of the tortilla with cheese. Add chopped tomato and onion. Top with cilantro and hot salsa, if desired. Fold uncovered half of tortilla over toppings. Place on a baking sheet. Bake until cheese is melted. Cut into pie-shaped wedges. Arrange in a fan pattern on a round plate with a mound of Guacamole in the center. Garnish Guacamole with tomato wedges and an olive. Makes 1 serving.

Garnachas
Open-Face Snacks

Beans adhere better to a chilled tortilla, so refrigerate baked tortillas overnight.

1 cup instant masa
1/2 cup water
Frijoles Refritos made with black beans,
    page 149
Salsa Roja for Picadas, page 103,
Salsa Verde for Picadas, page 103,
    heated
3 medium boiling potatoes

Boiling salted water
Milk
Oil for frying
1 small onion, sliced, cut into slivers
12 oz. queso fresco, or farmer cheese,
    crumbled, or 6 oz. Monterey Jack
    cheese, shredded (1-1/2 cups)

The day before, mix instant masa and water with your fingers in a small bowl. Add more water if needed to make a smooth dough. Line bottom of tortilla press with plastic wrap. Preheat an ungreased griddle over medium heat. Divide dough into 12 pieces. Shape each piece into a ball. Place on tortilla press. Place another piece of plastic wrap on top of dough. Press with the palm of your hand to flatten slightly. Close tortilla press firmly and then open. Tortilla should be about 4 inches in diameter. Peel plastic from top and bottom of tortilla. Bake on hot griddle until each side is lightly spotted with brown. Wrap tortillas and refrigerate overnight. Prepare Frijoles Refritos and salsas. The next day, peel potatoes and cook in boiling salted water until tender, about 30 minutes. Drain, peel and mash potatoes. Beat in a little milk to hold potatoes together. Just before serving, pour oil 1/4 inch deep into a large skillet. Heat to 365°F (185°C). Spread each garnacha base with beans and top with mashed potato. Fry potato-side up in hot oil until garnacha bases are browned, splashing a little oil onto tops. Drain on paper towels. Top with Salsa Roja or Salsa Verde, a few onion slivers and a little cheese. Makes 12 garnachas.

Quesadilla del Mercado
Cheese Crisp Market-Style

Sandwiches don't have to be made with bread!

1 oz. Monterey Jack cheese, shredded
    (1/4 cup)
2 corn tortillas
2 thin slices tomato

1 thin onion slice
1/4 cup finely shredded lettuce
Homemade or canned hot salsa
1 slice avocado

Preheat a lightly greased griddle over medium-high heat. Sprinkle cheese on a tortilla and top with another tortilla. Cook on each side on hot griddle until tortillas are hot and cheese is melted. Place on a plate. Lift up top tortilla. Place tomato slices, onion, lettuce, salsa and avocado inside. Replace top; serve immediately. Makes 1 serving.

Picadas
Filled Tortilla Cups

In Veracruz, picadas are served as snacks with fruit and a soft drink.

Salsa Roja, see below
Salsa Verde, see below
1 cup instant masa
1/2 cup water
Oil for frying
1 small onion, sliced, cut into
   slivers

4 oz. queso fresco or farmer cheese,
   crumbled, or 2 oz. Monterey Jack
   cheese, shredded (1/2 cup)
1/2 cup chopped cilantro leaves,
   if desired

Salsa Roja (Red Sauce):
1 or 2 serrano chiles or other small
   hot chiles
2 small tomatoes (1/2 lb.)
1 small garlic clove

1/4 small onion
1 teaspoon vegetable oil
Salt

Salsa Verde (Green Sauce):
3 or 4 serrano chiles or other small
   hot chiles
1/2 lb. tomatillos or 3/4 cup canned
   tomatillos, drained
1/2 small onion

1 large garlic clove
1/2 cup loosely packed chopped cilantro
   leaves with some sprigs
1 teaspoon vegetable oil
Salt

Prepare Salsa Roja and Salsa Verde; keep warm. Mix masa and water with your fingers in a small bowl. Add a little more water if needed to make a smooth dough. Line bottom of tortilla press with plastic wrap. Preheat an ungreased griddle over medium-high heat. Divide dough into 8 pieces. Shape each piece into a ball. Place on tortilla press. Place another piece of plastic wrap on top of dough. Press with the palm of your hand to flatten slightly. Close tortilla press firmly and then open. Peel plastic from top and bottom of tortilla. Bake picada bases one at a time on hot griddle 10 seconds on each side or until partially cooked but not dry. Remove from griddle and immediately fold up edges, pressing and pinching to form a firm rim 1/3 to 1/2 inch high. Use a cloth towel if tortilla is too hot. Pour oil 1/4-inch deep in a medium skillet. Heat to 365°F (185°C). Fry picada bases on both sides until lightly browned and crisp. Drain on paper towels. Fill picadas with Salsa Roja or Salsa Verde. Add a few onion shreds and 1 tablespoon cheese. Garnish with cilantro, if desired. Serve immediately. Makes 8 picadas.

Salsa Roja (Red Sauce):
Roast chiles on griddle over medium heat until blistered on all sides. Cut off stems but do not peel. Cut tomatoes in half and cut out stem portions. Place roasted chiles, halved tomatoes, garlic and onion in blender or food processor and process until pureed. Heat oil in a small saucepan over moderate heat. Add chile mixture. Bring to a boil. Add salt to taste. Makes about 1 cup.

Salsa Verde (Green Sauce):
Roast chiles on griddle over medium heat until blistered on all sides. Cut off stems but do not peel. Remove papery husks from fresh tomatillos; wash. Cut tomatillos in half. Place roasted chiles, halved tomatillos or drained canned tomatillos, onion, garlic and cilantro in blender or food processor and process until pureed. Heat oil in a small saucepan over moderate heat. Add chile mixture. Bring to a boil. Add salt to taste. Makes about 1 cup.

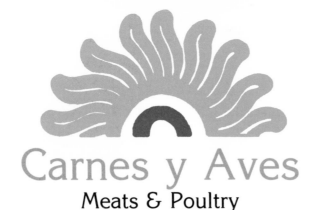

Carnes y Aves
Meats & Poultry

The Aztecs were eating flavorful *moles*—pronounced *moh-lays*—when the Spaniards arrived in the 16th century. The most famous *mole* was developed in the convent of Santa Rosa in Puebla toward the end of the 17th century in honor of a visiting viceroy. After spending days in Puebla sampling different versions of the dish, visiting the kitchen of the convent and examining old recipes, I was able to duplicate authentic chocolate-colored *Mole Poblano* (*Mole* Puebla-Style). It is complicated to make but the flavor is extraordinary. Just as sumptuous as *Mole Poblano* (*Mole* Puebla-Style) but much easier to prepare is *Pavo en Relleno Blanco* (Turkey with White Stuffing). It's stuffed with a mixture of ground pork, almonds, olives, capers and raisins. Serve it with two sauces: a white sauce containing virtually no fat and a tomato sauce flavored with the same ingredients as the pork stuffing. Although this version is made with a turkey breast, you could try it with a whole turkey for a large gathering.

Carne asada, or grilled steak, is popular throughout Mexico. The recipe for *Carne Asada Tampiqueña* (Grilled Steak Tampico-Style) comes from the El Conquistador Hotel in Tijuana.

When a *fiesta* is about to take place, your host may butcher a hog. Chunks of pork are deep-fried in big copper cauldrons to make *Carnitas a la Casera* (Home-Style Meats). These are eaten plain or shredded for *tacos* and *tostadas*. The pig's skin is fried to make *chicharrones*, a crisp snack to enjoy with beer. This same pig also yields lard, Mexico's traditional cooking agent. Home-rendered lard is exceptionally tasty and must be used to give certain dishes their proper flavor.

Nuts and seeds contribute subtle flavors to many meat and chicken dishes. Ground squash seeds flavor *Mole Verde de Puerco* (Green *Mole* with Pork), a Oaxacan recipe. Ground sesame seeds are added to *Mole Colorado de Oaxaca* (Oaxacan Red *Mole*). Squash seeds and sesame seeds enhance *Pollo en Pipián* (Chicken in Squash Seed Sauce). Almonds and sesame seeds go into *Mole Poblano* (*Mole* Puebla-Style).

In the southwestern United States, meat dishes such as *Chile Verde a la Fay* (Green *Chile* Stew), *Chile Colorado con Carne* (Red *Chile* with Meat) and *Bistec Picado* (Steak Strips with Vegetables) are often used as filling for *tacos, burritos* and sandwiches.

YUCATÁN FIESTA

Carne Asada a la Tampiqueña
Grilled Steak Tampico-Style

Begin this full-course meal one or two days in advance.

2 garlic cloves
1 cup vegetable oil
4 (10-oz.) tender steaks such as
   top sirloin or rib steak
2 teaspoons dried leaf oregano,
   crushed
Salt and coarsely ground pepper

2 cups canned or homemade refried beans
Totopos, page 30
4 Enchiladas de Pollo en Mole, page 78
Guacamole del Conquistador, page 40
Rajas de Chile, see below
Shredded Monterey Jack or Cheddar cheese

Rajas de Chile (Chile Strips):
2 tablespoons reserved garlic oil
1 large onion, cut lengthwise,
   thinly sliced
1/2 teaspoon dried leaf oregano,
   crushed

4 California chiles, roasted, peeled,
   cut in long strips, or 4 canned
   whole green chiles, cut in strips
Salt

Begin 1 or 2 days in advance by lightly crushing garlic cloves and combining with oil in a jar. Cover tightly and let stand to flavor oil. Garlic oil not used in preparing steak and Rajas may be used to refry beans. Several hours before cooking, marinate steaks in 1/2 cup garlic oil, oregano and salt and pepper to taste. Refrigerate. Bring to room temperature before cooking. Prepare refried beans, Totopos, Enchiladas de Pollo en Mole, Guacamole del Conquistador and Rajas de Chile. Grill steaks over coals as desired or cook in a very hot skillet greased with garlic oil. For each serving, place 1 steak on a heated platter. Place Rajas de Chile on top or at one side of each steak. Add a serving of refried beans. Sprinkle beans with cheese and garnish with a totopo. Add an enchilada and a spoonful of guacamole. Makes 4 servings.

Rajas de Chile (Chile Strips):
Heat reserved garlic oil in a medium skillet. Add onion. Cook until tender but not browned. Add oregano and chiles. Cook and stir gently until heated through. Season with salt to taste.

Bistec Picado
Steak Strips with Vegetables

Serve these robustly flavored steak strips with rice or roll them up in flour tortillas.

1-3/4 lbs. round steak
3 tablespoons vegetable oil
1 medium green pepper, diced
1 small onion, chopped
1 güero chile, finely chopped,
   or hot pepper sauce to taste

1 large garlic clove, minced
1 (8-1/4-oz.) can stewed tomatoes
1 teaspoon Worcestershire sauce
1 teaspoon dried leaf oregano, crushed
Salt and pepper

Cut meat in 1-1/2" x 1/4" strips. Heat oil in a large heavy skillet over high heat. Add meat strips. Cook until browned. Reduce heat. Add green pepper, onion, chile or hot pepper sauce and garlic. Cook until vegetables are limp. Add tomatoes, Worcestershire sauce, oregano and salt and pepper to taste. Cover and simmer 1 hour or until meat is tender. Makes 6 servings.

Carne Asada
Grilled Steak

Serve steak with beans and rice for a hearty meal or slice it thinly for a taco filling.

1 (1-lb. 4-oz.) top sirloin steak	1/4 teaspoon coarsely ground pepper
2 tablespoons vegetable oil	1/4 cup orange juice
1/2 teaspoon dried leaf oregano, crushed	1 tablespoon lime juice
	2 teaspoons cider vinegar
1/2 teaspoon salt	2 orange slices, cut 1/2 inch thick

Place steak in a shallow glass baking dish. Rub oil on each side of steak. Sprinkle with oregano, salt and pepper. Sprinkle orange juice, lime juice and vinegar over steak. Cover and refrigerate overnight for best flavor or several hours, turning occasionally. To cook, bring meat to room temperature. Prepare and preheat charcoal grill. Drain meat, reserving marinade. Place steak on grill over hot coals. Top with orange slices. Occasionally spoon reserved marinade over steaks as they cook. Grill 3 to 4 minutes on each side, or until medium-rare. Cook longer, if desired. Remove orange slices to turn steak. Replace orange slices on top of steak. Makes 4 servings.

Chile Colorado con Carne
Red Chile with Meat

This is the way they make chile in northern Mexico.

2 lbs. beef stew-meat	1 teaspoon salt
2 tablespoons vegetable oil	1 tablespoon vegetable oil
1-3/4 cups water	1 onion, finely chopped
5 dried California chiles	1 tablespoon all-purpose flour
1 dried New Mexico chile	1 teaspoon dried leaf oregano, crushed
Water	1/4 teaspoon ground cumin
2 garlic cloves	

Cut meat into bite-size pieces. Heat 2 tablespoons oil in a large heavy skillet or Dutch oven. Add meat. Cook until browned. Add water. Cover and simmer 1 hour. While meat is cooking, place both California and New Mexico chiles in a medium saucepan. Add water to cover generously. Cover and bring to a boil. Remove from heat and let stand until softened, 45 minutes to 1 hour. Drain chiles. Discard stems and seeds. Place chiles in blender with about 1/2 cup cooking broth from meat. Blend until pureed. Press puree through a sieve to remove bits of peel. Add sieved puree to meat and broth. Mash garlic with salt to make a paste. Heat 1 tablespoon oil in a medium skillet. Add garlic paste and onion. Cook until onion is very tender but not browned. Add flour. Cook and stir 1 minute. Add onion mixture, oregano and cumin to meat mixture. Cover and simmer 1-1/2 hours. Taste and add more salt if needed. Makes 4 to 6 servings.

Variation

For a hotter dish, substitute as many New Mexico chiles as desired for California chiles. If dried whole chiles are not available, substitute 1/4 to 1/3 cup chili powder.

Carne de Res Guisada en Jitomate
Beef Stewed with Tomatoes

Spicy seasonings are typical of the tropical east coast of Mexico.

2 lbs. beef chuck steak or rump roast	1 bay leaf
1 cup water	1/4 teaspoon whole allspice
Salt	6 peppercorns
4 small tomatoes, peeled (1 lb.)	1/4 teaspoon sugar
1 medium onion, quartered	12 to 15 pimiento-stuffed green olives
1 large garlic clove	1 teaspoon capers
1 tablespoon vegetable oil	Salt

Cut meat in 1" x 1/4" slices. Place in a large saucepan. Add water and salt to taste. Bring to a boil; reduce heat. Cover and simmer 1 hour. Combine tomatoes, onion and garlic in blender or food processor. Blend until pureed. Heat oil in a medium saucepan. Add tomato puree, bay leaf, allspice, peppercorns and sugar. Bring to a boil; reduce heat. Simmer uncovered 15 minutes. Add hot tomato puree, olives, capers and salt to taste to beef. Cover and simmer 1 hour. Uncover and simmer 1/2 hour longer. Makes 4 to 6 servings.

Variation

Add 1 large sliced or cubed cooked potato to meat during last 1/2 hour of cooking time. Add 3/4 cup canned or frozen peas during last 7 minutes of cooking.

Picadillo
Minced Meat

Serve this piquant mixture with rice or use it as a filling for Empanadas de Picadillo, page 31.

2 tablespoons vegetable oil	2 tablespoons chopped blanched almonds
1/2 lb. ground beef	2 tablespoons raisins, soaked in hot
1/2 lb. ground pork	water until softened
1/2 small onion, chopped	6 Spanish-style green olives, pitted,
1 large garlic clove, minced	chopped
1 medium tomato, peeled, chopped	2 teaspoons capers
2 tablespoons chopped fresh parsley	1/4 teaspoon salt

Heat oil in a large skillet. Add beef and pork. Cook until meat is no longer pink, stirring to keep crumbly. Add onion, garlic, tomato, parsley, almonds, raisins, olives and capers. Cook over medium heat 8 minutes, stirring frequently. Stir in salt. Makes 4 servings.

Bistec a la Maya
Steak Mayan-Style

The orange-lemon juice blend is a substitute for the sour orange juice used in Yucatán.

Juice of 1 orange (6 to 8 tablespoons)
2 tablespoons lemon juice
1-1/2 lbs. chuck or round steak
Salt
2 tablespoons lard

1/2 medium onion, sliced
1 garlic clove, minced
1/2 green pepper, cut in strips
2 tomatoes, sliced
Salt

Combine orange and lemon juices. Trim fat from meat. Cut meat in thin strips and place on a platter. Sprinkle with half the juice mixture, about 1/4 cup, and salt. Let stand 30 minutes. Heat lard in a large heavy skillet. Add meat. Cook until meat has browned and liquid has evaporated. Add onion, garlic, green pepper, tomatoes and 2 tablespoons of the reserved juice mixture. Season with salt to taste. Cover and simmer 45 minutes or until meat is tender. Makes 4 servings.

Carne Deshebrada   Photo on pages 86 and 87.
Shredded Meat

Mexican home cooking is simple and always tasty.

1 lb. beef stew-meat
1-1/2 cups water
Salt
2 tablespoons vegetable oil
1/2 medium onion, thinly sliced
1 garlic clove, minced
4 small tomatoes, peeled, chopped
   (1 lb.)

2 medium green peppers, cut in thin
   strips (1/2 lb.)
1 serrano chile or other small hot
   chile, minced, if desired
Salt and pepper
Cooked white rice

Combine beef, water and salt to taste in a large saucepan. Bring to a boil; reduce heat. Cover and simmer until meat is tender, about 2 hours. Cool meat in broth. Drain meat, reserving broth. Use 2 forks to shred meat. Heat oil in a large skillet. Add onion and garlic. Cook until tender but not browned. Add tomatoes. Simmer until tomatoes are cooked, 5 to 10 minutes. Stir in green peppers, meat and chile, if desired. Add 1/2 cup broth and salt and pepper to taste. Cover and simmer until green pepper is tender, about 15 minutes. Serve with rice. Makes 4 servings.

Variation

For a drier mixture, reduce quantity of broth or eliminate broth entirely. Mixture may then be used as burrito filling.

Salpicón
Cold Meat Salad

If you can't find Maggi seasoning, ask your supermarket manager to order some.

2 lbs. flank steak
2 cups water
l/4 small onion
2 or 3 garlic cloves
1/4 teaspoon dried leaf oregano,
  crushed
1/4 teaspoon dried leaf spearmint
  or mint, crushed
1 teaspoon salt
3 or 4 peppercorns
3 medium boiling potatoes (1 lb.)
Boiling salted water
3 poblano chiles, roasted, peeled, or
  3 whole canned green chiles, cut
  in thin strips

1/2 cup olive oil
1/4 cup white vinegar
1 teaspoon Maggi seasoning
Salt and freshly ground pepper
1/4 cup olive oil, if desired
2 tablespoons vinegar, if desired
10 large romaine lettuce leaves
1 to 2 tablespoons olive oil
2 tablespoons white vinegar,
  if desired
2 medium tomatoes, cut in wedges (3/4 lb.)
1 small avocado, peeled, sliced
1 small red onion, thinly sliced
Strips of queso fresco, Monterey Jack or
  Swiss cheese

Place steak in a large saucepan. Add water, onion , garlic, oregano, spearmint or mint, 1 teaspoon salt and peppercorns. Cover and simmer until meat is tender, about 1 hour 45 minutes. Let cool. Drain, reserving broth for another use. Cut meat across grain into 2-inch long pieces. Use 2 forks to shred meat. Peel potatoes and cook in boiling salted water until tender, about 30 minutes. Drain; cool and cut into 1/2-inch cubes. Combine meat, cooked potatoes and chiles in a large bowl. Mix 1/2 cup olive oil, 1/4 cup vinegar and Maggi seasoning. Add to meat mixture with salt and freshly ground pepper to taste. Toss gently. Taste and add more seasoning, if needed. If more dressing is desired, add 1/4 cup olive oil and 2 tablespoons vinegar. Wash lettuce leaves and slice crosswise into 1/2-inch pieces. Place lettuce on a large platter. Sprinkle lightly with 1 to 2 tablespoons olive oil; toss. Arrange meat mixture on lettuce. Garnish with tomato wedges, avocado slices, red onion slices and cheese strips. Serve at room temperature. Makes 8 servings.

Chile Verde a la Fay
Fay's Green Chile Stew

This version of chile verde features pork. You'll enjoy it with flour tortillas.

2 lbs. boneless pork butt
2 tablespoons vegetable oil
1 onion, chopped
1 large garlic clove, minced
2 teaspoons all-purpose flour

1 (8-1/4-oz.) can stewed tomatoes
1 (7-oz.) can chopped green chiles
1 (10-oz.) can tomatoes with hot green
  chiles
Salt and freshly ground pepper

Trim off fat and cut pork into 1-inch cubes. Heat oil in a large heavy pot or Dutch oven. Add pork and cook until browned. Add onion and garlic. Cook until tender. Stir in flour. Cook and stir 1 to 2 minutes. Add stewed tomatoes, chopped chiles and tomatoes with hot chiles, breaking up tomatoes with a spoon. Season with salt and pepper to taste. Cover and simmer gently 1-1/2 hours or until meat is tender. Makes 4 servings.

Birria con Vino Tinto
Lamb with Red Wine

Restaurateur Antonio Gutierrez steams lamb and chile until the meat is so tender it falls off the bone.

3 dried California chiles
3 dried pasilla chiles
Water
1 cup dry red wine
2 thin slices fresh ginger, peeled,
  or 1/4 teaspoon ground ginger
2 garlic cloves

1 teaspoon ground cumin
1 teaspoon dried leaf oregano, crushed
1/2 teaspoon salt
4 lbs. lamb shanks
1 or 2 onions, chopped
Canned or homemade salsa

Place both California and pasilla chiles in a saucepan. Cover with water. Bring to a boil. Remove from heat and let stand covered until softened, 45 minutes to 1 hour. Drain chiles. Discard stems and seeds. Place softened chiles, wine, ginger, garlic, cumin, oregano and salt in blender or food processor; puree. Press through a sieve to eliminate bits of peel. Place lamb shanks in a baking pan. Coat with chile mixture, cover and marinate in refrigerator overnight or at least 4 hours. Bring to room temperature before cooking. Preheat oven to 350°F (175°C). Cover lamb shanks tightly with foil. Bake 2-1/2 hours, or until very tender. Turn meat in marinade every hour, covering tightly each time. When meat is cool enough to handle, remove from bones; discard bones. Serve meat with chopped onion and salsa on the side. Makes 4 to 6 servings.

Variation

If dried whole chiles are not available, substitute about 1/3 cup chili powder.

Lomo de Puerco al Horno
Baked Pork Loin

Mexicans not only drink Coca Cola, they cook with it!

2 dried chipotle chiles
2 garlic cloves
1/2 teaspoon dried leaf oregano,
  crushed

1 (16-oz.) bottle Coca Cola
1 (3- to 3-1/2-lb.) pork loin roast
Salt and pepper
3 tablespoons vegetable oil or lard

Place chiles in a small saucepan. Cover with water. Bring to a boil and let stand until softened, about 30 minutes. Drain chiles. Remove stems, seeds and veins. Process chiles with garlic, oregano and 1/4 bottle of Coca Cola in blender or food processor. Preheat oven to 350°F (175°C). Sprinkle pork roast evenly with salt and pepper. Heat oil or lard in a large heavy skillet. Add pork; brown on all sides. Drain meat and place in a baking pan. Spread chile mixture over meat. Add remaining Coca Cola to meat. Bake uncovered 2 to 2-1/2 hours or until meat thermometer reads 170°F (75°C), basting often with Coca Cola in pan. Let meat stand 15 minutes before slicing. Serve remaining pan liquid separately as a sauce. Makes 4 to 6 servings.

Variation

If dried chipotle chiles are not available, substitute 2 canned chipotle chiles or 1 tablespoon chili powder.

Mole Colorado de Oaxaca
Oaxacan Red Mole

Spicy enough for most of us without the extra-hot guajillo chiles.

6 dried ancho chiles
5 dried guajillo chiles, if desired
1/2 lb. pork spareribs, cut in 2-inch
   lengths
2 lbs. pork butt
4 cups water
1/4 large onion
1/2 teaspoon salt
1/3 cup sesame seeds, toasted
2 whole cloves

3 peppercorns
1 small cinnamon stick
1/2 teaspoon dried leaf oregano
1/8 teaspoon dried leaf thyme
1 medium onion, quartered
1 medium tomato, peeled, halved
1 tablespoon lard
2 teaspoons sugar
3/4 teaspoon salt

Place dried chiles in a large saucepan. Add water to cover generously. Bring to a boil. Remove from heat and let stand 1 hour or until softened. Separate pork ribs. Trim fat from pork butt and cut meat in 1- to 1-1/2-inch cubes. Place ribs and cubed meat in another large saucepan. Add water, 1/4 onion and 1/2 teaspoon salt. Bring to a boil; reduce heat. Cover and simmer 1 hour. Remove meat and strain broth; set aside. Grind sesame seeds, cloves, peppercorns, cinnamon stick, oregano and thyme in blender until pulverized. Remove and set aside. Drain soaked chiles and remove stems and seeds. Puree chiles in blender. Press through a sieve into a medium bowl to remove peel. Without washing blender, puree onion and tomato. Heat lard in a large skillet. Add meat. Sauté quickly until partially browned. Place browned meat in a large saucepan. Add pureed tomato mixture and pureed chiles to drippings in skillet. Cook over medium heat about 7 minutes, stirring occasionally. Stir in sesame seed mixture. Add 1-1/2 cups reserved broth, sugar and 3/4 teaspoon salt. Add chile sauce to meat. Cover and simmer 30 minutes. Add more broth if needed for desired consistency. Makes about 6 servings.

Variation

If dried chiles are not available, substitute about 1/3 cup chili powder.

Chorizo
Spiced Pork Sausage

Mild chili powder is labeled California chili. Hot chili powder is New Mexico chili.

1 large garlic clove
1 teaspoon salt
2 tablespoons mild chili powder
2 to 3 teaspoons hot chili powder

1/2 teaspoon dried leaf oregano
2 tablespoons vinegar
1 tablespoon water
1 lb. boneless pork

In a small bowl, mash garlic with salt to make a paste. Add chili powders. Crush oregano to fine crumbs and add to garlic mixture with vinegar and water. Grind pork with fine blade of meat grinder or food processor. Add garlic mixture; mix well. Cover tightly and refrigerate 24 hours to blend flavors. Chorizo may be stored in refrigerator 3 or 4 days before cooking. Freeze for longer storage. Makes 1 pound of chorizo.

Mole Verde de Puerco
Green Mole with Pork

Use a jalapeño chile in place of the California chile to make this Oaxaca-style mole hotter!

1-1/2 lbs. pork butt
3 cups water
1 small onion, cut in half
2 garlic cloves
1/2 teaspoon salt
1/4 cup hulled squash seeds
3/4 lb. fresh tomatillos or
  1 (13-oz.) can tomatillos
Boiling water

1 large California chile, roasted,
  peeled, seeded, or 1 canned whole
  green chile
5 romaine lettuce leaves
1/4 cup parsley leaves
2 tablespoons cilantro leaves
1 tablespoon vegetable oil
1/2 teaspoon salt
1/4 teaspoon ground cumin

Trim fat from pork butt and cut meat into 1-inch pieces. Place in a large saucepan with 3 cups water, 1/2 onion, 1 garlic clove and 1/2 teaspoon salt. Bring to a boil. Skim foam from surface. Reduce heat. Cover and simmer 1 hour. Toast squash seeds in a small skillet until lightly browned, stirring constantly. Cool slightly. Place in a blender and grind until pulverized; set aside. If using fresh tomatillos, remove papery husks. Place fresh tomatillos in a medium saucepan. Cover with boiling water. Cover and cook 10 minutes. Drain and cool. If using canned tomatillos, drain. Combine tomatillos, chile, lettuce, remaining garlic clove, remaining onion half, parsley and cilantro in blender or food processor. Blend until finely ground. Drain cooked meat. Strain and reserve broth. Return meat to saucepan. Heat oil in a large skillet. Add pulverized squash seeds. Sauté over low heat 2 minutes. Do not burn. Add ground tomatillo mixture. Stir over low heat 5 minutes. Stir in 1 cup reserved broth. Pour mixture over meat. Add 1/2 teaspoon salt and cumin. Simmer gently uncovered 20 to 30 minutes. Add more broth if sauce becomes too thick. Makes 4 servings.

Poc-Chuc
Grilled Pork

Los Almendros Restaurant in Mérida serves this charcoal-grilled pork dish.

1-1/2 lbs. boneless pork loin sirloin
  chops or pork steaks
Cold water
1-1/2 teaspoons salt
4 medium or 3 large red onions, peeled (1 lb.)
4 small tomatoes (1 lb.)

1/2 teaspoon salt
1 jalapeño chile or other small
  hot chile, finely chopped,
  if desired
1-1/2 tablespoons white vinegar
1/4 teaspoon salt

Place pork chops in a shallow dish. Add 4 cups cold water and 1-1/2 teaspoons salt. Let stand 1 hour. Drain chops; cover with fresh cold water and let stand until ready to cook. Heat and oil grill. Cook whole onions on grill about 40 minutes, turning until softened and charred on all sides. Cook tomatoes on grill 15 to 20 minutes, until tender. Drain pork; pat dry with paper towels. Cook pork on grill 15 minutes, turning once. Remove and keep warm. Peel and core grilled tomatoes. Discard cores. Place peeled and cored tomatoes in a bowl. Mash with a fork. Stir in 1/2 teaspoon salt. If desired, add chile to taste; set aside. Remove outer charred portions of onions. Cut onions into medium pieces. Place in a medium bowl. Stir in vinegar and 1/4 teaspoon salt. To serve, top each portion of pork with tomato sauce, then with onion mixture. Makes 4 servings.

Mole de Puerco
Pork Mole

Serve this Michoacán stew with corn tortillas. Or use it as a taco filling.

2 lbs. boneless pork	1 tablespoon lard
3 cups water	3 garlic cloves
1/4 medium onion	1/4 teaspoon ground cinnamon
1 bay leaf	1/8 teaspoon ground cloves
6 peppercorns	1/4 teaspoon freshly ground pepper
5 dried guajillo chiles or 3 dried	1 tablespoon lard
California or New Mexico chiles	1-1/2 teaspoons salt
Water	2 teaspoons vinegar
1 slice white bread	2 teaspoons sugar

Trim fat from meat and cut in large pieces. Place in a large saucepan with 3 cups water, onion, bay leaf and peppercorns. Bring to a boil. Skim foam from surface. Reduce heat. Cover and simmer 45 minutes. Drain meat, reserving broth. Place chiles in a medium saucepan. Cover with water; bring to a boil. Let stand until softened, about 1 hour. Drain chiles. Remove stems and seeds. Place in blender or food processor but do not process; set aside. In a large pot or Dutch oven, fry bread in 1 tablespoon lard until golden brown on each side. Add fried bread, garlic and about 2 tablespoons reserved broth to chiles. Puree; add more broth if needed. Press through a sieve to eliminate chile peel. Stir in cinnamon, cloves and pepper. Heat 1 tablespoon lard in same pot or Dutch oven. Stir in chile puree. Sauté 1 to 2 minutes. Stir in cooked pork pieces. Strain 2 cups reserved broth into pork mixture. Add salt, vinegar and sugar. Bring to a boil; reduce heat. Cover and simmer 45 minutes. If sauce is not thick enough, uncover and simmer 10 to 15 minutes longer. Serve in soup bowls. Makes 4 to 8 servings.

Variation

If dried whole chiles are not available, substitute 1/4 to 1/3 cup chili powder.

Relleno de Puerco
Pork Stuffing

Gourmet stuffing for any fowl, this is especially good with Pavo en Relleno Blanco, page 121.

2 tablespoons vegetable oil	2 tablespoons raisins
1 lb. ground lean pork	1 tablespoon drained capers
3 tablespoons chopped blanched almonds	1/4 teaspoon salt
4 Spanish-style green olives, pitted,	Pinch pepper
chopped	

Heat 2 tablespoons oil in a medium skillet. Add pork. Cook until no longer pink, stirring to crumble. Add almonds, olives, raisins and capers. Cook gently 5 minutes. Add salt and pinch of pepper. Remove from heat. Makes about 2-1/2 cups of stuffing.

Carnitas a la Casera
Home-Style Meats

Pork cooked this way is used for tacos, burritos, tostadas and sandwiches.

1-3/4 to 2 lbs. pork butt
Water
1/2 medium onion, cut in half
1 large garlic clove

1 teaspoon salt
1/4 teaspoon dried leaf oregano, crushed
1/4 teaspoon ground cumin
Salt or garlic salt

Place meat in a 3-quart saucepan. Add water to cover, onion, garlic, salt, oregano and cumin. Bring to a boil; reduce heat. Cover and simmer 2 hours. Preheat oven to 350°F (175°C). Drain meat, reserving broth for another use. Place meat in a baking pan. Sprinkle meat evenly with salt or garlic salt. Bake 45 minutes. Remove from oven. While still warm, use 2 forks to shred meat. Makes about 4 cups of shredded meat.

How To Make
Carnitas a la Casera

Sprinkle boiled drained meat with salt or garlic salt before baking.

Shred warm baked meat with two forks.

Recado Colorado
Seasoned Achiote Paste

Packages of achiote seeds are available in markets featuring Mexican food.

**1 tablespoon crushed achiote seeds
  or New Mexico chili powder**
Pinch turmeric

**2 tablespoons lime juice, lemon
  juice or vinegar**

Combine all ingredients and mash to make a paste. Makes about 3 tablespoons.

Mole Poblano
Mole Puebla-Style

Authentic Mole Poblano is complicated to make but worth the effort.

**2 (3-lb.) broiler-fryers, cut in
  serving pieces**
Water
1 onion, cut in half
1 bay leaf
4 peppercorns
Salt
2 dried ancho chiles
4 dried mulato chiles
3 dried pasilla chiles
3 tablespoons vegetable oil
About 3/4 cup water
1 onion, coarsely chopped
2 garlic cloves
1 small tomato, peeled
1 tablespoon vegetable oil
1/2 slice white bread

1/2 corn tortilla
2 tablespoons blanched almonds
2 tablespoons toasted sesame seeds
**2 tablespoons raisins, softened in hot
  water, drained**
2 whole cloves
3 peppercorns
1/4 teaspoon anise seeds
1/4 teaspoon ground cinnamon
2 tablespoons vegetable oil
**2 oz. Mexican spiced chocolate or
  2 oz. semisweet chocolate, 4 teaspoons
  sugar, 1/8 teaspoon cinnamon and
  2 or 3 drops vanilla extract**
1 tablespoon sugar
Salt
Sesame seeds for garnish

Place chicken pieces in a large pot or Dutch oven. Add water to cover, onion halves, bay leaf, 4 peppercorns and salt to taste. Bring to a boil; reduce heat. Cover and simmer 1 hour. Rinse chiles; pat dry with paper towels. Heat 3 tablespoons oil in large pot or Dutch oven. Add chiles. Fry 5 minutes, turning constantly. Drain on paper towels. Process chiles and about 3/4 cup water in blender until pureed, adding more water if needed. Press through a sieve to eliminate peel. Process chopped onion, garlic and tomato in blender until smooth. Heat 1 tablespoon oil in the same pot or Dutch oven. Stir bread, tortilla and almonds in oil until browned but not burned. Add browned bread mixture, sesame seeds, raisins, cloves, 3 peppercorns, anise seeds and cinnamon to onion mixture. Process until pureed, adding about 2 tablespoons water or broth from chicken as needed. Heat 2 tablespoons oil in clean pot or Dutch oven. Add pureed onion mixture. Stir over medium heat 10 minutes. Add chile puree. Cook and stir 5 minutes. Gradually stir in 4 cups broth from chicken. Stir in chocolate and sugar until dissolved. Add salt to taste. Cover and simmer 1 hour 45 minutes. Uncover and cook 30 minutes longer or until thickened slightly. Add chicken pieces. Simmer 30 minutes. To serve, place a piece of chicken on each plate. Cover with sauce; garnish with sesame seeds. Makes 6 to 8 servings.

Pollo a la Vinagreta
Chicken Vinaigrette

A spectacular company dish from Veracruz.

2 (3- to 3-1/2-lb.) broiler-fryers
1 cup water
Salt
3 bay leaves
12 peppercorns
1/4 cup prepared mustard
1/2 cup white vinegar
6 to 8 small tomatoes, peeled, sliced
  (2 lbs.)

2 medium onions, sliced
4 small boiling potatoes, peeled (1 lb.)
Boiling salted water
Romaine or other leaf lettuce
2 or 3 hard-cooked eggs, quartered
1/2 (8-oz.) can peas, drained, heated

Cut up chickens. Separate thighs from legs. Cut off wings and discard wing tips. Cut breasts and backs in half crosswise. Place chicken pieces in a large pot or Dutch oven. Add 1 cup water, salt to taste, bay leaves and peppercorns. Bring to a boil; reduce heat. Cover and simmer 30 minutes. Blend mustard and vinegar. Stir into chicken broth. Top chicken pieces with tomatoes and onions. Cover and simmer until vegetables are tender, about 30 minutes. While tomatoes and onions cook, simmer potatoes in boiling salted water until tender, about 30 minutes. Line a large platter with lettuce leaves. Carefully lift chicken pieces from broth with a slotted spoon and arrange on lettuce. Top chicken with cooked tomato and onion. Cut cooked potatoes in half and arrange around platter. Place egg quarters between potatoes and on top of chicken. Top with peas. Pour some of the pan juices over chicken and vegetables. Remainder may be strained and served separately as a sauce. Makes 8 servings.

Pollo Estofado
Stewed Chicken

Mexicans serve this with rice or boiled potatoes to soak up the juices.

1 (3-1/2-lb.) broiler-fryer
1 large garlic clove
1/2 teaspoon salt
1/8 teaspoon coarsely ground pepper
3 tablespoons white vinegar
3 tablespoons vegetable oil
2 tablespoons sweet sherry
1 medium onion, chopped

4 small tomatoes, peeled, chopped
  (1 lb.)
12 Spanish-style green olives
2 teaspoons capers
1/2 teaspoon dried leaf oregano, crushed
1 bay leaf
1 teaspoon salt

Quarter chicken, wash and pat dry. Mash garlic with 1/2 teaspoon salt to make a paste. Mix garlic paste, pepper and vinegar. Rub chicken all over with garlic mixture. Let stand at least 1 hour before cooking. Heat oil in large skillet. Add chicken quarters 2 at a time and brown on both sides. Place browned chicken in a large pot or Dutch oven. Add sherry, onion, tomatoes, olives, capers, oregano, bay leaf and 1 teaspoon salt. Bring to a boil; reduce heat. Cover and simmer 1 hour, turning chicken pieces in sauce. Makes 4 servings.

Pollo en Pipián
Chicken in Squash Seed Sauce

Unusual nutty sauce makes this Guadalajaran dish exceptional.

5 dried ancho chiles	1/4 lb. hulled squash seeds
Water	1/2 cup sesame seeds
2 (3-lb.) chickens, cut up	1 tablespoon uncooked long-grain rice
Water	1 tablespoon lard
1/2 onion	1 slice white bread, broken up
1 bay leaf	1 corn tortilla, torn in pieces
8 peppercorns	1 tablespoon lard
Salt	1 teaspoon salt

Place chiles in a medium saucepan and add water to cover generously. Bring to a boil. Remove from heat and let stand until softened, about 1 hour. Place chicken pieces in a large pot or Dutch oven with water to cover. Add onion, bay leaf, peppercorns and salt to taste. Bring to a boil; reduce heat. Cover and simmer 45 minutes. Drain chicken, reserving broth. Toast squash seeds in an ungreased, heavy skillet until lightly browned, stirring often. Remove from skillet; set aside. Add sesame seeds and rice to skillet. Cook and stir until browned. Add to toasted squash seeds. Heat 1 tablespoon lard in skillet. Add broken bread and tortilla. Cook until browned. Add to squash seed mixture. Grind toasted ingredients 1/2 cup at a time in blender, stirring with a rubber spatula so blender does not become clogged. Toasted ingredients may be ground all at once in food processor. Mixture should be very fine. Drain chiles. Remove stems and seeds. Place in blender or food processor. Puree, adding a little chicken broth if needed. Press through a sieve to eliminate peel. Heat 1 tablespoon lard in a large pot or Dutch oven. Add ground seed mixture and chile puree. Cook 1 minute. Stir in 4 cups reserved chicken broth and 1 teaspoon salt. Add chicken pieces. Simmer 15 minutes. Taste and add more salt if needed. Sauce should be a medium consistency. Thin with more broth, if needed. Makes 6 servings.

Variation
If dried ancho chiles are not available, substitute about 5 tablespoons chili powder.

Pollo Yucateco
Yucatecan Chicken

Serve this red-coated chicken with rice or shred it and use to top Panuchos Mérida, page 100.

1 (3-1/2-lb.) broiler-fryer	3 or 4 spearmint leaves
5 cups water	6 peppercorns
1/2 onion	Salt
1 garlic clove	Recado Colorado, made with white
3 cilantro sprigs, including stems	vinegar, page 116

Place whole chicken breast-side down in a large pot or Dutch oven. Add water, onion, garlic, cilantro, spearmint, peppercorns and salt to taste. Bring to a boil; reduce heat. Cover and simmer 30 minutes. Remove chicken, reserving broth for another use. Let chicken cool slightly. Preheat oven to 350°F (175°C). Prepare Recado Colorado. If too thick, add a little water. Daub mixture over chicken. Place chicken in a baking dish. Bake 30 minutes or until cooked but not dry. Makes 4 servings.

Arroz con Pollo
Chicken & Rice

Tasty but subtle seasonings make this an ideal party casserole.

2 whole chicken breasts
1 qt. water
1/4 medium onion
1 large garlic clove
Salt
8 peppercorns
1 (8-1/2-oz.) can peas, drained
18 large Spanish-style green olives

1/2 teaspoon dried leaf oregano, crushed
1 teaspoon salt
Pepper
1 tablespoon bacon drippings
1 cup uncooked long-grain rice,
  rinsed, drained
1 cup canned tomatoes, undrained

Place chicken breasts in a large pot or Dutch oven. Add water, onion, garlic, salt to taste and peppercorns. Bring to a boil; reduce heat. Cover and simmer until tender, about 45 minutes. Drain chicken, reserving broth. Coarsely shred meat with 2 forks or your fingers. Add peas, olives, oregano, 1 teaspoon salt and pepper to taste; set aside. Preheat oven to 350°F (175°C). Heat bacon drippings in a large skillet. Add rice. Sauté until lightly browned. Add tomatoes; press into rice with a spoon. Simmer 3 to 5 minutes. Turn into a 2-1/2- to 3-quart casserole. Add chicken mixture; mix gently. Strain 2-1/2 cups broth into mixture. Add more if needed to cover mixture. Cover and bake 1 hour. Let stand covered a few minutes before serving. Makes 6 servings.

Variation

To make 12 servings, double all ingredients. Use 1 (16-oz.) can whole tomatoes and 1 (5-oz.) jar Spanish-style green olives.

Pollo con Piña a la Barbacoa
Barbecued Chicken With Pineapple

Choose a fairly firm, heavy, light-colored pineapple that has plump, glossy eyes.

1 medium, fresh pineapple
1/4 cup honey
1 (1-lb.) can tomato puree
1/4 cup canned pineapple juice
2 tablespoons vegetable oil
1 tablespoon sugar
1 tablespoon chopped fresh parsley

1 teaspoon salt
1/2 teaspoon chili powder
1/8 teaspoon hot pepper sauce
1/8 teaspoon pepper
1 (3- to 3-1/2-lb.) broiler-fryer
1 whole chicken breast

Remove pineapple crown. Cut pineapple lengthwise in 8 sections. Cut core from each section but leave shell on. Place in a rectangular baking dish. Brush cut surfaces with honey. Let stand 1 hour, turning occasionally to coat thoroughly with honey. Prepare grill. Combine tomato puree, pineapple juice, oil, sugar, parsley, salt, chili powder, hot pepper sauce and pepper. Cut chicken into serving pieces, splitting breasts, if desired. Place chicken on grill over hot coals. Brush with tomato-pineapple sauce. Cook 45 minutes to 1 hour, turning several times and brushing with sauce each time. Place pineapple wedges shell-side down on grill and cook 15 minutes or until heated through. Serve chicken with pineapple on the side. Makes 4 or 5 servings.

Pollo Pibil
Baked Chicken

If you don't have banana leaves for this Yucatán specialty, use foil only.

Recado Colorado made with lime juice
   or lemon juice, page 116
1 garlic clove
3 tablespoons vegetable oil
1 medium onion, sliced

4 large sections banana leaf, including
   center rib
1 (3-lb.) chicken, quartered
Salt

Prepare Recado Colorado. Add garlic. Mash to blend; set aside. Heat 1 tablespoon oil in a medium skillet. Add onion. Cook until tender but not browned; set aside. Preheat oven to 350°F (175°C). Cut four 20-inch sheets of aluminum foil. Place 1 sheet of foil on a flat surface. Place banana leaf in center of foil. Rub 1 chicken quarter with some of the remaining oil. Place chicken on banana leaf. Spread 1/4 of the Recado Colorado mixture over chicken with back of a spoon. Sprinkle with salt. Add 1/4 of the cooked onion. Wrap banana leaf around chicken to cover. Fold foil over banana leaf and crimp to close securely. If you use small pieces of banana leaf, overlap them to enclose chicken completely. Continue until all chicken quarters are seasoned and wrapped. Place in a single layer in a large baking pan. Bake 1 hour. Remove foil and drain off excess juices. Serve chicken wrapped in the leaves. Makes 4 servings.

How To Make
Pollo Pibil

Place a chicken quarter on a banana leaf or foil, then smear chicken with Recado Colorado.

Sprinkle chicken with salt and top with 1/4 of the cooked onions. Wrap in banana leaves, then in foil.

Pavo en Relleno Blanco
Turkey with White Stuffing

Sumptuous stuffed turkey breast is from Los Almendros Restaurant in Mérida.

1 (5-lb.) turkey breast	Relleno Puerco, page 114
Cold water	2 tablespoons vegetable oil
3 medium or 2 large garlic cloves	Tomato Sauce, see below
1 teaspoon salt	White Sauce, see below
1/2 teaspoon white pepper	Grated Parmesan cheese
2 tablespoons white vinegar	

Tomato Sauce:

2 tablespoons vegetable oil	2 tablespoons raisins
2 small onions, chopped (1/2 lb.)	4 Spanish-style green olives, pitted,
2 small green peppers, chopped	chopped
4 small tomatoes, peeled, chopped (1 lb.)	1 tablespoon drained capers
3 tablespoons chopped blanched almonds	Salt

White Sauce:

1/2 cup all-purpose flour	3/4 cup Tomato Sauce, see above
3 cups chicken or turkey broth, room temperature	

One hour before roasting, remove turkey breast from refrigerator. Rinse with cold water and pat dry with paper towels. Mash garlic with 1 teaspoon salt to make a paste. Add pepper and vinegar; mix well. Rub surface of turkey breast with garlic mixture. Let stand at room temperature until ready to cook. Prepare Relleno Puerco. Preheat oven to 325°F (165°C). Place a piece of heavy foil slightly larger than base of turkey in a shallow roasting pan. Stuff a little of the pork stuffing into turkey breast. Mound remaining stuffing in center of foil. Place stuffed turkey breast, cavity-side down over stuffing mound. Crimp foil tightly around turkey. Coat top of turkey with 2 tablespoons oil. Cover with a loose tent of additional foil. Roast 2 hours. Remove foil tent; roast 1 hour longer. Prepare Tomato Sauce; set aside. Remove turkey breast from oven. Grasp 2 opposite sides of foil and lift from pan onto a warm platter. Place platter in oven with heat off and door open. Let stand in open oven 25 to 30 minutes before slicing. Prepare White Sauce. Reheat remaining Tomato Sauce. Before serving, lift turkey and foil from platter; place on a baking sheet. Drain off any drippings from stuffing. Spoon stuffing from foil and turkey cavity onto platter; mix gently. Place turkey breast on top of stuffing. To serve, slice turkey; top each serving with some stuffing, a generous amount of White Sauce and a spoonful of Tomato Sauce. Sprinkle with grated Parmesan cheese. Makes 8 servings.

Tomato Sauce:
Heat oil in a small skillet. Add onions and green peppers. Cook until onions are very tender. Add tomatoes, almonds, raisins, olives and capers. Cook over low heat 15 minutes, stirring occasionally. Season with salt to taste. Makes 3 cups.

White Sauce:
Place flour in a jar with a tight-fitting lid. Add 1 cup broth. Cover and shake until blended. Strain into a 2-quart saucepan. Add remaining 2 cups broth. Bring to a boil, stirring constantly. Add 3/4 cup Tomato Sauce. Simmer gently 15 minutes. Makes about 4 cups.

Entertain with a Yucatán Fiesta. Pavo en Relleno Blanco (Turkey with White Stuffing) is in the center with bowls of White Sauce and Tomato Sauce. Clockwise from top right: Ensalada Mixta Uxmal (Uxmal Mixed Salad), page 56; Panuchos Mérida (Panuchos Mérida-Style), page 100; Sopa de Lima (Lime & Tortilla Soup), page 45; and Torta de Cielo (Heavenly Torte), page 180.

Pescados y Mariscos
Fish & Shellfish

Two long coastlines and numerous lakes and rivers provide Mexicans with a variety of fish and shellfish. Because it's never far from the coast to any point in the center of the country, you can have good seafood almost anywhere in Mexico. But freshly caught fish cooked and served at once with the surf whispering in the background is an exceptional treat. You can eat grilled fish on a stick at Puerto Vallarta or have a sizzling whole fish brought to you under a palm thatch at Zihuatanejo.

At most beach resorts, you can also order *ceviche*, an appetizer of raw fish soaked in lime juice. This soaking procedure cooks the fish just as thoroughly as if it had been heated, so don't hesitate to try it. *Ceviche de Alberto* (Alberto's Marinated Fish) is a simple mixture served as a first course at a restaurant in Mérida. A few slight changes and it becomes *ceviche* as served at the Chato Moya, a rustic seafood cafe near the docks in Veracruz.

Mariscos, or shellfish, are much loved in Mexico and a seafood cocktail is a popular way to start a meal. Choose a shrimp, crab or oyster cocktail or try a mixture of shellfish—usually shrimp and oysters—called *Campechana* in honor of the coastal state of Campeche.

An attractive first course is *Camarones en Salpicón* (Shrimp Salad). My recipe is from Horacio, a workman in Mexico City. This shrimp salad is served on lettuce with mayonnaise on the side and lime juice squeezed over it.

The best-known place for seafood in Mexico is probably Boca del Rio, a small town on the outskirts of Veracruz. Here you will find a wide variety of seafood and the lively music of Veracruz. Always on the menu is *Huachinango a la Veracruzana* (Red Snapper Veracruz-Style), one of Mexico's most famous fish dishes. One Veracruz chef adds wine and consommé. Others add *jalapeño* chiles, but the dish usually has a mild flavor. The simple but authentic recipe here comes from Bertha Delfín de Rodriguez of Veracruz.

GULF COAST DINNER

Ceviche de Alberto
Alberto's Marinated Fish

Marinating fish in lime juice several hours or overnight is almost like cooking it!

**1 lb. white fish fillets such as
   haddock or sole
1/2 cup lime juice**

**1 medium tomato, chopped
1/4 cup finely chopped onion
1/2 teaspoon salt**

Wash fish and pat dry with paper towels. Cut in 1/3- to 1/2-inch square pieces. Place in a medium bowl. Add lime juice; stir. Cover and refrigerate several hours or overnight until fish becomes opaque. Turn fish into a colander; drain. Rinse lightly with cold water, but not enough to wash out the lime. Drain. Return fish to bowl. Stir in tomato, onion and salt. Refrigerate at least 30 minutes for flavors to blend. Serve in seafood cocktail glasses as a first course. Makes 6 servings.

Variation

Ceviche Chato Moya (Marinated Fish from the Chato Moya Restaurant): When stirring in tomato, add a dash of pepper and thin slices of a serrano chile or other small hot chile to taste. Serve on individual plates or in cocktail glasses.

How To Make
Ceviche de Alberto

Cut raw fish into 1/3- to 1/2-inch squares. Marinate in lime juice several hours or overnight.

Drain marinated fish, rinse slightly and mix with tomato, onion and salt. Refrigerate 30 minutes.

Coctel de Camarones Mazatlán

Shrimp Cocktail Mazatlán-Style

A treat from the beaches of western Mexico.

1 lb. unshelled small shrimp	4 teaspoons chopped cilantro leaves
1 qt. water	1/4 cup diced cucumber
2 onion slices	1/2 cup ketchup
1 bay leaf	1/4 cup lime juice
1 tablespoon lime juice	Few drops hot chile salsa or hot pepper
8 peppercorns	sauce
1/2 teaspoon salt	Freshly ground pepper
1/4 cup chopped onion	Whole cilantro leaves

Wash shrimp well; drain. Do not peel. Combine water, onion slices, bay leaf, 1 tablespoon lime juice, peppercorns and salt in a large saucepan. Bring to a boil. Drop shrimp into boiling water. Cook 4 minutes. Remove shrimp. Strain and reserve liquid. Peel shrimp; slit backs and remove sand veins. Place in a large bowl. Cover with reserved liquid; chill. In a medium bowl, combine chopped onion, cilantro, cucumber, ketchup, 1/2 cup reserved shrimp liquid, 1/4 cup lime juice, hot chile salsa or hot pepper sauce to taste and pepper to taste. Drain shrimp, discarding remaining liquid. Stir drained shrimp into onion mixture. Spoon into 4 seafood cocktail glasses. Garnish with whole cilantro leaves. Makes 4 servings.

Variation

Reduce shrimp liquid to 1/4 cup. Add 1/4 cup white wine. Reduce lime juice to 2-1/2 teaspoons.

Coctel de Camarones

Shrimp Cocktail

You'll find this version of shrimp cocktail in Progreso, the port city of Yucatán.

1/2 lb. peeled cooked small shrimp	1/4 cup chopped onion
1/2 cup water	About 8 teaspoons mayonnaise
2/3 cup ketchup	Freshly ground pepper
2 tablespoons coarsely chopped	Drained canned or cooked fresh peas
cilantro leaves	2 limes, cut in half

Divide shrimp among 4 seafood cocktail glasses. Stir water into ketchup and spoon equally over shrimp. Add 1-1/2 teaspoons cilantro and 1 tablespoon onion to each glass. Stir lightly. Top each cocktail with about 2 teaspoons mayonnaise. Sprinkle with pepper and garnish with a few peas. Serve limes on the side. Makes 4 servings.

Variation

Coctel Campechana (Seafood Cocktail Campeche-Style): Substitute a mixture of seafood such as shrimp and oysters or shrimp, oysters and crabmeat for the shrimp.

Camarones en Salpicón
Shrimp Salad

A fresh and lively first course.

1 lb. fresh unshelled medium shrimp
1 qt. water
1 tablespoon lime juice
1 bay leaf
6 peppercorns
1/2 teaspoon salt
1 large California chile, roasted,
  peeled, chopped or 1/4 cup canned
  chopped green chiles

1 small tomato, chopped
4 green onions, chopped
2 tablespoons chopped cilantro leaves
1 tablespoon lime juice
Salt and pepper
4 large lettuce leaves
4 tablespoons mayonnaise
4 lime wedges

Wash shrimp thoroughly. Bring water to a boil in large saucepan. Add 1 tablespoon lime juice, bay leaf, peppercorns and 1/2 teaspoon salt. Drop shrimp into boiling water. Cook 4 minutes. Drain shrimp, reserving liquid. Peel shrimp; slit backs and remove sand veins. Place shrimp in a large bowl. Cover with reserved liquid; chill. Before serving, drain shrimp thoroughly. Mix drained shrimp with chile, tomato, green onions and cilantro. Sprinkle with 1 tablespoon lime juice and salt and pepper to taste; stir. Arrange lettuce leaves on 4 plates. Spoon shrimp mixture evenly onto lettuce leaves. Mound 1 tablespoon of mayonnaise beside shrimp. Garnish with a lime wedge. Makes 4 servings.

How To Make
Camarones en Salpicón

Peel cooked shrimp; slit backs and remove sand veins.

Combine chilled, drained shrimp with chile, tomato, green onions and cilantro leaves.

Pescado al Mojo de Ajo
Fish in Garlic Sauce

For those who love garlic!

1 small lime	1/4 cup olive oil
1 lb. white fish fillets such as	3 garlic cloves, chopped
haddock or sole	1/4 cup vegetable oil
Salt and pepper	Chopped parsley

Squeeze lime juice over fish. Sprinkle with salt and pepper to taste. Let stand while preparing garlic oil. Heat olive oil and garlic in a small skillet or saucepan over medium heat until olive oil is fragrant and garlic just starts to brown lightly. Keep garlic oil warm. Heat vegetable oil in a large skillet. Add fish fillets. Sauté until fish flakes easily when tested with a fork, 7 to 10 minutes, depending upon thickness of fish. Turn once. Divide fish into 4 serving portions. Spoon some of the garlic oil onto each portion. Sprinkle with parsley. Makes 4 servings.

Huachinango a la Veracruzana
Red Snapper Veracruz-Style

An authentic version of the famous Veracruz dish.

3 tablespoons olive oil	2 tablespoons capers
1 medium onion, chopped	3 bay leaves
3 garlic cloves, minced	6 peppercorns
5 medium tomatoes, peeled, chopped	Salt
(1-1/2 lbs.)	2 lbs. red snapper fillets or other
10 Spanish-style green olives, pitted,	white fish fillets
chopped	Salt

Heat olive oil in a large saucepan. Add onion and garlic. Cook until tender but not browned. Add tomatoes, olives, capers, bay leaves, peppercorns and salt to taste. Bring to a boil; reduce heat. Simmer gently uncovered 10 minutes. Place fish fillets in a large skillet and sprinkle with salt. Pour sauce over fish. Bring to a boil; reduce heat. Cover and simmer 10 minutes or until fish flakes easily when tested with a fork. Makes 6 servings.

Pescado Capeado en Caldillo
Fish in Gravy

Many fish markets write their recipe-of-the-day on a blackboard. I saw this one in Veracruz.

Tomato Sauce, see below
2 eggs, separated
1 lb. white fish fillets such as
   haddock or sole

1/3 cup vegetable oil
Salt
1/3 cup all-purpose flour

Tomato Sauce:
6 to 8 small tomatoes, peeled (2 lbs.)
1/2 medium onion
2 garlic cloves
1 tablespoon vegetable oil

3 jalapeño chiles or other
   small hot chiles
1 (2-inch) piece cinnamon stick
1 teaspoon salt

Prepare Tomato Sauce; set aside. Beat egg whites in a medium bowl until stiff. Add egg yolks and beat until blended; set aside. Cut fish into 4 serving-size pieces. Heat oil in a large skillet. Sprinkle salt on each side of fish. Coat with flour, then dip in beaten eggs. Fry in oil until lightly browned on both sides. Add Tomato Sauce. Cover and simmer 5 minutes. Makes 4 servings.

Tomato Sauce:
Combine tomatoes, onion and garlic in blender or food processor and process until pureed. Heat oil in a large sucepan. Add tomato mixture, chiles, cinnamon stick and salt. Bring to a boil; reduce heat. Simmer gently uncovered 30 minutes; keep hot. Remove chiles and cinnamon stick before serving. Makes about 4 cups.

How To Make
Pescado Capeado en Caldillo

Dip salted, floured fish into beaten egg mixture.

Fry coated fish pieces in hot oil until golden brown.

Camarones a la Veracruzana
Shrimp Veracruz-Style

Shrimp cooked too long or left to stand in hot sauce will become tough.

1 lb. fresh medium shrimp	**1-1/2 teaspoons capers**
1 large green pepper	**1 bay leaf**
1 tablespoon vegetable oil	**1/2 teaspoon sugar**
1 small onion, chopped	**1/2 teaspoon salt**
5 small tomatoes, peeled, chopped	**2 tablespoons vegetable oil**
(1-1/4 lbs.)	**Lime juice**
12 pimiento-stuffed green olives	

Peel shrimp; slit backs and remove sand veins. Set aside. Cut green pepper into 1-1/2"x1/2" strips. Heat 1 tablespoon oil on a large saucepan. Add onion and green pepper strips. Cook until onion is tender but not browned. Add tomatoes, olives, capers, bay leaf, sugar and salt. Bring to a boil; reduce heat. Cover and simmer 20 minutes. Taste sauce and add more salt if needed. Heat 2 tablespoons oil in another large skillet. Add cleaned shrimp. Cook over medium heat until pink, about 3 minutes. Sprinkle a few drops of lime juice over shrimp. Add sauce. Cook and stir 3 to 4 minutes longer. Serve immediately. Makes 4 servings.

Pescado con Salsa de Aguacate
Fish with Avocado Sauce

Mellow velvety Avocado Sauce is superb!

1-1/2 lbs. red snapper or other white	**3 or 4 onion slices**
fish fillets	**Juice of 1/2 small lime or lemon (1-1/2**
Water	**to 2 teaspoons)**
6 peppercorns	**Avocado Sauce, see below**
1/4 teaspoon salt	**Parsley**
1 bay leaf, crumbled	

Avocado Sauce:	
1 large avocado	**1/2 teaspoon Worcestershire sauce**
1/2 cup whipping cream	**1/2 teaspoon salt**
1/2 cup milk	**Dash white pepper**
1 teaspoon lime juice	**2 or 3 parsley sprigs**
3/4 teaspoon Maggi seasoning	

Place fish in a large skillet. Add water to cover, peppercorns, salt, bay leaf, onion slices and lime juice or lemon juice. Bring to a boil; reduce heat. Cover and simmer 10 minutes or until fish flakes easily when tested with a fork. Prepare Avocado Sauce. Drain fish. Place on a warm platter and keep warm. Pour over fish. Garnish with parsley; serve immediately. Makes 6 servings.

Avocado Sauce:
Peel avocado and slice into blender. Add remaining ingredients. Cover and blend until smooth. Pour into a saucepan. Heat over medium heat. stirring frequently; do not boil.

Camarones a la Veracruzana (Shrimp Veracruz-Style)

Pescado Alemán
Fish German-Style

Mustard and potatoes represent the German influence.

1 large boiling potato, peeled
Boiling salted water
1-1/2 to 2 lbs. fresh tuna or white
   fish fillets such as haddock
Water
Salt
8 peppercorns
Juice of 1/2 small lime or lemon
   (1-1/2 to 2 teaspoons)
3 or 4 onion slices
3 tablespoons butter

1 medium onion, cut in half
   lengthwise, sliced
3 tablespoons all-purpose flour
2 teaspoons Dijon-style mustard
1/2 cup milk
1 bay leaf
1/8 teaspoon dried leaf oregano,
   crushed
1/8 teaspoon dried leaf thyme, crushed
Salt
Pinch white pepper

Cook potato in boiling salted water 35 minutes or until tender. Drain; set aside. Place fish in a large skillet. Add water almost to cover. Add salt to taste, peppercorns, lime juice or lemon juice and 3 or 4 onion slices. Bring to a boil; reduce heat. Cover and simmer 10 minutes or until fish flakes easily when tested with a fork. Drain fish. Place on a warm platter and keep warm. Strain fish stock, reserving 1-1/2 cups. Melt butter in a medium saucepan. Add sliced medium onion. Cook until tender but not browned. Stir in flour and mustard. Gradually stir in reserved fish stock. Add remaining ingredients. Cook and stir until mixture boils and thickens. Slice cooked potato. Add to sauce; heat through. Pour over fish. Serve immediately. Makes 6 to 8 servings.

Pescado en Salsa Verde
Fish in Green Sauce

Green tomatoes are not identical to tomatillos, but you can try them as a substitute

1 lb. fresh tomatillos or 1-3/4 cups
   drained canned tomatillos
3 green onions, with some green tops
1 garlic clove
1 tablespoon chopped parsley leaves
1 small California chile, roasted,
   peeled, seeded, or 1 canned whole
   green chile

2 teaspoons vegetable oil
Salt
1-1/2 lbs. white fish fillets such as
   haddock or sole
3 tablespoons lime juice
1/2 teaspoon salt
3 tablespoons vegetable oil

Remove papery husks from tomatillos. Wash tomatillos. Pour water 1/2 inch deep into a medium saucepan. Add fresh tomatillos. Bring to a boil; reduce heat. Cover and cook 10 minutes or until tender. Drain and cool. Do not cook canned tomatillos. Place tomatillos, green onions, garlic, parsley and chile in blender or food processor; process until pureed. Heat 2 teaspoons oil in a medium saucepan. Add puree and salt to taste. Bring to a boil; reduce heat. Simmer gently uncovered 15 minutes. Set sauce aside and keep warm. Sprinkle fish with lime juice and 1/2 teaspoon salt. Let stand 3 to 5 minutes. Heat 3 tablespoons oil in a large skillet. Add fish. Cook 1 minute on each side. Add sauce. Cover and simmer 5 minutes or until fish flakes easily when tested with a fork. Makes 6 servings.

Huevos
Eggs

Eggs gain spicy character and lots of color when cooked with Mexican ingredients. Delicious combinations of tomatoes, *chiles*, *tortillas* and eggs are endless.

Fry a *tortilla* until it's crisp, top it with a fried egg and tomato *salsa* for *Huevos Rancheros* (Eggs Ranch-Style). Switch from a red to a green *salsa* made with *tomatillos* for a dish with a different flavor and appearance. Sandwich fried eggs between two *tortillas*, place them on a mound of refried black beans and pour tomato sauce over them. It's called *Huevos Motuleños* (Eggs Motul-Style). The trademark of this dish is fried banana slices on the side.

If eggs are hard-cooked, wrapped in a *tortilla* and topped with a sauce, they are *Papadzules* (Egg-Filled *Enchiladas*), page 81. The sauce is usually made of ground squash seeds, but you can also serve them with a tomato sauce.

Sometimes eggs are baked in a tomato sauce as in *Huevos a la Malagueña* (Eggs Málaga-Style). A specialty of the Gran Café de la Parroquia in Veracruz, the recipe includes ham, bacon, asparagus and a whole *chile*.

In the pleasant little patio of the Hotel Colón in Mérida, I ordered *Huevos Revueltos Albañil* (Stonemason's Scrambled Eggs). They are scrambled with beans. A sweet roll and Mexican coffee added up to a thoroughly delightful breakfast. You can also stir *chorizo*, spicy Mexican sausage, into scrambled eggs, serve them on a plate or roll them up in a flour *tortilla* for a quick and easy breakfast *burrito*.

Incidentally, you may see the word *tortilla* listed under eggs on a restaurant menu in Mexico. *Tortilla* is the Spanish word for omelet as well as for the flat bread made of corn flour used to make *tacos*, *enchiladas* and other typical dishes.

SUNDAY BRUNCH

Huevos Motuleños
Eggs Motul-Style

This egg dish from a town in Yucatán is a good way to use leftover refried beans.

3/4 cup Tomato Sauce for Pescado
   Capeado en Caldillo, page 129
1/4 cup Frijoles Refritos made with
   black beans, page 149
Vegetable oil for frying
2 corn tortiilas

3 diagonal slices banana or plantain
2 eggs
1/2 thin slice of cooked ham, diced
2 tablespoons drained canned or cooked
   fresh peas, room temperature

Prepare Tomato Sauce; keep hot. Heat beans; keep hot. Pour oil 1/4 inch deep into a medium skillet. Heat to 365°F (185°C). Fry each tortilla until crisp and lightly browned. Drain on paper towels, reserving oil in skillet. Keep tortillas warm. Fry banana or plantain slices in reserved oil until browned. Drain on paper towels, reserving oil in skillet. Keep fried banana or plantain warm. In the same skillet, fry eggs sunny-side up. To asssemble dish, spread some of the Tomato Sauce on a warm plate. Place heated beans in the center. Top beans with 1 cooked tortilla. Place fried eggs side-by-side on the tortilla. Top eggs with a second cooked tortilla. Pour remaining Tomato Sauce over tortilla. Sprinkle with ham and peas. Arrange cooked banana or plantain slices on top. Serve immediately. Makes 1 serving.

How To Make
Huevos Motuleños

Spread some tomato sauce on a plate. Top with black beans and a fried tortilla.

Continue layering with fried eggs, a second tortilla, tomato sauce, ham, peas and banana or plantain slices.

Huevos Rancheros
Eggs Ranch-Style

Sprinkle refried beans with shredded cheese and serve on the side.

Salsa Picante de Carmen, page 36   **6 corn tortillas**
Vegetable oil for frying   **12 eggs**

Prepare salsa, reducing chiles to 1 or 2 if a milder sauce is desired; keep hot. Pour oil 1/4 inch deep into a medium skillet. Heat to 365°F (185°C). Fry tortillas until crisp and lightly browned. Drain on paper towels; keep warm. Remove all but a little oil from skillet. Fry eggs sunny-side up. Place 2 eggs on each tortilla. Top with 1/3 cup salsa. Serve immediately. Makes 6 servings.

Huevos al Vallejo
Eggs Vallejo-Style

Named for an old California family, this recipe has its origins in Spain.

1 tablespoon butter   **1 (16-oz.) can whole tomatoes, undrained**
1 small onion, sliced   **Salt and pepper**
2 California chiles, roasted, peeled,   **6 eggs**
** or 2 canned whole green chiles,**
** cut into short strips**

Heat butter in a large skillet. Add onion. Cook until tender but not browned. Stir in chile strips and tomatoes. Cook 5 minutes, breaking up tomatoes with a spoon. Add salt and pepper to taste. Break eggs one at a time into a saucer and slide into hot tomato mixture. Cover and simmer 5 minutes or until egg whites are set; spoon sauce over eggs as they cook. Makes 6 servings.

Variation
When eggs are almost set, top each with a slice of Monterey Jack cheese. Cover and cook until cheese is melted.

Huevos Revueltos Albañil
Stonemason's Scrambled Eggs

Bolillos (French Rolls), page 161, or plain white rolls are usually served with this hearty breakfast.

1 teaspoon butter or vegetable oil   **2 tablespoons finely mashed Frijoles Refritos**
2 eggs, beaten   **   made with black beans, page 149**

Heat butter or oil in skillet over medium-high heat. Add eggs. Cook and stir until set. Stir in beans. Cook until heated through. Makes 1 serving.

Huevos a la Malagueña

Eggs Málaga-Style

The name may be Spanish, but the chiles indicate this dish is Mexican.

3 cups Salsa Roja for Picadas,
  omitting hot chiles, page 103
4 California chiles, roasted, peeled,
  or 4 canned whole green chiles
2 thin slices cooked ham, diced

1/4 cup drained canned, cooked fresh,
  or thawed frozen peas
8 eggs
4 slices bacon, cooked
4 canned asparagus spears

Prepare Salsa Roja, omitting hot chiles. Cut stems from chiles. Cut as small a slit as possible in each chile and remove seeds and veins, leaving chiles whole. Preheat oven to 375°F (190°C). Place 3/4 cup Salsa Roja in each of 4 shallow individual baking dishes. Add a fourth of the ham and 1 tablespoon peas to each dish; stir. Break an egg into a saucer; slide egg gently into one baking dish without breaking yolk. Break another egg into saucer; slide it carefully into same baking dish. Repeat, placing 2 eggs side-by-side in each dish. Top with a bacon slice, a whole chile and an asparagus spear. Bake 15 minutes or until eggs are set as desired. Makes 4 servings.

Huevos Revueltos a la Mexicana

Mexican Scrambled Eggs

For several servings, remove vegetables before cooking eggs. Stir in vegetables as directed.

1 teaspoon vegetable oil
1 serrano chile or other small hot
  chile, seeded, chopped
1/2 small tomato, chopped

1/4 small onion, chopped
2 eggs, beaten
Salt

Heat oil in large skillet over medium-high heat. Add chile, tomato and onion. Stir-fry just until vegetables are heated through. Vegetables should remain crisp. Push vegetables to one side of skillet. Add eggs. Cook and stir until eggs are almost set, then stir in vegetables and cook 1 to 2 minutes longer. Season with salt to taste. Makes 1 serving.

Soufflé de Elote

Corn Soufflé

Sprinkling the baking dish with flour prevents soufflé from sticking.

1 (1-lb. 1-oz.) can whole-kernel corn
1/2 medium onion, finely chopped
3 tablespoons butter
3 eggs, separated

1/2 cup chopped, peeled, roasted
  California chiles or canned
  chopped green chiles
1/2 teaspoon salt

Preheat oven to 375°F (190°C). Butter a 1-1/2-quart baking dish. Sprinkle lightly with flour; set aside. Drain corn. In a medium skillet, cook onion in butter until tender. Combine drained corn, cooked onion and egg yolks in blender or food processor. Process until corn is fine. Turn out into a medium bowl. Stir in chiles and salt. Beat egg whites in a small bowl until stiff. Fold gently but thoroughly into corn mixture. Turn into prepared baking dish. Bake 10 minutes. Reduce heat to 350°F (175°C) and bake 20 to 30 minutes longer until soufflé is lightly browned and a knife inserted off-center comes out clean. Cut into wedges. Makes 4 to 6 servings.

Huevos a la Malagueña (Eggs Málaga-Style)

Huevos con Papas y Chorizo
Eggs with Potatoes & Chorizo

Wake up to a hearty Mexican breakfast!

2 large baking potatoes, peeled	**4 eggs**
1/2 lb. chorizo	**1 avocado, sliced**
1/2 cup finely chopped onion	**Cilantro or parsley sprigs, if desired**

Cut potatoes into 1/4-inch thick slices and then into 1/4-inch dice. Remove chorizo from casing and place in a large skillet. Cook and mash chorizo until lightly browned and fat has melted. Add diced potatoes and onion. Cover and cook over medium heat until potatoes are tender, about 15 minutes. Remove lid. With the back of a large spoon, press 4 indentations in mixture. Break an egg into each indentation. Cover and cook until eggs are set, about 5 minutes. To serve, garnish with avocado slices and cilantro or parsley sprigs, if desired. Makes 4 servings.

How To Make
Huevos con Papas y Chorizo

Cut potatoes into 1/4-inch thick slices, then 1/4-inch thick sticks before dicing.

Break eggs into indentations that have been made with a spoon. Cover and cook until eggs are set.

Arroz y Frijoles
Rice & Beans

It's difficult to imagine a Mexican meal without rice and beans. They are often served separately—rice preceding the meat and beans following the meat.

Mexican cooks are famous for their tender, dry, flaky rice—easy to duplicate once you know the cooking method. Rice is often tinted red with tomato, but that's only the beginning. Its flavor can vary from lightly seasoned *Arroz Blanco* (White Rice) to rich mixtures with sausage, seafood and meat. Sometimes the rice course is called *Sopa Seca de Arroz* (Dry Rice Soup) which is confusing to tourists not accustomed to Mexican culinary terms. *Sopa* here means a *dry soup*, not a wet one.

For authentic Mexican rice, use long-grain rice prepared according to the method described in the following pages.

In a typical Mexican home, a pot of beans is always on the stove. Beans are served whole in their broth, plain or topped with garnishes such as chopped onion and *chile*. Served this way they are *Frijoles de la Olla* (Beans from the Pot). Or they may be fried and mashed in lard or oil to make *Frijoles Refritos* (Refried Beans). Broth from beans is occasionally used to make soup or as a substitute for water or broth when making rice. While beans and rice are usually served separately, my Veracruz friends mix black beans and white rice and call the dish *casamiento*, or *marriage*, the combining of the two ingredients.

Many types of beans are grown in Mexico. Some of their names are *bayo gordo*, *parraleño*, *ojo de liebre*, *flor de mayo* and *canario*. Each bean type differs in appearance. In southern Mexico, black beans predominate. Elsewhere, pinto beans are common. Unless I specify another type of bean, use pinto beans with the recipes in this book.

LUNCH AT THE BORDER

Guacamole (Guacamole)	page 40
Totopos (Corn Chips)	page 30
Enchiladas de Queso (Cheese Enchiladas)	page 78
Arroz Rojo (Red Rice)	page 142
Frijoles Refritos (Refried Beans)	page 149
Helado o Nieve (Ice Cream or Sherbet)	

HOW TO COOK RICE

This method is only for long-grain rice—not converted or instant rice.

Use 2 cups of cooking liquid to 1 cup of rice. If you use tomato sauce or pureed tomatoes, measure them with the cooking liquid so you won't have too much liquid.

Rinsing—Rice is enriched by coating the grains with nutrients. Although these nutrients are removed when rice is rinsed, the method described here is commonly used in Mexico. With other methods, the rice will be starchier than Mexican rice. Place the rice in a large bowl and cover with *very hot* tap water. Let it stand 10 to 15 minutes. Then rub and squeeze rice with your fingers until the water is cloudy. Drain the rice in a strainer. Return the rice to the bowl. Cover it with *cold* water. Rub and squeeze it again, then drain. Repeat the cold water and draining process once more or as many times as it takes to get the water fairly clear. Drain the rice thoroughly and spread it on a platter to dry. You can use rice while it is still wet, but there is danger of spattering hot oil when wet rice is added to the skillet. Rice usually takes 1 hour or more to dry.

Frying—When you are ready to cook rice, heat the lard, oil or butter and oil in a large pot, Dutch oven or deep skillet with a tight-fitting lid. Add the rice. Stir it frequently until it is lightly browned. If you are using onion and garlic, add them to the pot as the rice begins to brown. Continue to stir often.

Cooking Liquid—While the rice is browning, heat the cooking liquid to minimize the danger of spattering and steaming when it contacts hot rice. When all the rice is lightly browned, carefully pour the hot cooking liquid into the pot. Cover and boil vigorously for 3 to 5 minutes, until the liquid is absorbed by the rice but the rice is still quite moist.

Steaming—Place the pot over very low heat. If necessary, place an asbestos *heat diffuser* on the burner to reduce the heat. Let the rice steam until it is tender, 30 to 45 minutes. Fluff steamed rice with a fork before serving.

Arroz a la Mexicana
Rice Mexican-Style

Traditional Mexican rice is colored with tomato and other vegetables.

1 cup long-grain rice	1 cup water
1 garlic clove	1 cup chicken broth
1/2 teaspoon salt	1/3 cup frozen peas, thawed
2 tablespoons lard or vegetable oil	1 small carrot, peeled, cooked, diced
1 small onion, chopped	1/2 teaspoon salt
2 tomatoes, peeled, chopped (1/2 lb.)	

Rinse rice according to the directions above. Mash garlic with 1/2 teaspoon salt to make a paste; set aside. Heat lard or vegetable oil in a large pot or Dutch oven. Add rice. Cook and stir over medium heat until lightly browned. Add onion and garlic paste. Cook and stir until onion is tender. Add tomatoes. Cook and stir until tomatoes are softened and blended into rice mixture. Add water. Cover and simmer until water is absorbed. Stir in broth, peas, carrot and 1/2 teaspoon salt. Cover and simmer until most of the liquid is absorbed, 3 to 5 minutes. Reduce heat to very low and steam 30 to 45 minutes until rice is tender. Makes 4 servings.

Soak rice in hot water, then rub between your fingers. The water will become milky.

How To Cook Rice

Draining rice and spreading in a thin layer to dry reduces spattering when rice is fried.

Fry and stir rice in oil, butter or lard until browned.

Arroz Chicano
Rice Chicano-Style

A Mexican-American cook's shortcut for Arroz a la Mexicana.

1 cup long-grain rice
2 tablespoons vegetable oil
2 cups hot water
1 (10-1/2-oz.) can vegetable beef soup

1 teaspoon onion salt
1/4 teaspoon onion powder
1/4 teaspoon dried leaf oregano,
   crushed

Rinse rice according to How to Cook Rice, page 140. Heat oil in a large pot or Dutch oven. Add rice. Cook and stir over medium heat until browned. Add 1 cup hot water and soup. Rinse soup can with remaining 1 cup hot water and add to rice with onion salt, onion powder and oregano. Stir well. Cover and simmer until most of the liquid is absorbed. Reduce heat to very low and steam 30 to 45 minutes, until rice is tender. Makes 4 servings.

Arroz Instante
Quick Mexican Rice

When you don't have time to cook rice from scratch, try this.

1 medium onion
1 garlic clove
1/2 teaspoon salt
1 tablespoon bacon drippings
1 (8-1/4-oz.) can stewed tomatoes

1/2 cup chicken broth
1/2 teaspoon chili powder
1/8 teaspoon ground cumin
1 cup instant rice

Cut onion in half. Finely chop 1 half. Cut the other half in very thin slices. Mash garlic with salt to make a paste. Heat bacon drippings in a medium saucepan. Add chopped onion and garlic paste. Cook and stir until onion is tender. Add stewed tomatoes, chicken broth, chili powder and cumin. Mash tomatoes with a masher or the back of a spoon. Bring mixture to a boil. Stir in rice and sliced onion. Cover and let stand over very low heat 15 to 20 minutes or until liquid is absorbed. Use an asbestos heat diffuser if necessary to maintain very low heat. Makes 4 servings.

Arroz Rojo
Red Rice

If the cooked rice is dry, sprinkle it with a little warm broth or water.

1-1/2 cups long-grain rice
1 garlic clove
3/4 teaspoon salt
3 tablespoons vegetable oil

1/2 medium onion, finely chopped
1 (8-oz.) can tomato sauce
2 cups chicken broth

Rinse rice according to How to Cook Rice, page 140. Mash garlic with salt to make a paste. Heat oil in a large pot or Dutch oven. Add rice. Cook and stir over medium heat until lightly browned. Add onion and garlic paste. Cook and stir until onion is tender. Stir in tomato sauce and chicken broth. Cover and simmer until most of the liquid is absorbed. Reduce heat to very low and steam 30 to 45 minutes until rice is tender. Makes 6 servings.

Sopa Seca de Arroz
Dry Rice Soup

Sopas secas, or dry soups, are rice or pasta dishes served without broth or other liquid.

1 cup long-grain rice
1 garlic clove
1/2 teaspoon salt
2 tablespoons butter
2 tablespoons vegetable oil

1 small onion, chopped
2 cups chicken broth
2 tablespoons chopped fresh parsley
1/2 teaspoon chopped fresh marjoram or
   oregano, if desired.

Rinse rice according to How to Cook Rice, page 140. Mash garlic with 1/2 teaspoon salt to make a paste; set aside. Heat butter and oil in a large pot or Dutch oven. Add rice. Cook and stir over medium heat until lightly browned. Add onion and garlic paste. Cook and stir until onion is tender. Add chicken broth, parsley and marjoram or oregano, if desired. Cover and simmer until most of the liquid is absorbed. Taste and add more salt, if needed. Reduce heat to very low and steam 30 to 45 minutes, until rice is tender. Makes 4 servings.

Arroz con Chiles
Rice with Chiles

Rice with cheese and chiles as served at a restaurant in Guanajuato.

1 cup long-grain rice
2 California chiles, roasted, peeled,
   or 2 canned whole green chiles
1 garlic clove
1/2 teaspoon salt

3 tablespoons vegetable oil
1 small onion, finely chopped
2 cups chicken broth
2 oz. Monterey Jack cheese, shredded
   (1/2 cup)

Rinse rice according to How to Cook Rice, page 140. Cut chiles into thin strips 1 to 1-1/2 inches long. Mash garlic in 1/2 teaspoon salt to form a paste. Heat oil in a large pot or Dutch oven. Add rice. Cook and stir until lightly browned. Add onion and garlic paste. Cook and stir until onion is tender. Add chile strips and broth. Cover and simmer until most of the liquid is absorbed. Reduce heat to very low; steam 30 to 45 minutes, until rice is tender. Taste and add more salt if needed. Before serving, toss rice with a fork and stir in cheese. Cover and steam over very low heat until cheese is melted, about 5 minutes. Makes 4 servings.

Arroz con Chorizo
Rice with Chorizo

Use the oil below only with homemade Chorizo, page 112. Other chorizo has a lot of fat.

1 cup long-grain rice	**1/4 cup frozen peas**
1/4 lb. chorizo	**2 cups chicken broth**
1/4 cup vegetable oil	**Salt**
1/3 cup chopped onion	**Avocado slices, if desired**
1 medium tomato, peeled, chopped	**Tomato wedges, if desired**

Rinse rice according to How to Cook Rice, page 140. Remove casing from chorizo; discard casing. Heat 2 tablespoons oil in a large pot or Dutch oven. Add chorizo. Fry over medium heat until browned, stirring to keep crumbly. Remove chorizo from pot, set aside. Add remaining 2 tablespoons oil to pot. Add rice. Cook and stir over medium heat 3 to 5 minutes. Add onion. Cook and stir until onion is tender. Add tomato. Cook and stir until tomato can be mashed into rice. Add browned chorizo, peas and broth. Cover and simmer until most of the liquid is absorbed. Reduce heat to very low and steam 30 to 45 minutes, until rice is tender. Taste and add salt, if neded. Garnish with avocado slices and tomato wedges, if desired. Makes 4 servings.

Arroz Catalina
Rice Catalina-Style

You won't be able to taste the mint, but it brings out the flavor of the rice.

1-1/2 cups long-grain rice	**1 mint sprig or 1/4 teaspoon crushed**
3 tablespoons butter	**dried leaf mint**
1 medium onion, finely chopped	**Salt**
3 cups strong chicken broth	

Rinse rice according to How to Cook Rice, page 140. Heat butter in a large pot or Dutch oven. Add rice. Cook and stir over medium heat until lightly browned. Add onion. Cook and stir until onion is tender. Add broth, mint and salt to taste. Cover and simmer until most of the liquid is absorbed. Reduce heat and steam 30 to 45 minutes, until rice is tender. Remove mint sprig; fluff rice with a fork. Makes 6 servings.

Arroz Guisado
Seasoned Rice

Cloves and cinnamon add a pleasing and different taste.

1 cup long-grain rice	2 tablespoons bacon drippings
2 small tomatoes, peeled (1/2 lb.)	1 tablespoon vegetable oil
1/2 medium onion	1-1/2 cups pork broth
1 garlic clove	1 teaspoon salt
Pinch ground cloves	1/3 cup frozen peas, thawed
1/8 teaspoon ground cinnamon	1/2 cup diced, peeled potato

Rinse rice according to How to Cook Rice, page 140. Combine tomatoes, onion, garlic, cloves and cinnamon in blender or food processor; puree. Heat bacon drippings and oil in a large pot or Dutch oven. Add rice. Cook and stir over medium heat until lightly browned. Add tomato mixture. Cook and stir 3 minutes. Add broth and salt. Cover and simmer until most of the liquid is absorbed. Stir in peas and potato. Reduce heat to very low. Cover and steam 30 to 45 minutes, until rice is tender. Makes 6 servings.

Arroz a la Veracruzana
Rice Veracruz-Style

If you cannot reduce the heat to very low, place an asbestos heat diffuser under the pot.

1 cup long-grain rice	1 thin strip jalapeño chile or
1 large garlic clove	other small hot chile
1/2 teaspoon salt	1 tablespoon chopped fresh parsley
2 tablespoons vegetable oil	2 cups beef broth
1 medium onion, finely chopped	

Rinse rice according to How to Cook Rice, page 140. Mash garlic with salt to make a paste. Heat oil in a large pot or Dutch oven. Add rice. Cook and stir over medium heat until lightly browned. Add onion and garlic paste. Cook and stir until onion is tender. Add chile strip, parsley and broth. Cover and simmer until most of the liquid is absorbed. Reduce heat to very low. Steam 30 to 45 minutes, until rice is tender. Add more salt, if needed. Makes 4 servings.

Arroz Verde de Zihuatanejo
Green Rice from Zihuatanejo.

Green pepper and parsley provide color.

1 cup long-grain rice
1 large green pepper
1/2 medium onion
2 garlic cloves

1/4 cup fresh parsley leaves
3 tablespoons vegetable oil
2 cups chicken broth
1/2 teaspoon salt

Rinse rice according to How to Cook Rice, page 140. Remove stem and seeds from green pepper. Process green pepper, onion, garlic and parsley in blender or food processor until finely ground. Heat 1 tablespoon oil in a small saucepan. Add green pepper mixture. Cook and stir 2 to 3 minutes. Heat 2 tablespoons oil in a large pot or Dutch oven. Add rice. Cook and stir over medium heat until lightly browned. Stir in sautéed green pepper mixture, broth and salt. Cover and simmer until most of the liquid is absorbed. Reduce heat to very low. Steam 30 to 45 minutes, until rice is tender. Taste and add more salt, if needed. Makes 4 to 6 servings.

Arroz Blanco
White Rice

Serve plain white rice with spicy foods or dishes that have a lot of sauce.

1 cup long-grain rice
1-1/2 tablespoons lard
2 medium garlic cloves, crushed

2 cups water or chicken broth
1 teaspoon salt

Rinse rice according to How to Cook Rice, page 140. Heat lard in a large pot or Dutch oven. Add garlic. Cook until browned. Remove garlic; discard. Add rice. Cook and stir over medium heat until golden. Add water or broth and salt. Cover and simmer until most of the liquid is absorbed. Reduce heat to very low. Steam 30 to 45 minutes, until rice is tender. Makes 4 servings.

Variation

Arroz Negro (Black Rice): Sauté 1/2 small onion, chopped, with the rice. Substitute black bean cooking liquid for water or broth.

ARROZ CON PLÁTANOS (RICE WITH BANANAS)

Mexico produces many banana varieties, generally called *plátanos. Arroz con Plátanos* (Rice with Bananas) is popular in the Veracruz area. There are two ways you can make this dish. The easiest way is to slice bananas directly on top of cooked rice as a garnish. Another method is to cut bananas lengthwise into thin slices, sauté them in butter or oil until they are browned, then place the sautéed bananas on top of cooked rice.

HOW TO COOK BEANS

Sorting & Soaking—Sort beans carefully to remove small stones, dirt and other foreign matter. Place the beans in a large pot, deep saucepan or Dutch oven. Cover them generously with very hot water. Let them soak overnight. If you don't have time to let them soak overnight, cover them with water and bring to a boil. Continue to boil for 2 minutes. Remove the pot from the heat and let it stand for 1 hour.

Soaking Liquid—Bean soaking liquid may be discarded or used as cooking liquid. More nutrients will be retained if beans are cooked in their soaking liquid. If you choose this method, rinse the beans thoroughly before soaking and cover them loosely to keep out dust and other foreign matter.

Cooking—Be sure beans are covered with liquid. Bring them to a boil. If the recipe calls for garlic and onion, add them at this point. Reduce the heat. Place the lid slightly ajar on the pot. Simmer 4 to 6 hours or until beans are completely tender when pierced with a fork. Add hot water as needed to keep beans covered. Stir them occasionally to prevent sticking and burning.

Salt—There is no absolute rule to follow for adding salt to beans. Salt has a reputation for making beans tough so some cooks do not add salt until the beans are almost cooked. Others add salt during cooking, and a few cooks salt the beans when they put them in the pot.

Lard—Many cooks add a spoonful of lard to beans as they cook to add flavor. It also reduces the foam. Most Mexican cooks use home-rendered lard, which has more flavor than the processed supermarket product.

Frijoles Sencillos
Basic Beans

Follow this method to cook any type of dried beans.

1 cup dried pinto beans, black beans
   or other beans
Hot water
1/4 medium onion, if desired

1 garlic clove, if desired
1 tablesoon lard or bacon drippings
Salt

Sort beans to remove rocks and other foreign matter. Place beans in a large saucepan. Add hot water to cover. Let stand covered overnight or at least 8 hours. Drain beans. Rinse; cover with fresh hot water. Bring to a boil. Add onion and garlic if desired. Cover with lid ajar and simmer gently 2 hours. Add lard or bacon drippings and salt to taste. Cook 2 to 4 hours longer or until beans are very tender. Add more hot water if needed to keep beans covered. Makes 4 servings.

Frijoles de la Olla
Beans from the Pot

Serve with warm flour tortillas or Totopos, page 30.

Frijoles Sencillos, above
Salsa Mexicana, page 33, or
   other salsa

1 onion, chopped

Prepare Basic Beans and salsa. Serve beans with their cooking liquid in individual soup bowls. Serve chopped onion and salsa separately. Makes 4 servings.

Frijoles Refritos   **Photo on pages 86 and 87.**
Refried Beans

Topped with grated cheese and Totopos, page 30, Refried Beans are a traditional side dish.

Frijoles Sencillos, page 148   **Salt**
1-1/2 tablespoons lard, bacon
 drippings or vegetable oil

Prepare Frijoles Sencillos. Heat lard, bacon drippings or vegetable oil in a large heavy skillet until very hot. Use a slotted spoon to place beans in skillet. Add a little cooking liquid. Mash beans with a potato masher or the back of a large spoon. Beans may be partially or completely mashed. Add salt to taste. Simmer beans to desired consistency, adding more cooking liquid, if needed. Stir beans frequently. Makes 4 servings.

Variation

Fry beans as directed above until fairly dry. Season to taste with chili powder.

Frijoles al Horno
Baked Beans

Look what happened to Boston baked beans in Mexico!

1 lb. dried Great Northern beans   **2 teaspoons salt**
Hot water   **6 peppercorns**
1 (8-oz.) pork shoulder steak   **4 whole allspice**
Water   **2 whole cloves**
1 tablespoon vegetable oil   **1 (1-inch) piece cinnamon stick**
1/4 lb. cooked ham   **1/2 teaspoon dry mustard**
3 slices bacon   **1/2 teaspoon Worcestershire sauce**
2 small tomatoes, peeled (1/2 lb.)   **1 bay leaf**
1/4 cup white vinegar   **1 medium onion**
2 tablespoons sugar

Sort beans to remove rocks and other foreign matter. Place beans in a large saucepan. Add hot water to cover. Let stand covered overnight or at least 8 hours. Drain beans and rinse well. Add fresh hot water to cover generously. Bring to a boil; reduce heat. Cover with lid ajar and simmer 1 hour. Remove bone from pork steak. Place boned pork in a medium saucepan. Cover with water. Cover and cook 20 minutes. Drain, adding broth to beans. Heat oil in a skillet. Add cooked pork. Saute until browned and crisp on the outside. Cut cooked and browned pork into small pieces. Dice ham and bacon; set aside. Puree tomatoes in blender or food processor. Combine tomato puree, vinegar, sugar, salt, peppercorns, allspice, cloves, cinnamon, dry mustard, Worchestershire sauce and bay leaf in a medium saucepan. Bring to a boil; remove from heat. Preheat oven to 350°F (175°C). Drain beans, reserving cooking liquid. Place beans in a large bean pot. Stir in tomato puree mixture, pork, ham and bacon. Place onion in center of beans. Add reserved bean liquid to cover. Cover and bake 3 to 4 hours, adding more bean liquid if needed. If there is too much liquid, uncover and bake 15 to 20 minutes longer until liquid is reduced. Makes 10 servings.

Frijoles Especiales
Special Beans

Richly seasoned beans are popular in central Mexico.

2 cups dried pinto beans
Hot water
1 small onion, cut in wedges
1 large garlic clove
1 slice bacon, diced
2 teaspoons salt

Totopos, page 30
2 tablespoons chili powder
1/2 teaspoon ground cumin
2 tablespoons lard or vegetable oil
1 (5.33-oz.) can evaporated milk
Grated Parmesan cheese

Sort beans to remove rocks and other foreign matter. Place beans in a large saucepan. Add hot water to cover. Let stand covered overnight or at least 8 hours. Drain beans and rinse well. Add fresh hot water to cover generously. Bring to a boil; reduce heat. Add onion, garlic and bacon. Cover with lid ajar and simmer 2 hours. Add salt. Simmer 4 hours longer or until beans are very tender. Add hot water as needed to keep beans covered. Prepare Totopos; set aside. Mix chili powder and cumin in a small bowl. Remove 1/4 cup bean cooking liquid from saucepan. Add to chili powder mixture. Mix well and set aside. Heat lard or vegetable oil in a large heavy skillet. Use a slotted spoon to place beans in skillet. Mash until partially or completed pureed. Stir in chili powder mixture. Add milk. Cook and stir until beans are as thick as desired. To serve, sprinkle with cheese and garnish with Totopos. Makes 6 to 8 servings.

How To Make Frijoles Especiales

Blend chili powder and cumin with bean cooking liquid.

Garnish beans with Totopos and sprinkle with grated cheese.

Frijoles con Puerco
Beans with Pork

To cook these Yucatán beans without soaking overnight, see How to Cook Beans, page 148.

1-1/2 cups dried black beans
Hot water
1 small onion
2 garlic cloves
1 lb. boneless pork

About 2 tablespoons lime juice
Salt
2 tablespoons lard
1-1/2 teaspoons salt
Garnishes, see below

Garnishes:
Salsa Roja for Picadas, page 103. or
  other hot salsa
6 green onions, with some tops,
  chopped
Lime wedges

6 radishes, diced
2 tomatoes, chopped (1/2 lb.)
2 fresh or pickled jalapeño chiles,
  sliced
1/2 cup coarsely chopped cilantro leaves

Sort beans to remove rocks and other foreign matter. Place beans in a large saucepan. Add hot water to cover. Let stand covered overnight or at least 8 hours. Drain beans and rinse well. Add fresh hot water to cover generously. Bring to a boil. Add onion and garlic. Cover with lid ajar and simmer 2 hours. Cut pork in medium chunks. Rub each chunk with lime juice and sprinkle lightly with salt. Heat lard in a large heavy skillet. Add seasoned pork. Cook until browned, about 5 minutes. Drain browned pork. Add to beans with 1-1/2 teaspoons salt. Cover and simmer 3 hours longer or until beans are tender. Add hot water as needed to keep beans covered. To serve, spoon pork and beans into shallow soup bowls. Serve garnishes separately to be added to pork and beans as desired. Makes 4 main-dish servings or 6 side-dish servings.

Garnishes:
Prepare Salsa Roja. Arrange green onions, lime wedges, radishes, tomatoes, chiles, cilantro, and salsa in separate bowls.

Frijoles Negros
Black Beans

It's typical of Mexican cooking to flavor the lard or oil with onion.

1 cup dried black beans
Hot water
1/2 small onion

3 tablespoons lard
1 teaspoon salt
1/3 cup coarsely chopped onion

Sort beans to remove rocks and other foreign matter. Place beans in a large saucepan. Add hot water to cover. Let stand covered overnight or at least 8 hours. Drain beans and rinse well. Add fresh hot water to cover generously. Bring to a boil; reduce heat. Add onion half and 2 tablespoons lard. Cover and simmer 2 hours. Add salt. Cover and simmer 2 hours longer or until beans are tender. Add hot water as needed to keep beans covered. Heat remaining 1 tablespoon lard in a large skillet. Add chopped onion. Cook until browned. Remove onion from skillet; discard onion. Add beans and their cooking liquid to skillet. Mash to purree some but not all beans. Cook until thickened but not dry. Makes 4 servings.

Frijoles con Chorizo
Beans with Chorizo

To make your own Chorizo, see page 112.

1 cup dried pinto beans   **Salt**
Hot water   **Totopos, page 30**
1/2 small onion   **1/4 lb. chorizo**
1 large garlic clove   **Grated Parmesan cheese**

Sort beans to remove rocks and other foreign matter. Place beans in a large saucepan. Add hot water to cover. Let stand covered overnight or at least 8 hours. Drain beans and rinse well. Add fresh hot water to cover generously. Bring to a boil; reduce heat. Add onion and garlic. Cover with lid ajar and simmer 2 hours. Add salt to taste. Simmer 2 to 4 hours longer or until beans are very tender. Add hot water as needed to keep beans covered. Prepare Totopos; set aside. Remove casing from chorizo. Fry chorizo in a large skillet until browned and crumbly. Use a slotted spoon to add beans. Add a little cooking liquid. Mash beans into cooked chorizo with a Mexican masher or potato masher. Continue cooking to desired consistency. To serve, sprinkle with cheese and garnish with Totopos. Makes 4 servings.

How To Make
Frijoles con Chorizo

Remove casing from chorizo and fry until crumbly.

Mash cooked beans into chorizo with a Mexican masher or potato masher.

Frijoles Colados
Strained Beans

Soupy black beans are often served with the main course in Yucatán.

1 cup dried black beans	**1/2 cup finely chopped onion**
Hot water	**1 jalapeño chile or other small**
1/2 teaspoon salt	**hot chile**
1 tablespoon vegetable oil	

Sort beans to remove rocks and other foreign matter. Place beans in a large saucepan. Add hot water to cover. Let stand covered overnight or at least 8 hours. Drain beans and rinse well. Add fresh hot water to cover generously. Bring to a boil; reduce heat. Cover and simmer 2 hours. Add salt; cover and simmer 2 hours longer or until tender. Let cool. Turn beans with cooking liquid into blender; puree. Strain through a sieve. Heat oil in a medium saucepan. Add onion. Cook until onion is tender. Add pureed beans and chile. Bring to a boil; reduce heat. Simmer uncovered 15 minutes or until beans have thickened slightly. Taste and add more salt if needed. Remove chile. Serve beans in small bowls as a side dish. Makes 4 to 6 servings.

Frijoles Rancheros
Beans Ranch-Style

These beans are delicious spooned over Arroz Blanco, page 147.

1 cup dried black beans	**1 tablespoon vegetable oil**
Hot water	**1/4 small onion, finely chopped**
1/4 small onion	**3 or 4 thin slices jalapeño**
1 teaspoon salt	**chile or other small hot chile**

Sort beans to remove rocks and other foreign matter. Place beans in a large saucepan. Add hot water to cover. Let stand covered overnight or at least 8 hours. Drain beans and rinse well. Add fresh hot water to cover generously. Bring to a boil; reduce heat. Add onion quarter. Cover and simmer 2 hours. Add salt. Cover and simmer 2 to 4 hours longer or until beans are tender. Add hot water as needed to keep beans covered. Heat oil in a large skillet. Add chopped onion and chile. Cook over medium heat until onion is tender. Add beans and enough cooking liquid to almost cover. Mash down through beans a few times to thicken liquid. Leave most of the beans whole. Simmer until thickened but still soupy. Makes 4 to 6 servings.

Panes
Breads

Corn *tortillas* are the national bread of Mexico. They are as basic to a meal as salt and *salsa*. But they are far from the only bread eaten in Mexico—as any tourist knows. Directions for making corn and flour *tortillas* are on pages 74 to 76.

Especially popular are *Bolillos* (French Rolls). They are softer and sweeter than European-style French rolls. Restaurants in Mexico usually serve *bolillos* with meals, while Mexican restaurants outside the country stress *tortillas*.

Then there is the imaginative array of sweet rolls, loaves, cakes and cookies known collectively as *pan dulce*, or sweet bread. Each whimsically fashioned sweet bread has its own name. I have included *Peineta* (Comb Bread), *Cuernos* (Horns) and *Puros* (Cigar-Shaped Rolls) and many others in this section.

Hotels and cafes usually offer some type of *pan dulce* for breakfast, but it is more fun to go the *panadería*, or bakery. To shop in a *panadería*, you take a tray and tongs, then make your selection from trays heaped with bread. The entrancing variety makes it hard to choose. You are likely to end up with more than you can possibly eat!

Markets are good places to see regional breads.

Roomfuls of bread at the old market near the center of Oaxaca and at the newer *Mercado de Abastos* are astonishing! Particularly charming are round egg breads, each decorated with a painted face made of what looks like flour paste.

Some breads are associated with important holidays. *Pan de Muertos* (Bread of the Dead) is baked for the Day of the Dead, celebrated November 1 and 2. These breads are fancifully decorated with skulls, knobs, bones and tears made of dough.

For Christmas, the Mexicans make *Buñuelos* (Fried Bread) by rolling out the dough as thin as possible and then stretching it even thinner. *Buñuelos de Molde* (Molded Fritters) are made by dipping a hot iron into batter and then into hot oil. The irons come in varied shapes and can be bought in cookware departments. You can also use Scandinavian *rosette irons*.

Traditional for Twelfth Night—January 6—is *Rosca de los Reyes* (Ring of the Kings), a ring-shaped bread with a tiny favor baked inside. According to one custom, the person who gets a slice of bread containing the favor must give a party on February 2, a religious holiday.

HOLIDAY BRUNCH

Pan de Muertos
Bread of the Dead

Quaint dough sculpture decorates bread traditionally served on All Soul's Day.

1 cup milk
1/2 cup butter, softened
1/2 cup sugar
1-1/2 teaspoons salt
1 teaspoon finely grated orange peel
1/2 teaspoon anise seeds, ground
1 envelope active dry yeast
   (1 tablespoon)

Pinch sugar
1/4 cup warm water
2 whole eggs
3 egg yolks
1 teaspoon water
5-1/4 to 5-1/2 cups all-purpose flour
2 tablespoons sugar

Scald milk by heating to just under boiling point, about 180°F (80°C). Pour over butter, 1/2 cup sugar, salt, orange peel and ground anise seeds in a large bowl. Stir until sugar is dissolved. Let cool. Stir yeast and pinch of sugar into 1/4 cup warm water. Let stand until yeast is softened. Beat whole eggs and egg yolks in a small bowl. Spoon 2 tablespoons beaten eggs into another small bowl or a custard cup. Stir in 1 teaspoon water. Refrigerate and use for glaze. Stir softened yeast and remaining beaten eggs into milk mixture. Stir enough flour into milk mixture to make a stiff dough. Turn out onto a lightly floured surface. Knead until smooth and elastic, at least 10 minutes, adding more flour is needed. Clean and grease bowl. Place dough in bowl, turning to grease all sides. Cover with a dry cloth towel. Let stand in a warm place free from drafts until doubled in bulk, about 1 hour. Punch down dough and turn out onto surface. Let rest while greasing 2 small baking sheets. Divide dough in half. Set aside about 1/3 cup from each half. Shape large pieces of dough into smooth round loaves. Place on prepared baking sheets. Brush with some of reserved egg mixture. Divide 1 of the small pieces of dough into 3 equal pieces. Roll 2 pieces into 8- to 9-inch ropes. Shape ends of ropes to resemble knobs on bones. Cross bone shapes over top of one loaf, stretching to reach bottom of each side. Shape third piece of dough into a ball. Moisten bottom with egg mixture. Place in center of crossbones, pressing firmly. Repeat with remaining small piece of dough and remaining loaf. Cover loosely with towels. Let stand in a warm place until doubled in bulk, about 45 minutes. Preheat oven to 350°F (175°C). Brush loaves evenly with egg mixture. Sprinkle each loaf with 1 tablespoon sugar. Bake 30 to 35 minutes or until browned. Remove from baking sheet; cool on racks. Makes 2 loaves.

How To Make
Pan de Muertos

**Flatten ends of ropes to resemble knobs on bones.
Cross and stretch ropes over top of loaf.**

Rosca de los Reyes
Ring of the Kings

Ring-shaped sweet bread is usually served on Twelfth Night.

1/3 cup water
1 teaspoon anise seeds
1 envelope active dry yeast
   (1 tablespoon)
Pinch granulated sugar
1/3 cup warm milk
About 4 cups all-purpose flour
2 whole eggs

4 egg yolks
1 teaspoon water
1/4 lb. butter, softened
1/4 cup granulated sugar
1/2 teaspoon salt
1/4 lb. mixed candied fruit, chopped
2 to 3 tablespoons powdered sugar

Bring water and anise seeds to a boil in a small saucepan. Remove from heat; let cool. Strain; discard seeds. Reheat water until warm to your fingers. Stir in yeast and pinch of granulated sugar. Let stand until yeast is softened. Combine softened yeast, milk and 1 cup flour in a medium bowl, beating until blended. Cover and let stand until mixture rises and becomes spongy. Beat whole eggs and egg yolks in a small bowl. Spoon 2 tablespoons beaten eggs into another small bowl or a custard cup. Stir in 1 teaspoon water. Refrigerate and use to glaze bread before baking. In a large bowl, beat butter, remaining beaten eggs, 1/4 cup granulated sugar and salt to combine. Stir in sponge mixture. Add enough remaining flour to make a stiff dough. Turn out onto a lightly floured surface. Knead at least 10 minutes or until smooth and elastic. Add additional flour if needed. Clean and grease bowl. Place dough in bowl, turning to grease all sides. Cover with a dry cloth towel. Let stand in a warm place free from drafts until doubled in bulk, about 1 hour. Punch down dough. Turn out onto surface and knead 5 times. Let rest while greasing a large baking sheet. Roll out dough to a 24" x 10" rectangle. Sprinkle evenly with candied fruit, leaving edges clear. Roll up jelly-roll fashion from long edge. Place on prepared baking sheet seam-side down, bringing ends together to form a ring. Pinch ends to seal. Lightly cover with towel. Let stand until almost doubled in bulk, about 1 hour. Preheat oven to 350°F (175°C). Before baking, brush loaf evenly with reserved egg mixture. Sift powdered sugar over loaf. Bake 35 to 45 minutes or until browned. If loaf becomes dark brown before 35 minutes, cover loosely with foil to prevent additional browning. Remove from baking sheet immediately. Cool on a rack. Makes 1 loaf.

Semas
Semas

Like tortillas, these sweet round loaves have no equivalent name in English.

1 cup milk	Pinch sugar
6 tablespoons butter, softened	1/4 cup warm water
1/2 cup sugar	About 4-1/2 cups all-purpose flour
1 teaspoon salt	2 egg yolks
1 teaspoon vanilla extract	1 egg, separated
1 envelope active dry yeast	2 teaspoons water
(1 tablespoon)	

Scald milk by heating to just under boiling point about 180°F (80°C). Pour hot scalded milk over butter, 1/2 cup sugar and salt in a large bowl. Stir to dissolve sugar. Cool to lukewarm. Stir in vanilla. Stir yeast and pinch of sugar into 1/4 cup warm water. Let stand until yeast is softened. Beat 2 cups of flour into cooled milk mixture. Beat in softened yeast and 3 egg yolks Refrigerate egg white. Add enough remaining flour to milk mixture to make a stiff dough. Turn out onto a lightly floured surface. Knead until smooth and elastic, at least 10 minutes. Add more flour if needed. Clean and grease bowl. Place dough in bowl, turning to grease all sides. Cover with a dry cloth towel. Let stand in a warm place free from drafts until doubled in bulk, about 1 hour. Punch down dough. Turn out onto surface and knead 5 times. Let dough rest while greasing 2 baking sheets. Divide dough in half. Knead each half 5 times. Roll out 1 piece of dough to an 8-inch circle. Use a razor blade or very sharp knife to make four 1/2-inch deep slashes 4 inches long, marking a 4-inch square in center of loaf. Repeat with remaining dough. Place loaves on prepared baking sheets. Cover loosely with towels. Let stand in a warm place until doubled in bulk, about 45 minutes. Preheat oven to 350°F (175°C). Beat reserved egg white with 2 teaspoons water. Brush loaves evenly with egg white mixture. Bake 25 to 30 minutes or until browned and loaves sound hollow when tapped on top. Remove from baking sheets. Cool on racks. Makes 2 loaves.

Churros
Mexican Crullers

Brought to Mexico by the Spaniards, these crullers are often served with hot chocolate.

Oil for frying	1 cup all-purpose flour
1 cup water	3 eggs
6 tablespoons butter	1/4 teaspoon cinnamon or nutmeg
1/8 teaspoon salt	About 1 cup powdered sugar

Pour oil 1 inch deep into a 10-inch skillet. Heat to 370°F (190°C). Bring water to a boil in a 2-quart saucepan. Add butter and salt. Heat until butter is melted. Add flour all at once; remove from heat. Beat until mixture is smooth and is the consistency of mashed potatoes. Beat in one egg at a time. When smooth, beat in cinnamon or nutmeg. Turn mixture into a pastry bag fitted with a star tip. Squeeze directly into hot oil, making churros about 8 inches long. Cook 3 or 4 at a time until a deep golden brown; turn occasionally. Drain over skillet, then on paper towels. Sift powdered sugar over churros. Serve immediately. Do not store. Makes 16 churros.

Peineta
Comb Bread

The shape of this bread inspired the name peineta, which means a large, fancy comb.

1 cup milk
1/2 cup vegetable shortening
2 tablespoons sugar
2 teaspoons salt
3/4 cup hot tap water
Pinch sugar

1 envelope active dry yeast
 (1 tablespoon)
1/4 cup warm water
About 5-3/4 cups all-purpose flour
1 egg

Scald milk by heating to just under boiling point, about 180°F (80°C). Pour hot scalded milk over shortening, 2 tablespoons sugar and salt in a large bowl. Stir until sugar is dissolved. Stir in 3/4 cup hot tap water; shortening does not need to melt. Cool to lukewarm. Stir pinch of sugar and yeast into 1/4 cup warm water. Let stand until yeast is softened. Beat 2 cups flour into cooled milk mixture. Beat in softened yeast and egg. Add enough remaining flour to make a stiff dough. Turn out onto a lightly floured surface. Knead until smooth and elastic, at least 10 minutes. Add more flour if needed. Clean and grease bowl. Place dough in bowl, turning to grease all sides. Cover with a dry cloth towel. Let stand in a warm place free from drafts until doubled in bulk, about 1 hour. Punch down dough. Turn out onto surface. Knead 5 times. Let dough rest while greasing 1 large and 1 small baking sheet. Divide dough into 3 pieces. Roll out 1 piece of dough to a 9-inch circle. Use sharp kitchen shears or a sharp knife to make 3/4-inch long cuts every 1/2 inch around edge of circle. Fold circle in half, bringing upper edge even with ends of cuts in bottom edge of dough. Repeat with remaining dough. Place 2 loaves on prepared large baking sheet and 1 loaf on prepared small baking sheet. Shape folded side of each loaf making a sharp crescent with cut edges on the outside. Cover with towel. Let stand in a warm place until doubled in bulk, about 45 minutes. Preheat oven to 350°F (175°C). Place 1 baking sheet in oven at a time. Bake 25 minutes or until loaves are browned and sound hollow when tapped on top. Remove bread from baking sheets immediately. Cool on racks. Makes 3 loaves.

How To Make Peineta

Make 3/4-inch long cuts every 1/2 inch around edge of dough. Fold nearly in half; shape like a curved comb.

Semitas **Photo on page 160.**

Whole-Wheat Rolls

Sugary toppings add to the appeal of these rich, dark rolls.

3/4 cup milk	1 envelope active dry yeast (1 tablespoon)
1 (3-inch) cinnamon stick	Pinch granulated sugar
1/2 cup packed dark brown sugar	1/4 cup warm water
1 teaspoon salt	2-1/2 cups all-purpose flour,
1/4 cup vegetable shortening	2-1/2 cups whole-wheat flour
3/4 cup warm water	Brown Sugar Glaze, see below

Brown Sugar Glaze:
1/2 cup packed dark brown sugar
1/4 cup water

Scald milk by heating to just under boiling point, about 180°F (80°C). Place cinnamon stick in blender and process at high speed until finely ground. Cinnamon will be flakes—not powder. Pour hot scalded milk over 1 teaspoon flaked cinnamon, brown sugar, salt and shortening in a large bowl. Reserve remaining cinnamon for another use. Stir until sugar is dissolved and shortening is softened; shortening does not need to melt. Add 3/4 cup warm water. Let stand until cooled. Stir yeast and pinch granulated sugar into 1/4 cup warm water. Let stand until yeast is softened. Stir softened yeast into cooled milk mixture. Stir all-purpose flour into milk mixture to make a thick batter; beat well. Cover with a dry cloth towel. Let stand in a warm place free from drafts until batter rises and becomes spongy. Beat again. Stir in enough whole-wheat flour to make a stiff dough. Turn out onto a surface sprinkled with whole-wheat flour. Knead dough until smooth and elastic, at least 10 minutes. Add more whole-wheat flour if needed. Clean and grease bowl. Place dough in bowl, turning to grease all sides. Cover with towel. Let stand in a warm place until doubled in bulk, about 1 hour. Punch down dough. Turn out onto surface and knead 5 times. Let rest while greasing 2 baking sheets. Divide dough into 18 pieces. Shape each piece into a smooth ball. Place balls on prepared baking sheets. Press down with heel of hand to flatten. Cover loosely with towel. Let stand in a warm place until doubled in bulk, about 45 minutes. Preheat oven to 350°F (175°C). Bake 20 minutes or until rolls are golden brown. Prepare Brown Sugar Glaze; keep warm. Brush hot baked rolls with glaze. Remove glazed rolls from baking sheets. Cool on racks. Makes 18 rolls.

Brown Sugar Glaze:
Bring sugar and water to a boil in a small saucepan. Boil about 1 minute.

Variations

Mound 1/2 teaspoon brown sugar on center top of each roll before baking. Bake 20 minutes. Brush bare portions of rolls with warm glaze.

Mound 3/4 teaspoon brown sugar on top of each baked roll. Carefully drop 1 or 2 drops water onto sugar. Bake 2 minutes. Do not glaze. Cool on racks.

Bolillos
French Rolls

Mexican-style French rolls should not be overbaked or they'll become hard.

1-1/2 cups boiling water	Pinch sugar
1/4 cup lard	1/4 cup warm water
2 tablespoons sugar	About 5 cups all-purpose flour
1-1/2 teaspoons salt	1/2 teaspoon salt dissolved in 4
1 envelope active dry yeast	teaspoons water
(1 tablespoon)	

Pour 1-1/2 cups boiling water over lard, 2 tablespoons sugar and 1-1/2 teaspoons salt in a large bowl. Stir until sugar and salt are dissolved. Let stand until lard melts and mixture cools. Stir yeast and pinch of sugar into 1/4 cup warm water. Let stand until yeast is softened. Add softened yeast to cooled lard mixture. Beat in 2-1/2 cups flour to make a stiff batter. Cover and let stand in a warm place until batter rises and becomes spongy. Stir in enough flour to make a stiff dough. Turn out onto a lightly floured surface. Knead until smooth and elastic, about 10 minutes. Add additional flour if needed. Clean and grease bowl. Place dough in bowl, turning to grease all sides. Cover with a dry cloth towel. Let stand in a warm place free from drafts until doubled in bulk, about 1 hour. Punch down dough. Turn out onto surface and knead 5 times. Let rest while greasing 2 baking sheets. Divide dough into 10 pieces. Shape each piece of dough into a rectangle, pinching and pulling ends into points. Place rolls on prepared baking sheets. Cover loosely with towel. Let rise until doubled in bulk, about 45 minutes. Preheat oven to 375°F (190°C). Before baking, brush each roll lightly with salt water. Bake 20 to 25 minutes or until browned and crusty. Remove from baking sheets. Cool on racks. Makes 10 rolls.

Torrejas
Bread Fritters

Prepare the syrup the night before, then serve Torrejas like French toast.

3 Bolillos, above, or French rolls	2 tablespoons brandy
1/2 lb. piloncillo or 1 cup plus	3 eggs, separated
2 tablespoons packed brown sugar	Milk
1-1/2 cups water	Oil for deep-frying
1 teaspoon anise seeds	

Stir pilconcillo or brown sugar, water and anise seeds in a medium saucepan over medium heat until a syrup forms. Remove from heat. Stir in brandy; cool. Strain syrup; discard seeds. Cut off pointed ends of each bolillo or French roll. Cut vertically in 1/3-inch thick slices. Beat egg whites in a medium bowl until stiff. Beat egg yolks in a small bowl. Stir into beaten egg white until just blended. Pour oil about 1/2 inch deep into a large skillet. Heat oil to 365°F (185°F). Dip each bread slice in milk. Drain slightly. Use a spatula to spread egg mixture over both sides of bread. Fry bread slices in hot oil until golden brown on each side. Drain on paper towels, then arrange on platter. Heat syrup and spoon over slices. Let stand until syrup is absorbed. Makes 4 servings.

On the silver bread tray from left to right are Pan de Naranja (Orange Bread), page 163; Bolillos (French Rolls), above; Picones (Oval Rolls), page 164, and Semitas (Whole-Wheat Rolls), page 159.

Puros
Cigar-Shaped Rolls

Raspberry jam is the surprise filling.

3/4 cup milk	Pinch granulated sugar
1 tablespoon molasses	1/4 cup warm water
1/4 cup packed dark brown sugar	2 cups whole-wheat flour
1/4 cup vegetable shortening	1 egg
1 teaspoon salt	About 3-1/3 cups all-purpose flour
3/4 cup hot water	About 1/3 cup raspberry jam
1 envelope active dry yeast	1 egg, beaten with 1 tablespoon water
(1 tablespoon)	Sesame seeds

Scald milk by heating to just under boiling point, about 180°F (80°C). Pour hot scalded milk over molasses, brown sugar, shortening and salt in a large bowl. Stir until brown sugar dissolves; shortening does not need to melt. Add 3/4 cup hot water. Let mixture stand until lukewarm. Stir yeast and pinch of granulated sugar into 1/4 cup warm water. Let stand until yeast is softened. Beat whole-wheat flour into milk mixture. Beat in softened yeast and 1 egg. Stir in enough all-purpose flour to make a stiff dough. Turn out onto a lightly floured surface. Knead until smooth and elastic, about 10 minutes. Add additional flour if needed. Clean and grease bowl. Place dough in bowl, turning to grease all sides. Cover with a dry cloth towel. Let stand in a warm place free from drafts until doubled in bulk, about 1 hour. Line 2 large baking sheets with foil. Grease foil; set aside. Punch down dough. Turn out onto surface and knead 5 times. Divide dough into 3 parts. Work with 1 part at a time, keeping rest of dough covered. Divide 1 part into 7 pieces. On a lightly floured board, roll out each piece to a 6'' x 3-1/2'' oval. Spread 3/4 teaspoon jam off-center down length of each oval, keeping ends clear. Starting from long side of dough nearest jam, roll up jelly-roll fashion. Place seam-side down on prepared baking sheets. Repeat with remaining dough. Cover rolls loosely with towel. Let stand in a warm place until just doubled in bulk, about 45 minutes. Preheat oven to 350°F (175°C). Before baking, brush rolls with egg-water mixture. Sprinkle lightly with sesame seeds. Bake 20 minutes or until browned well and rolls sound hollow when tapped on top. Remove from baking sheets immediately. Cool on racks. Makes 21 rolls.

How To Make Puros

Spread jam off-center down length of each oval; roll up. Place seam-side down on prepared baking sheets.

Pan de Naranja **Photo on page 160.**
Orange Bread

You'll love these tender, orange-flavored sweet rolls.

1/2 cup milk	Pinch sugar
1/2 cup sugar	1/2 cup warm water
1 teaspoon salt	5-1/2 to 5-3/4 cups all-purpose flour
1/4 cup lard or butter	3 eggs
1 teaspoon grated orange peel	1 tablespoon orange juice
1/4 cup orange juice	Granulated sugar
1 envelope active dry yeast	
(1 tablespoon)	

Scald milk by heating to just under boiling point, about 180°F (80°C). Pour hot scalded milk over 1/2 cup sugar, salt, lard or butter and orange peel in a large bowl. Stir until sugar is dissolved. Let stand until lard is almost melted. Stir in 1/4 cup orange juice. Let cool to lukewarm. Stir yeast and pinch of sugar into warm water. Let stand until yeast is softened. Add softened yeast to milk mixture. Beat in enough flour to make a thick batter, about 2-1/2 cups. Cover and let stand until mixture rises and becomes spongy. Beat eggs in a small bowl. Spoon 1 tablespoon beaten eggs into another small bowl or a custard cup; refrigerate. Stir down sponge. Stir beaten eggs into sponge. Add enough remaining flour to make a stiff dough. Turn dough out onto a lightly floured surface. Knead until smooth and elastic, about 10 minutes. Add additional flour if needed. Clean and grease bowl. Place dough in bowl, turning to grease all sides. Cover with a dry cloth towel. Let stand in a warm place free from drafts until doubled in bulk, about 1 hour. Punch down dough. Turn out onto surface and knead 5 times. Let rest while greasing 2 or 3 baking sheets. Divide dough into 18 pieces. Gently roll each piece of dough into a 12- to 14-inch rope, keeping hands lightly greased with lard while rolling. Shape each rope into a coil, tucking end underneath. Place on baking sheets. Cover loosely with towels. Let stand in a warm place until doubled in bulk, about 45 minutes. Preheat oven to 350°F (175°C). Stir 1 tablespoon orange juice into reserved beaten eggs. Brush rolls lightly with egg mixture, then sprinkle evenly with granulated sugar. Bake 15 minutes or until lightly browned. Remove from baking sheets immediately. Cool on racks. Makes 18 large rolls.

Picones   **Photo on page 160.**

Oval Rolls

Look for red sugar crystals in the cake decorating section of the supermarket.

1 cup milk
6 tablespoons butter, softened
1/2 cup sugar
1 teaspoon salt
1 envelope active dry yeast,
   (1 tablespoon)
Pinch sugar

1/4 cup warm water
About 4-1/2 cups all-purpose flour
3 egg yolks
Topping, see below
Beaten egg, reserved from topping
1 to 2 teaspoons red sugar crystals

Topping:
4 tablespoons butter
1/2 cup sugar

2 eggs, beaten
1/2 cup all-purpose flour

Scald milk by heating to just under boiling point, about 180°F (80°C). Pour hot scalded milk over butter, 1/2 cup sugar and salt in a large bowl. Stir until sugar dissolves. Let stand until cooled. Stir yeast and pinch of sugar into warm water. Let stand until yeast is softened. Beat 2 cups of flour into cooled milk mixture. Beat in egg yolks 1 at a time. Stir in softened yeast. Add enough remaining flour to make a stiff dough. Turn out onto a lightly floured surface. Knead until smooth and elastic, at least 10 minutes. Add more flour if needed. Clean and grease bowl. Place dough in bowl, turning to grease all sides. Cover with a dry cloth towel. Let stand in a warm place free from drafts until doubled in bulk, about 1 hour. Punch down dough. Turn out onto surface and knead 5 times. Let rest while greasing 2 baking sheets. Divide dough into 12 pieces. Shape each piece into an oval, pinching and pulling ends into points. Place on baking sheets, pressing with heel of hand to flatten. Cover loosely with a towel. Let stand in a warm place until doubled in bulk, about 45 minutes. Preheat oven to 350°F (175°C). Prepare Topping. When rolls have risen, brush with reserved egg from Topping. Divide topping into 12 parts. Shape each part into a flat oval. Place 1 oval on center top of each roll. Sprinkle rolls and topping with red sugar crystals. Bake 20 to 25 minutes or until rolls are browned. Remove from baking sheets. Cool on racks. Makes 12 rolls.

Topping:
Cream butter and sugar in a small bowl. Stir 2 teaspoons beaten egg into butter mixture. Reserve remaining beaten egg to glaze rolls before baking. Use a fork to press flour into butter mixture until smooth.

Cuernos
Horns

Crescent-shaped loaves are made with an unusual cut-out design.

1 cup milk	**Pinch sugar**
6 tablespoons butter, softened	**1/4 cup warm water**
2 tablespoons sugar	**About 5-1/4 cups all-purpose flour**
1-1/2 teaspoons salt	**4 eggs**
1 envelope active dry yeast	**1 teaspoon water**
(1 tablespoon)	

Scald milk by heating to just under boiling point, about 180°F (80°C). Pour hot scalded milk over butter, sugar and salt in a large bowl. Stir until sugar and salt are dissolved. Let stand to cool. Mix yeast and pinch of sugar with 1/4 cup warm water. Let stand until yeast is softened. Beat 1-1/2 cups flour into milk mixture. Beat in 3 eggs one at a time. Reserve 1 egg. Add softened yeast to milk mixture. Stir in enough flour to make a stiff dough. Turn out onto a lightly floured surface. Knead until smooth and elastic. Add additional flour if needed. Clean and grease bowl. Place dough in bowl, turning to grease all sides. Cover with a dry cloth towel. Let stand in a warm place away from drafts until doubled in bulk, about 1 hour. Punch down dough. Turn out onto surface and knead 5 times. Let rest while greasing 2 baking sheets. Divide dough in 3 parts. Roll out 1 part to a 10-inch circle. Cut circle in half, then cut each half into 3 triangles. From center of each triangle, cut out a small triangle about 2-1/2 inches long; start cutting about 3/4 inch in from tip. Leave sides of large triangle at least 1/2 inch wide and curved edge about 1-1/4 inches wide. Place cut out dough back in bowl. Pat and shape each large triangle to make smooth and even. Roll up from curved edge to tip. Curve slightly to make ends look like horns. Place on prepared baking sheets. Repeat with remaining balls of dough. Knead center cut-outs and roll out to a circle. If circle is smaller than those rolled previously, cut into 4 triangles. Cut dough as directed and roll up. Shape any remaining cut-out centers into a bun. Cover rolls loosely with towel. Let stand in a warm place until doubled in bulk, about 45 minutes. Preheat oven to 350°F (175°C). Beat reserved egg with 1 teaspoon water. Brush rolls with egg mixture. Bake 15 minutes or until golden brown. Remove from baking sheets. Cool on racks. Makes 22 to 24 rolls.

How To Make Cuernos

Cut a small triangle from the center of each larger triangle. Roll up from curved edge to tip.

Sopaipillas
Fried Breads with Honey

Golden fried puffs are usually served with honey for dessert. Try them with cinnamon and sugar.

2 cups all-purpose flour
1/2 teaspoon salt
2 teaspoons baking powder
1 tablespoon shortening

3/4 cup warm water
Oil for deep-frying
Honey

In a medium bowl, mix flour, salt and baking powder. Cut in shortening with 2 knives until mixture resembles cornmeal. Stir in warm water until all ingredients are moist. Turn dough out onto a lightly floured surface. Knead until smooth, about 5 minutes. Cover dough with plastic wrap or a dry towel. Let rest at least 30 minutes. For later use, dough may be placed in a plastic bag and refrigerated 24 hours. Cut dough in half. On a lightly floured surface, roll out dough about 1/4 inch thick. Cut into 3- or 4-inch squares. Pour oil 3 inches deep into a saucepan or deep fryer. Heat to 400°F (205°C). Carefully drop dough squares 1 at a time into hot oil. Cook until puffed and golden brown, turning once. If sopaipillas do not puff immediately, oil is not hot enough. Drain cooked sopaipillas on paper towels. Serve immediately with honey. Makes 35 to 40.

Buñuelos
Fried Bread

Sugar-sprinkled fried pastries are traditional for Christmas and fiestas.

About 1-1/4 cups all-purpose flour
2 teaspoons sugar
1/4 teaspoon baking powder
1/4 teaspoon salt
1 egg

1/4 cup milk
1-1/2 tablespoons butter, melted
1/2 cup sugar
1/2 teaspoon cinnamon
Oil for frying

Combine 1 cup flour, sugar, baking powder and salt in a large bowl. Beat egg and milk in a small bowl. Stir in butter. Add milk mixture to flour mixture, stirring until smooth. Turn out onto a lightly floured surface. Knead in about 2 tablespoons additional flour to make a very soft dough. Knead until smooth. Divide dough into 8 parts. Shape each part into a ball. Return to bowl and cover with a dry cloth towel. Let rest 20 minutes. Mix 1/2 cup sugar and cinnamon; set aside. Place 1 ball of dough on a lightly floured surface. Press into a flat circle. Roll out into as large a circle as possible. Pick up circle and stretch gently all around to make as thin as possible. Repeat with remaining dough. Let circles rest about 5 minutes before frying. Pour oil 1 inch deep into a 10- or 12-inch skillet. Heat to 360°F (180°C). Carefully place 1 buñuelo at a time in oil. Fry until underside is lightly browned. Press each buñuelo down into oil and scoop oil over top. Turn buñuelos with tongs and fry other side until crisp. Drain on paper towels. Sprinkle hot buñuelos immediately with cinnamon-sugar mixture. Continue until all buñuelos are fried. Store in an airtight container. Makes 8 buñuelos.

Buñuelos de Molde
Molded Fritters

If you don't have a buñuelo iron, make these feather-light pastries with a rosette iron.

2 eggs	1/2 teaspoon salt
1 cup milk	Oil for frying
1/4 teaspoon vanilla extract	1/2 cup sugar
1 cup sifted all-purpose flour	1/2 teaspoon cinnamon
1 tablespoon sugar	

Beat eggs in a deep medium bowl. Beat in milk and vanilla. Combine flour, 1 tablespoon sugar and salt in sifter. Sift into egg mixture. Beat thoroughly. Let stand while heating oil. Pour oil 3/4 inch deep into a medium saucepan. Heat to 365°F (185°C). Combine 1/2 cup sugar and cinnamon in a small bowl; set aside. Hold buñuelo iron or rosette iron in hot oil until heated. Drain well, then quickly dip in batter. Let batter come all the way up sides of iron but not over top or buñuelos will cling to iron. Remove immediately from batter and place again in hot oil. As soon as batter firms slightly, pry buñuelo from iron with a sharp knife; set iron aside. Fry buñuelo in hot oil until golden. Lift from oil with a fork; drain over saucepan then place on paper towels. Sprinkle immediately with cinnamon-sugar. Repeat with remaining batter. Serve immediately or store in an airtight container. Makes about sixty 4-inch buñuelos.

How To Make
Buñuelos de Molde

Heat iron in hot oil. Dip in batter to coat bottom of iron.

Place coated iron in hot oil. When batter becomes firm, carefully pry from iron and fry until golden brown.

Postres
Desserts

If you judge by restaurant menus, the most common Mexican desserts are *flan*, or caramel-coated custard; *arroz con leche*, or rice pudding; *chongos*, or sweetened curds and whey; canned fruit and ice cream. Good as they are, these desserts only hint at the vast number of sweets produced by native artistry and inventiveness.

Some desserts are seasonal. During Lent, you must have *capirotada*, or bread pudding. Margarita Jimenez, from San Juan de Los Lagos in the state of Jalisco, makes an extravagant dessert using *pan dulce*, or sweet bread. I've included it in this book as *Capirotada de Margarita* (Margarita's Bread Pudding). A more common version, *Capirotada con Queso* (Bread Pudding with Cheese), is made with leftover *bolillos*, or French rolls, sliced and layered with cheese, nuts and raisins, then drenched with syrup made from *piloncillo*, or brown sugar.

Cinnamon is a popular flavoring for Mexican desserts. All markets sell bundles of cinnamon sticks, which are more widely used than the ground spice.

Strong vanilla extract from Papantla in the state of Veracruz flavors *flan* and other desserts. In the city of Veracruz, you may see Indians in baggy white pants and voluminous white shirts. These are the Totonac Indians who come from Papantla bringing vanilla to sell on the streets. Vanilla is available in supermarkets throughout Mexico.

Many desserts reflect foreign influence. French pastries are fashionable. The best pecan pie I've tasted is *Pie de Pacana* served at the Restaurant Los Portales, a Lebanese restaurant in Mérida. *Pie de Limón* (Lime Pie) comes from Culiacán, the capital of the state of Sinaloa.

Cajeta de Celaya (Caramel Candy from Celaya), a soft brown candy resembling caramel topping, is exquisite over ice cream or as a filling for crepes. At a christening party, I had *cajeta* spread on soda crackers—an excellent combination. A specialty of Celaya in the state of Guanajuato, *cajeta* is made by boiling goat's milk, cow's milk and sugar in an unlined copper pot. However, it can be made entirely with cow's milk, and an ordinary saucepan will do if you don't have the traditional Mexican copper pot. Making *cajeta* is a lesson in patience because it must be stirred continuously, but it is delicious and worth the effort. You can buy *cajeta* in several flavors in Mexican grocery stores.

CHRISTMAS EVE DINNER

HOW TO MAKE FLAN

Caramelizing the Mold—Allow 1/2 cup sugar for a 1-quart mold. For a 1-1/2- to 2-quart mold, use 2/3 to 3/4 cup sugar.

Place the sugar in a 7-inch skillet. Heat over medium-high heat until the sugar begins to melt. Reduce the heat to medium. Heat until the sugar is melted and golden brown, stirring occasionally. If your skillet or burner has a "hot spot," stirring will equalize the heat and help prevent the caramel from burning. Immediately spoon hot caramel over the sides and bottom of the mold; cool. Add the *flan* mixture.

Baking—Place the mold containing the *flan* in a large baking pan. Place the baking pan on the middle or lower rack of your oven. Pour hot water into the baking pan at least half way up the mold. Bake until a knife inserted off-center comes out clean. To prevent overcooking, test the *flan* before the end of the baking time, then test at intervals.

Remove the *flan* at once from its hot-water bath and place it on a rack to cool. Refrigerate cooled *flan* several hours or until it's firm enough to turn out onto a serving plate.

Flans in this book are baked at 325°F (165°C). Some cooks prefer to bake them at 350°F (175°C) for a shorter time. In either case, if it begins to brown too much before it is set, cover it loosely with foil.

Unmolding—To prepare a *flan* for unmolding, carefully run a thin sharp knife around top edge to be sure it's not sticking to the mold. Shake gently. Place a serving plate upside-down on top of the mold, then invert quickly. *Flan* and caramel will slide onto plate. Scrape additional caramel from mold and spoon onto *flan*. Serve at once. *Flan* can be unmolded in advance and refrigerated before serving.

Flan de Café

Coffee Flan

A silky custard with light coffee flavor.

1/2 cup sugar	1 cup milk
2 whole eggs	1 (14-oz.) can sweetened condensed milk
2 egg yolks	1 teaspoon instant coffee powder

Heat sugar in a 7-inch skillet over medium-high heat. When sugar begins to melt, reduce heat to medium. Continue to cook sugar, stirring occasionally. When sugar is melted and browned, immediately spoon over bottom and sides of a shallow 1-quart baking dish. Set aside for caramel to cool. Preheat oven to 325°F (165°C). Place whole eggs and egg yolks in blender. Process until smooth. Add milk, condensed milk and coffee powder. Blend thoroughly. Pour into baking dish lined with caramelized sugar. Place baking dish in a baking pan. Pour hot water into pan half way up sides of baking dish. Bake about 1-1/2 hours or until a knife inserted off-center comes out clean. Cover flan loosely with foil if necessary to prevent excessive browning. Remove baking dish from pan of hot water. Cool, then refrigerate at least 3 hours. To serve, run a knife around top edge and invert flan onto a serving plate. Makes 6 servings.

Flan Especial
Special Custard

You may want to caramelize sugar over slightly lower heat. Burned caramel tastes terrible!

1 medium orange	**Pinch salt**
1 lime	**3/4 cup sugar**
1 qt. milk	**6 eggs**
3/4 cup sugar	

Use a sharp knife or peeler to peel orange and lime in thin strips. Leave as much white pith as possible on the fruit. Reserve orange and lime for another use. Combine orange and lime peels, milk, 3/4 cup sugar and salt in a large saucepan. Bring to a boil and cook gently until liquid is reduced to 3 cups. Stir occasionally to break up any film that forms on the surface. Strain and cool slightly. Heat 3/4 cup sugar in a 7-inch skillet over medium-high heat. When sugar begins to melt, reduce heat to medium. Continue to cook sugar, stirring occasionally. When sugar is melted and brown, immediately spoon over bottom and sides of a shallow 1-1/2-quart baking dish. Set aside to cool. Preheat oven to 325°F (165°C). Beat eggs in a large bowl. Gradually add warm milk mixture to eggs; beat well. Pour into baking dish lined with caramelized sugar. Place baking dish in a baking pan. Pour hot water into pan halfway up sides of baking dish. Bake about 1-1/2 hours or until a knife inserted off-center comes out clean. Cover flan loosely with foil if necessary to prevent excessive browning. Remove baking dish from pan of hot water. Cool, then refrigerate at least 3 hours. To serve, run a knife around top edge and invert flan onto a serving plate. Makes 6 to 8 servings.

How To Make
Flan Especial

Cook sugar, stirring occasionally, until melted and brown.

Pour custard mixture into baking dish lined with carmelized sugar. Place in a pan of water to bake.

Flan Napolitano de Veracruz
Neapolitan Flan from Veracruz

Outstanding for its creamy smooth texture, and very rich.

3/4 cup sugar
1 (14-oz.) can sweetened condensed
  milk
1 cup whipping cream

1/2 cup milk
4 eggs
1 cinnamon stick

Heat sugar in a 7-inch skillet over medium-high heat. When sugar begins to melt, reduce heat to medium. Continue to cook sugar, stirring occasionally. When sugar is melted and browned, immediately spoon over bottom and sides of a shallow 1-1/2-quart baking dish. Set aside for caramel to cool. Preheat oven to 325°F (165°C). Combine condensed milk, cream, milk and eggs in blender. Process until thoroughly mixed. Pour into baking dish lined with caramelized sugar. Drop cinnamon stick into middle of mixture. Place baking dish in a baking pan. Pour hot water into pan halfway up sides of baking dish. Bake about 1 hour 50 minutes or until a knife inserted off-center comes out clean. Cover flan loosely with foil if necessary to prevent excessive browning. Remove baking dish from pan of hot water. Cool, then refrigerate at least 3 hours. To serve, run a knife around top edge and invert flan onto a serving plate. Makes 8 servings.

Chongos Zamoranos
Curds in Syrup

Use household-style rennet tablets to make these milk squares, or chongos, from Michoacán.

2 egg yolks
1 qt. milk
2 rennet tablets

1 tablespoon water
1 cup sugar
1 or 2 cinnamon sticks

In a small bowl, beat egg yolks with a little of the milk. Combine egg yolk mixture and remaining milk in a 10-inch skillet. Heat gently until lukewarm 110°F (45°C); remove from heat. While milk mixture is heating, place rennet tablets in 1 tablespoon water. Let stand until dissolved. Stir rennet solution into lukewarm milk mixture in skillet. Let stand about 45 minutes, or until mixture has set. With a sharp knife, cut through milk mixture to make 2-inch squares. Sprinkle sugar over cut squares; add cinnamon sticks. Cook gently without boiling over very low heat about 2 hours, until sugar and whey have formed a syrup and milk squares or chongos have become firm. Do not boil or chongos will break up. If necessary, place an asbestos heat diffuser under pan. Remove skillet from heat. With a slotted spoon, lift out chongos and place in a 2-quart casserole. Return skillet with syrup to heat and boil until slightly reduced. Strain and pour over chongos. Chill thoroughly. Makes 6 servings.

Variation

If substituting commercial cheese rennet for household rennet, use 1/4 tablet.

Arroz con Leche
Rice Pudding

Old-fashioned rice pudding spiced with cinnamon is a Mexican favorite.

1/3 cup rice
1-1/2 cups water
Pinch salt
2 cups hot milk
1/2 cup sugar

1 cinnamon stick
Pinch salt
2 egg yolks
3 tablespoons raisins plumped in hot water
Ground cinnamon

Prepare rice according to How To Cook Rice, page 140, but do not dry rice. Turn rice into a 2-quart saucepan. Add 1-1/2 cups water and a pinch of salt. Bring to a boil, reduce heat. Cover and boil gently about 20 minutes, until water is almost absorbed. Add hot milk, sugar, cinnamon stick and a pinch of salt to cooked rice. Cook and stir over medium heat until mixture is very thick but still soft and moist; do not overcook. Remove from heat. Remove cinnamon stick. With a large spoon, rapidly beat in egg yolks one at a time. Stir in raisins. To serve, turn into a 1-quart casserole and sprinkle with ground cinnamon. Let cool slightly but serve warm. Makes 6 servings.

Capirotada con Queso
Bread Pudding with Cheese

Capirotada is traditional for Lent. This version is layered with cheese, raisins, nuts and bananas.

1/2 (1-lb.) loaf French bread
4 tablespoons butter
4 cups water
8 oz. piloncillo or 1-1/2 cups
  packed brown sugar
2 cinnamon sticks
2 whole cloves
1 tablespoon butter

8 oz. Longhorn or mild Cheddar cheese,
  shredded (2 cups)
1/2 cup roasted unsalted peanuts
1/4 cup slivered blanched almonds
1/2 cup raisins
1 large banana, thinly sliced
Ground cinnamon

Preheat oven to 350°F (175°C). Cut a thin slice off heel of bread; reserve for another use. Cut remaining bread in 1/2-inch slices. Butter slices on 1 side with 4 tablespoons butter. Place buttered-side up in a single layer on 1 or 2 baking sheets. Bake 15 minutes, until lightly toasted and dry. Remove and cool. Combine water, piloncillo or brown sugar, cinnamon sticks and cloves in a large saucepan. Bring to a boil; reduce heat. Simmer syrup uncovered 20 minutes. Strain out cinnamon sticks and cloves; set syrup aside. Capirotada may be prepared in advance to this point and the bread left out overnight to dry. Grease a deep 2-1/2-quart baking dish with about 1/2 tablespoon butter. Reserve remaining 1/2 tablespoon butter, 1/4 cup cheese and 2 tablespoons peanuts for topping. In prepared baking dish, layer ingredients in the following order: a third of the toasted bread slices, half of the remaining peanuts, half of the almonds, half of the raisins and half of the banana slices. Cover with half of the remaining cheese. Pour 1 cup syrup evenly over cheese. Layer another third of the bread, remaining peanuts, almonds, raisins and banana slices. Cover with remaining cheese. Again pour 1 cup syrup evenly over cheese. Top with remaining bread. Sprinkle with reserved cheese and peanuts. Pour remaining syrup evenly over pudding. Dot with remaining butter and sprinkle lightly with ground cinnamon. Cover and bake 45 minutes. Let stand covered 30 minutes to 1 hour before serving. Makes 8 to 10 servings.

Capirotada de Margarita
Margarita's Bread Pudding

Candied cactus, or biznaga, may be found in Mexican food stores or gourmet shops.

1 loaf Sema, page 157
   or 1 (1-lb. 4-oz.) loaf sweet egg bread
1/4 cup butter
6 cups milk
1-3/4 cups sugar
2 cinnamon sticks
6 eggs, separated

1 cup raisins
1 cup shredded coconut
1 cup diced candied cactus (biznaga),
   citron or candied pineapple
1 (8-3/4-oz.) can fruit cocktail,
   drained
1/2 cup chopped pecans

Cut loaf into 1/2-inch thick slices. Trim crust from end pieces. Butter each slice lightly on one side, using about 3 tablepoons butter. With remaining butter, grease a shallow 4-quart square or rectangular baking dish; set aside. Combine milk, sugar and cinnamon sticks in a large saucepan. Bring to a boil. Boil gently 10 minutes, stirring until sugar is dissolved. Beat egg yolks in a small bowl. Gradually blend some of the hot mixture into egg yolks. Add egg yolk mixture to milk mixture. Remove sauce from heat immediately. Let cool slightly. Remove cinnamon sticks. Beat egg whites until stiff; fold into sauce. Make a layer of buttered bread in prepared baking dish. Top with half each of the raisins, coconut, candied cactus, citron or candied pineapple, fruit cocktail and pecans. Pour about a third of the sauce evenly over layers. Make another layer of bread, then top with remaining raisins, coconut, candied cactus, citron or candied pineapple, fruit cocktail and pecans. Pour another third of the sauce evenly over layers. Top with remaining bread and then remaining sauce. Let stand while preheating oven to 350°F (175°C). Bake pudding 45 minutes, until browned and puffy. Cool in baking dish on a rack. Serve warm. Makes 15 servings.

How To Make Capirotada de Margarita

Generously butter 1/2-inch thick slices of bread. Place in a buttered baking dish.

Add layers of fruit, coconut, raisins and nuts. Pour 1/3 of the custard over pudding. Repeat layering.

Almendrado
Almond Pudding

The colors of this delicate dessert represent the red, white and green Mexican flag.

1 envelope unflavored gelatin powder
1/2 cup water
6 egg whites
1/2 cup sugar
1 teaspoon almond extract

Red and green food coloring
1 (2-3/4 oz.) pkg. chopped almonds
  (3/4 cup), if desired
Natillas de Almendrado, page 184

Stir gelatin into water in a small saucepan. Stir gently over medium heat until gelatin dissolves. Remove from heat. Cool on a rack 15 minutes. Beat egg whites in a large bowl until frothy. Gradually beat dissolved gelatin into frothy egg whites. Slowly beat in sugar. Continue beating until mixture forms stiff peaks. Beat in almond extract. Divide mixture evenly into 3 medium bowls. Add red food coloring 1 drop at a time to 1/3 of the gelatin mixture to make bright pink. Add green food coloring 1 drop at a time to another third of the gelatin mixture to make bright green. Fold nuts into uncolored portion of gelatin mixture, if desired. Spread pink mixture evenly in a 2-quart loaf pan. Without disturbing pink layer, spread uncolored mixture over pink layer. Top with green mixture. Refrigerate until set, at least 2 hours. Prepare Natillas de Almendrado; refrigerate. Cut gelatin mixture into 8 crosswise slices. Place slices on dessert plates. Spoon Natillas de Almendrado over slices. Makes 8 servings.

Calabaza en Jarabe
Pumpkin in Syrup

Make this old-fashioned Mexican dessert for Halloween. Serve it with a little cream.

1 (2-lb) pumpkin
1 lb. piloncillo or 1/2 lb. each light
  and dark brown sugar
1 orange

1 cinnamon stick
1 bay leaf
1 cup water
Pinch salt

Cut pumpkin into wedges. Remove seeds and strings. Cut wedges into 1-1/2 to 2-inch pieces; peel. If necessary, place piloncillo or brown sugars inside a double plastic bag and pound with a hammer to break up. Cut off ends of orange, then cut into thin slices. In a 3-quart saucepan, layer peeled pumpkin pieces, broken up piloncillo or brown sugars and orange slices. Add cinnamon stick, bay leaf, water and salt. Bring to a boil; reduce heat. Cover and simmer gently 2 hours. Boil gently uncovered 30 to 45 minutes longer to reduce syrup. Do not stir. Serve in small bowls at room temperature or chilled. Makes 6 to 8 servings.

Pie de Limón
Lime Pie

The luscious and refreshing filling will not become as firm as fillings made with gelatin.

1-1/4 cups vanilla wafer crumbs
   (40 wafers)
6 tablespoons butter, melted
4 egg yolks
2-2/3 cups milk
3/4 cup sugar

3 tablespoons cornstarch
1 teaspoon grated lime peel
1/4 teaspoon salt
1/3 cup lime juice
Lime Meringue, see below

Lime Meringue:
4 egg whites
1/4 teaspoon cream of tartar

1/2 cup sugar
1-1/2 teaspoons lime juice

Preheat oven to 350°F (175°C). Mix wafer crumbs and butter. Pat over bottom and sides of a 9-inch pie plate. Bake 6 minutes. Cool thoroughly before adding filling. Combine egg yolks, milk, sugar, cornstarch, lime peel and salt in blender. Process until smooth. Pour into a medium saucepan. Cook and stir over medium heat until mixture boils, becomes very thick and separates when a spoon is drawn through it. Stir in lime juice. Cook and stir until mixture again becomes very thick. Remove from heat and cool thoroughly. Prepare Lime Meringue. Turn cooled filling into pie shell. Swirl meringue onto pie, spreading to edges and sealing to pie shell. Bake 12 to 15 minutes until meringue is browned. Cool pie. Chill before cutting. Makes one 9-inch pie.

Lime Meringue:
In a medium bowl, beat egg whites and cream of tartar until soft peaks form. While beating, add one tablespoon of sugar at a time. Beat until stiff. Beat in lime juice.

Pie de Piña
Pineapple Pie

Fresh and canned pineapple have very different flavors, but either one makes a delicious pie.

1 fresh medium pineapple or 1
   (1-lb. 4-oz.) can chunk pineapple
   packed in juice, drained
Pastry for 1 double-crust 8-inch pie
1/2 cup sugar
1 tablespoon cornstarch

Pinch salt
1 tablespoon butter
Pinch ground cinnamon
About 1 tablespoon whipping cream or
   milk
1-1/2 teaspoons sugar

Quarter pineapple lengthwise. Remove core from each quarter. Cut fruit from shell, using a curved, serrated pineapple knife or grapefruit knife. Dice pineapple. There should be about 3 cups. Drain off any juice. Preheat oven to 425°F (220°C). Prepare pastry; cut in half. Roll out half of pastry into a 10-1/2-inch circle. Line an 8-inch pie plate with rolled out pastry. Arrange drained pineapple evenly in pastry shell. In a small bowl, blend 1/2 cup sugar, cornstarch and salt, breaking up any lumps. Sprinkle evenly over pineapple. Dot with butter and sprinkle lightly with cinnamon. Roll out remaining half of pastry. Place over filling. Seal and flute edges. Cut slits in top of pie to let steam escape. Brush pie lightly with cream or milk; sprinkle with 1-1/2 teaspoons sugar. Bake 10 minutes. Reduce heat to 350°C (175°C) and bake 35 minutes longer. Cool in pie plate on a rack. Serve warm. Makes one 8-inch pie.

Pie de Jícama

Jícama Pie

Another word for pie in spanish is pastel.

1 (9-inch) pie shell, baked	3 egg yolks
1 (1/2-lb.) jícama, peeled, coarsely shredded (about 2 cups)	2 cups milk
	1 cinnamon stick
1/2 cup sherry	1-1/2 teaspoons butter
1/2 cup water	1/4 teaspoon ground cinnamon
3/4 cup sugar	2 teaspoons sugar
6 tablespoons all-purpose flour	1 teaspoon butter
1/4 teaspoon salt	

Prepare pie shell; set aside. Combine shredded jícama, sherry and water in a saucepan. Bring to a boil; reduce heat. Cover and boil gently 45 minutes or until most of liquid has evaporated. Drain thoroughly; set aside. Mix 3/4 cup sugar, flour and salt in a medium saucepan. Beat egg yolks and 1 cup milk in a small bowl. Stir into sugar mixture. Add remaining milk and cinnamon stick. Stir over medium heat until mixture boils, becomes very thick and separates when a spoon is drawn through it. Remove cinnamon stick. Add jícama mixture to milk mixture. Cook and stir 1 or 2 minutes longer, until very thick. Stir in 1-1/2 teaspoons butter. Remove from heat and cool slightly. Turn mixture into pie shell. Sprinkle lightly with ground cinnamon and 2 teaspoons sugar. Cut 1 teaspoon butter into small pieces. Place over filling. Broil 3 inches from heat until butter and sugar are melted and bubbly. Watch carefully and do not let crust burn. Cool pie slightly. Serve warm or at room temperature. Makes one 9-inch pie.

Panqué de Arroz

Rice Flour Cake

Call specialty shops in your area to find rice flour.

1/2 lb. butter, softened	2 teaspoons baking powder
1-1/4 cups sugar	2 oz. Edam or Monterey Jack cheese, shredded (l/2 cup)
5 eggs	
1-1/2 cups rice flour	1/2 cup milk

Preheat oven to 350°F (175°C). Grease and flour a 9-inch square baking pan; set aside. Beat butter until soft and creamy. Beat in sugar until mixture is fluffy. Add eggs one at a time, beating after each addition. In a sifter, combine rice flour and baking powder. Sift into butter mixture. Stir in cheese and milk. Turn into prepared pan. Bake about 40 minutes until surface springs back when touched with your fingers. Cool cake in pan on a rack 10 minutes. Remove cake from pan. Cool completely on rack. Makes one 9-inch cake.

Pie de Pacana
Pecan Pie

Extraordinary pecan pie is a specialty of the Restaurant Portales in Mérida.

2 cups all-purpose flour
Pinch salt
1/2 cup plus 2 tablespoons butter

1/3 cup sweetened condensed milk
2 egg yolks
Pecan Filling, see below

Pecan Filling:
1-1/2 cups shelled pecans
1/2 cup butter
1-1/3 cups sugar
1/4 cup maple-flavored syrup

3 whole eggs
2 egg whites
1/2 teaspoon vanilla extract

Combine flour and salt in a medium bowl. Cut in butter with 2 knives or a pastry blender until evenly blended. Add condensed milk and egg yolks. Mix well. Dough will be too soft to roll out. Turn into a 9-inch pie plate. Shape into a ball. Press dough from center out until pie plate is evenly covered and enough dough extends above plate to form a fluted rim. Flute edge. Cover with plastic wrap; refrigerate. Preheat oven to 350°F (175°C). Prepare Pecan Filling. Turn filling into prepared pie shell. Bake pie 20 minutes until fluted edge is lightly browned. Cut 4 curved strips of foil about 1-1/2 inches wide. Carefully fold foil strips over edge to prevent excessive browning. Do not let foil touch filling. Bake 20 to 25 minutes longer or until filling is set. Cool on a rack. Serve pie slightly warm or at room temperature. Makes one 9-inch pie.

Pecan Filling:
Grind pecans in blender or food processor until fine; set aside. Combine butter, sugar and syrup in a large saucepan. Bring to a boil over medium heat, stirring to blend. Beat whole eggs, egg whites and vanilla in a medium bowl. Gradually beat hot mixture into eggs. Stir in ground pecans.

Pie de Kahlúa
Kahlúa Pie

Kahlúa is the coffee liqueur produced in Mexico.

1 (9-inch) pie shell, baked
4 egg yolks
1/2 cup sugar
2 (1-oz.) squares semisweet chocolate
1/4 cup water
1 envelope unflavored gelatin powder

1/4 cup cold water
1/4 cup Kahlúa
1-1/4 cups whipping cream
2 tablespoons sugar
2 egg whites
Chopped toasted almonds

Prepare pie shell and set aside. Slightly beat egg yolks in top of a double boiler. Add 1/2 cups sugar. Place over simmering water. Cook and stir until sugar is dissolved. Melt chocolate with 1/4 cup water in a small saucepan. Stir melted chocolate mixture into egg yolks. Cook and stir until mixture begins to thicken. Soften gelatin in 1/4 cup cold water. Add to thickened chocolate mixture. Stir well and remove from heat. Add Kahlúa. Place pan with mixture in a bowl of ice water to cool. In a small bowl, beat cream with 2 tablespoons sugar until stiff. In another small bowl, beat egg whites until stiff. When chocolate mixture begins to thicken, fold in half of the whipped cream, then fold in stiffly beaten egg whites. Refrigerate remaining whipped cream. Turn chocolate mixture into pie shell; chill. Top pie with remaining whipped cream and almonds. Makes one 9-inch pie.

Pie de Kahlúa (Kahlúa Pie) is pictured on the following pages.

Torta de Cielo   **Photo on pages 122 and 123.**

Heavenly Torte

Refrigerate any leftover cake. It will taste even better a few days later.

1/2 lb. unblanched almonds	**1 tablespoon all-purpose flour**
Water	**1 tablespoon dark rum**
1-1/3 cups sugar	**1/4 teaspoon cream of tartar**
6 eggs, separated	**4 to 6 blanched almonds, coarsely chopped**
Pinch salt	

The night before, place 1/2 pound almonds in a medium saucepan. Cover with water and bring to a boil. Remove from heat and let stand 5 minutes; drain. Press soaked almonds between your fingers to remove skins. Return skinned almonds to saucepan. Cover with cold water and let stand overnight. Just before making torte, drain almonds and pat dry with paper towels. Grease a 9-1/2 inch springform pan. Line bottom with waxed paper. Grease paper; set pan aside. Preheat oven to 350°F (175°C). In blender or food processor, grind almonds with 2/3 cup sugar until very fine, almost a paste. In a large bowl, beat egg yolks, remaining 2/3 cup sugar and salt until light and creamy. Beat in flour, then rum. Beat in almond mixture. In a large bowl, beat egg whites with cream of tartar until stiff. Fold 1/3 of the egg whites into nut mixture, then fold in remaining egg whites lightly but thoroughly. Turn into prepared pan. Bake 35 minutes or until browned and cake has begun to shrink from side of pan. Cake will rise as it bakes, begin to settle in the center and settle further as it cools. Cool in pan on a rack. When torte is completely cool, run a knife around edge of pan to loosen. Remove side of pan. Cut in wedges and place on a serving plate. Decorate each wedge with a few pieces of coarsely chopped almonds. Makes 8 servings.

Pan Tity

Tity's Cake

Delightful served plain, you can also split this cake horizontally and fill it with jam.

2 eggs, separated	**1-1/2 teaspoons vanilla extract**
1 cup sugar	**1-1/2 cups all-purpose flour**
1/2 cup milk	**1 tablespoon baking powder**
1/2 cup vegetable oil	**1/4 teaspoon salt**

Grease and flour an 8-inch square baking pan; set aside. Preheat oven to 400°F (205°C). Place egg yolks, sugar, milk and oil in a medium bowl. Beat 1 minute with electric mixer on high speed. Add vanilla. In a sifter, combine flour, baking powder and salt. Sift into egg yolk mixture. Beat at low speed until thoroughly combined scraping sides of bowl with a rubber spatula. Beat egg whites in a small bowl until stiff. Fold beaten egg whites into batter. Turn batter into prepared pan. Place in oven and immediately reduce heat to 375°F (190°C). Bake until cake has doubled in size, about 10 minutes; reduce heat to 350°F (175°C). Bake about 30 minutes longer until a wooden pick inserted in center comes out clean. Cool cake in pan on a rack 10 minutes. Remove from pan and cool completely on rack. Makes one 8-inch square cake.

Pastel a la Federico
Federico's Chiffon Cake

A fluffy, citrus-flavored cake developed by a baker from Mérida.

1 cup all-purpose flour
1/2 cup cornstarch
1-1/2 cups sugar
1 tablespoon baking powder
1/2 teaspoon salt
3/4 cup vegetable oil
8 eggs, separated

1/4 cup fresh tangerine juice or
   orange juice
1/2 cup sugar
1/3 cup lime juice
Grated peel of 1 tangerine or 1 small
   orange (1-1/2 to 2 teaspoons)

Grease and flour a 10-inch tube pan; set aside. Preheat oven to 350°F (175°C). In a sifter, combine flour, cornstarch, 1-1/2 cups sugar, baking powder and salt. Sift into a large bowl. Add oil, egg yolks and tangerine juice or orange juice. Beat with electric mixer on high speed until thoroughly mixed. Beat egg whites in a large bowl until stiff. Fold batter into egg whites gently but thoroughly. Turn into prepared pan. Bake 40 minutes. Mix 1/2 cup sugar, lime juice and tangerine peel or orange peel. Spoon mixture evenly over cake and bake 5 minutes longer. Remove cake from oven and invert pan over the neck of a thin bottle. Let cake hang on bottle until thoroughly cooled, about 3 hours. If a bottle is not available, invert pan with edges resting on custard cups. Run a knife or spatula around sides of cake and tap bottom of pan on hard surface until cake is loosened. Invert onto a large plate, then invert again onto a serving plate. Do not frost. Makes one 10-inch tube cake.

Volteado de Piña
Pineapple Upside-Down Cake

A cooking demonstration by Lucy Lopez y Simon in Mérida yielded this recipe.

3/4 cup butter, softened
1/3 cup sugar
1 (1-lb. 4-oz.) can sliced pineapple
   in heavy syrup
Pitted prunes
Pecan halves

1 cup sugar
3 eggs
1/2 cup evaporated milk
2 cups all-purpose flour
2-1/2 teaspoons baking powder
1/4 teaspoon salt

Preheat oven to 350°F (175°C). Coat bottom and sides of a 9-1/2-inch springform pan with 3 tablespoons of the butter. Sprinkle with 1/3 cup sugar. Drain pineapple, reserving 1/2 cup syrup. Arrange pineapple slices in an attractive pattern to cover bottom of pan. Cut any extra slices in half and stand at sides of pan. Place a prune in the center of each pineapple slice. Fill in spaces between slices with pecan halves with rounded sides down. Set pan aside. Place remaining butter and 1 cup sugar in a large bowl. Beat with electric mixer on medium speed until mixture is light and creamy. Add eggs. Beat until fluffy. Add milk and reserved pineapple syrup. Beat until blended. In a sifter, combine flour, baking powder and salt. Sift in 3 parts into creamed mixture, beating after each addition until just blended. Beat at high speed 1 minute. Carefully pour batter over pineapple in prepared pan, spreading evenly. Bake 45 to 55 minutes, until a wooden pick inserted in center of cake comes out clean. Cool in pan on a rack. Remove side of pan. Invert cake on a serving plate. Remove pan bottom. Makes one 9-1/2-inch cake.

Mousse de Rompope
Rum Eggnog Mousse

This sophisticated dessert is lightly flavored with rum.

1 cup Rompope, page 16,
  room temperature
1 envelope unflavored gelatin powder
1/4 cup cold water

1/2 cup whipping cream
4 egg whites
Fresh strawberries mashed with sugar or
  crushed thawed frozen strawberries

Prepare Rompope. Pour gelatin onto cold water in measuring cup. Let stand 5 minutes to soften. Place measuring cup in a bowl of hot water. Stir gelatin mixture to dissolve. Gradually beat gelatin mixture into Rompope. Refrigerate only until mixture begins to thicken and has the consistency of unbeaten egg whites, 20 to 45 minutes. In a small bowl, whip cream until stiff. In another small bowl, beat egg whites until stiff. Fold whipped cream, then beaten egg whites into Rompope mixture. Refrigerate until firm. To serve, spoon mousse into dessert glasses. Top with strawberries. Makes 6 servings.

Mousse de Kahlúa
Kahlúa Mousse

Cream whips best when the bowl, beaters and the cream itself are ice-cold.

1 cup whipping cream
1/2 teaspoon instant coffee powder
1/4 cup Kahlúa
2 tablepoons sugar

1 egg white
2 teaspoons sugar
Chocolate sprinkles

Chill bowl and beater before beating cream. Combine cream and coffee powder in a medium bowl. Beat until stiff. Add Kahlúa and 2 tablespoons sugar. Beat until very stiff. In a small bowl, beat egg white to soft peaks. Add 2 teaspoons sugar. Beat until stiff. Fold egg white into whipped cream mixture. Cover and chill. To serve, mound in dessert glasses and decorate with chocolate sprinkles. Makes 6 servings.

Postre de Mango
Mango Dessert

Use your blender to prepare this unusual dessert.

1 (15-oz.) can sliced mangoes in heavy
  syrup
1 (14-oz.) can sweetened condensed
  milk
2 tablepoons dark rum

1 envelope unflavored gelatin powder
Whipped cream
Chopped walnuts
Maraschino cherries

Drain mangoes, reserving 1/4 cup syrup in a measuring cup. Combine drained mangoes, condensed milk and rum in blender; puree. Add gelatin to reserved 1/4 cup syrup. Let stand 5 minutes to soften. Place measuring cup in a bowl of hot water. Stir to dissolve gelatin. Add to mango mixture; blend. Pour into 6 small dessert glasses. Refrigerate until set. To serve, top with whipped cream and walnuts. Garnish with maraschino cherries. Makes 6 servings.

Budín de Zanahorias
Carrot Pudding

An incredibly rich, brandy-soaked carrot pudding.

3/4 cup butter
1 (14-oz.) can sweetened condensed
  milk
4 eggs
1 cup finely shredded raw carrots

5 tablespoons fine dry breadcrumbs
1/4 teaspoon vanilla extract
2/3 cup sugar
1/4 cup water
1/4 cup brandy

Preheat oven to 350°F (175°C). Butter and flour an 8-inch round glass cake pan; set aside. Cream butter until fluffy. Beat in condensed milk. Beat in eggs one at a time. Stir in carrots, breadcrumbs and vanilla. Mix well. Turn into prepared cake pan. Bake 30 to 35 minutes, until a knife inserted in center comes out clean. Cool completely in pan on a rack. Bring sugar and water to a boil in a small saucepan. Boil 2 minutes. Remove from heat; stir in brandy. Cool slightly. Spoon evenly over cooled carrot pudding. Refrigerate 1 hour. Cut into wedges. Makes 8 to 10 servings.

Natillas de Almendrado
Almond Custard

Top Almendrado, page 174, with this rich sauce.

6 egg yolks
1/8 teaspoon salt
1/4 cup sugar

2 cups hot milk
1/2 teaspoon almond extract sauce
1 (2-3/4 oz.) pkg. chopped almonds (3/4 cup)

In a medium bowl, beat egg yolks, salt and sugar until blended. Stirring constantly, slowly add hot milk. Pour into top of a double-boiler. Cook over simmering water until mixture coats a metal spoon, about 10 minutes. Remove from heat. Stir in almond extract and chopped almonds. Cool on a rack, then refrigerate at least 30 minutes. Makes about 3 cups.

Cajeta de Celaya
Caramel Candy from Celaya

A cajeta is a box. In Celaya, where this candy is made, it is packaged in wooden boxes.

2 cups cow's milk
2 cups goat's milk or additional
  cow's milk
2 teaspoons cornstarch
1/8 teaspoon baking soda

1-1/2 cups sugar
1 cinnamon stick
1 fig leaf, if available
1 tablespoon sweet sherry, if desired

In a small bowl, blend 1 tablespoon milk, cornstarch and baking soda. Combine remaining milk in a large saucepan. Bring to a boil. Stir in cornstarch mixture, sugar, cinnamon stick and fig leaf. Boil, stirring constantly, until mixture thickens and bottom of pan can be seen clearly when spoon is scraped across it, about 1 hour. After 30 minutes of boiling and stirring, remove cinnamon stick and fig leaf. When candy is very thick, stir in sherry. Cook 1 minute longer. Pour into a heatproof container or serving dish; cool. Candy should be soft but not runny. Serve in dessert dishes, or use as a soda cracker spread, dessert topping or crepe filling. Makes 1-1/2 cups.

Jamoncillo de Frutas
Milk Fudge with Fruit

Long boiling gives this confection a marvelous flavor. Make it the day before you plan to serve it.

1/4 lb. chopped mixed candied fruit	**3 cups sugar**
1/4 cup orange-flavored liqueur	**1/2 teaspoon vanilla extract**
1 qt. milk	**1/4 teaspoon baking soda**

Combine fruit and liqueur in a small bowl; stir. Let stand 3 to 5 hours until liqueur is absorbed, stirring occasionally. Butter an 8-inch square baking pan; set aside. Place milk in a deep medium saucepan. Add sugar, vanilla and baking soda. Bring to a boil. Continue to boil over medium-low heat until thickened, stirring occasionally. Stir thickened mixture constantly until mixture separates when a spoon is drawn through it. Remove from heat. Let cool slightly, then beat vigorously until candy stiffens. Stir in fruit mixture. Spread in prepared pan. Cover candy with plastic wrap or foil and let stand overnight. Candy will be quite soft, particularly if weather is warm. For firmer texture, refrigerate candy. To serve, cut into rectangles or shape into balls and place in fluted paper cups. Makes about 25 pieces.

Variation

Jamoncillo de Nuez (Milk Fudge with Nuts): Substitute 1/2 cup chopped walnuts for the candied fruit. Omit the liqueur.

How To Make
Jamoncillo de Frutas

Cook candy until bottom of pan can be seen when a spoon is drawn through mixture.

Beat candy until it stiffens, then stir in fruits. Spread mixture in a pan to cool.

Sevillanas
Seville Cookies

A friend in Tucson couldn't find pineapple flavoring, so she used lemon extract.

1/2 cup butter or shortening, softened	1/4 teaspoon salt
1 cup granulated sugar	1 teaspoon pineapple flavoring
1 whole egg	Yellow food coloring
1 egg yolk	1/2 teapoon vanilla extract
2 cups sifted all-purpose flour	Red food coloring
1 teaspoon baking powder	Powdered sugar

Cream butter or shortening and granulated sugar in a medium bowl until smooth. Add whole egg and egg yolk. Beat until fluffy. Add flour, baking powder and salt; mix well. Divide dough in half. To one half, add pineapple flavoring and enough yellow food coloring to make dough bright yellow. Knead flavoring and food coloring into dough by hand to blend evenly. To other half of dough, add vanilla and enough red food coloring to make dough pink. Knead to blend thoroughly. Wrap each half of colored dough in waxed paper or plastic wrap. Refrigerate until firm enough to roll out, at least 1 hour. Preheat oven to 325°F (165°C). Line baking sheets with foil; set aside. Work with 1 color dough at a time. On a lightly floured surface, roll out dough 1/8 inch thick, sprinkling with flour when necessary. Cut out cookies with a 2-1/2-inch round cutter. Cookies made with a larger cutter will be difficult to handle. Pick up scraps; knead and roll out again until all dough is used. Place cookies on prepared baking sheets and bake 10 to 15 minutes. Do not let edges brown. Remove immediately from foil with a large spatula and cool on racks. Sift powdered sugar over half the cookies. To serve, alternate sugar-topped and plain cookies in a circle on a serving plate. Makes about 36 cookies.

Besitos de Merengue
Meringue Kisses

Mexican spiced chocolate flavors exquisite meringue cookies.

1/2 circle Mexican spiced chocolate (1-1/2 oz.), or 1-1/2 oz. semisweet chocolate and pinch of cinnamon	1/8 teaspoon salt
	1/4 teaspoon cream of tartar
	1/4 teaspoon vanilla extract
2 egg whites	3/4 cup sugar

Preheat oven to 350°F (175°C). Grate chocolate or shave with a knife; set aside. Beat egg whites until frothy. Add salt and cream of tartar. Beat until stiff. Beat in cinnamon if semisweet chocolate is used. Add vanilla. Beat in sugar 1 tablespoon at a time. Beat until meringue is stiff and glossy. Stir in grated or shaved chocolate. Drop mixture by teaspoonfuls on ungreased baking sheets, swirling tops to a point. Place in oven and immediately turn off heat. Leave in oven 3 hours without opening door. Remove baking sheets and tap to loosen meringues. Remove and store in airtight containers. Makes 48 cookies.

Index

Index

Index

Index

Index

Index

The recipes for *Mole Poblano* (*Mole* Puebla-Style), *Frijoles con Puerco* (Beans with Pork), *Sopa de Lima* (Lime & *Tortilla* Soup), *Panuchos Mérida* (*Panuchos* Mérida-Style) and *Pescado en Salsa Verde* (Fish in Green Sauce) first appeared in *Home,* the magazine supplement of the *Los Angeles Times.* The recipe for *Tamal de Elote en Cazuela* (Green Corn Tamale Casserole) first appeared in "The Big Cheese News."

The author wishes to thank Richard Merrill, Instituto Moderno de Lenguas Extranjeras, Leon, Guanajuato; Maria Marquez de Merrill; Bertha Delfin de Rodriquez; Tity Rodriquez Delfin; Escuela Industrial Adolfo Lopez Mateos, Veracruz; Humphreys Family Center, Garfield Community Adult School, East Los Angeles, and the many cooks in Mexico and the southwestern United States who contributed to this book.

Books for Today's Cooks from HPBooks

Appliance

Crockery Cookery—Hoffman	$6.95
Food Processor Cookery—Draudt	8.95
More Wok Cookery—Dyer	7.95
Wok Cookery—Dyer	7.95

Baking

Baking: Easy & Elegant (hc)	$15.95
Best of Baking—Wolter & Teubner	9.95
Breads—Herbst	7.95
Chocolate Cookery—Hoffman	7.95
Cookies—Haughton	6.95
Crepe Cookery—Hoffman	7.95
Pies & Pastries—Pittman	7.95
Sourdough Cookery—Davenport	7.95

Creative Cuisine Series

Cooking for Fun—Ager	$4.95
Delicious Desserts—Suthering	4.95
Four Seasons Salads—Burrow	4.95
Main Dishes—Wadey	4.95
Make-Ahead Meals—Shepherd	4.95
Quick & Easy Cooking—Westland	4.95
Simple Chinese Cooking—Hsiung	4.95
Suppers & Snacks—Bowen	4.95

Entertaining

Appetizers—Hoffman	$8.95
Brunch Cookery—Jester	6.95
Cookery for Entertaining—Sorosky	7.95
Cocktails—Walker	7.95
Elegant Desserts (hc)	17.95
Ice Cream—Hoffman	7.95
Make-Ahead Entertaining—Hoffman	7.95
Popcorn—Kusche	7.95
Salads & Buffets—Teubner & Wolter	9.95
Today's Tips—Thomas	5.95
Wine Book—Cooper	7.95

General

30-Minute Meals—Draudt	$7.95
Best of Cold Foods (hc)	17.95
Complete Cook (hc)—Jester	17.95
Cookery for 1 or 2—Swain	6.95
Easy Suppers—Jester	7.95
New Ideas for Casseroles—Ojakangas	7.95

International

Basic French Cookery—Willan	$12.95
Chinese Cookery—Cheng & Morris	9.95
German Cooking—Meyer-Berkhout	12.95
International Cooking—Wolter & Teubner	9.95
Italian Cookery—Barrese	6.95
Mexican Cookery—Hansen	8.95
Middle Eastern Cooking—Dosti	12.95
Northern Italian Cooking—Caggiano	8.95
Polish Cookery—Olszewska	12.95
Scandinavian Cooking—Ojakangas	12.95

Microwave

Kids Cook Microwave—Emal & Kern	$4.95
Microwave Cookbook—Jester	14.95
Microwave Cookbook (rb)—Jester	22.50
Microwave Cookery—Deacon	7.95

Specialty

California Cooking—Hoffman	$7.95
Canning—Deeming	7.95
Cheese Cookery—Townsend	5.95
Chicken Cookery—Dyer	7.95
Fish & Shellfish—Walker	7.95
Herbs & Spices—Townsend	6.95
How to Dry Foods—DeLong	7.95
Make-A-Mix Cookery—Eliason	7.95
More Make-A-Mix—Eliason	7.95
Pasta Cookery—Kay	8.95
Soups & Sandwiches—Deeming	6.95
Vegetable Cookery—Pappas	7.95

(hc) = hard cover
(rb) = ring bound
All other books are paperback.

Books are available wherever fine cookbooks are sold, or order direct from the publisher. Send check or money order payable in U.S. funds to:

HPBooks, Inc., PO Box 5367, Dept. MP, Tucson, AZ 85703

Include $1.95 postage and handling for first book; $1.00 for each additional book. Arizona residents add 7% sales tax. Please allow 4-6 weeks for delivery. Prices subject to change without notice.

¡DELICIOSO!

Preparing fresh chiles, pages 8 and 9

Chayotes Rellenos (Stuffed Chayotes), page 69

Enchiladas de Queso (Cheese Enchiladas), page 78

Huevos Motuleños (Eggs Motul-Style), page 134

Capirotada de Margarita (Margarita's Bread Pudding), page 173

Now you can prepare authentic home-style Mexican food right in your own kitchen. It's easy, inexpensive, and you'll love the results. Serve *tacos, tortillas* and *enchiladas.* Serve genuine corn *tamales,* homemade *salsa* and delicious *carne asada.* Enjoy Mexican holiday breads, colorful fruit drinks and superb salads. Your family and friends will shout, *"¡Fantastico!"*

BIPAD 68112

ISBN 0-89586-038-4

$8.95

0

75478 00053